Women
Writers
Talking

Other books edited by Janet Todd

Be Good, Sweet Maid: An Anthology of *Women & Literature*
Gender and Literary Voice *(Women & Literature,* 1)
Men by Women *(Women & Literature,* 2)
Bibliography of Women in Literature, 1975–78

Women Writers Talking

Edited by
Janet Todd

Holmes & Meier, Publishers
New York **HM** London

Lines from her poetry used in the interview with May Sarton are reprinted by permission of the author and her publisher, W.W. Norton & Company, Inc., from the following books: *Selected Poems of May Sarton,* edited and with an Introduction by Serena Sue Hilsinger and Lois Brynes. W.W. Norton & Company, Inc. Copyright © 1978 by May Sarton. *Halfway to Silence, New Poems by May Sarton.* W.W. Norton & Company, Inc. Copyright © 1980 by May Sarton.

The poems by Joan Barton are reprinted by permission of the author.

First published in the United States of America 1983 by

Holmes & Meier Publishers, Inc.
30 Irving Place, New York, N.Y. 10003

Holmes & Meier Publishers, Ltd.
131 Trafalgar Road
Greenwich, London SE10 9TX

Copyright © 1983 by Holmes & Meier Publishers, Inc.

Library of Congress Cataloging in Publication Data
Main entry under title:

Women writers talking.

   1. Women authors, American — Interviews. 2. Women
authors, English — Interviews. 3. Women authors, French —
Interviews. 4. Authors, American — 20th century — Interviews. 5. Authors, English — 20th century — Interviews.
6. Authors, French — 20th century — Interviews. 7. Feminism and literature. I. Todd, Janet M., 1942–
PS151.W64   809'.89287   82-3100
ISBN 0-8419-0756-0   AACR2
ISBN 0-8419-0757-9 (pbk.)

Printed in the United States of America

For my parents

Contents

Preface

May Sarton once remarked that, for her, heaven was Bloomsbury. There is no equivalent now: a pocket or so of writers in New York's Greenwich Village or London's Hampstead, but too many are absent from each for heaven to be declared. There is no gathering to which the women interviewed here would come, leaving apartments in Paris, houses in Salisbury, or cottages in Maine. There is no place to meet them all, as May Sarton met Elizabeth Bowen and Virginia Woolf together over tea. This book of interviews is a surrogate, an effort to create Bloomsbury in pieces which the reader must fit together.

I think of *Women Writers Talking* as a party. Some of the invited guests, like June Jordan and Toni Cade Bambara, could or would not come; others brought friends. It is a noisy party, where conversations are between couples and overhearing is difficult. As in any gathering, some of the guests do not care for others and wonder why they have been invited; some are happy to know old friends are in the room.

The gathering is mixed. Grace Paley has come informally, A. S. Byatt formally. It is international and styles differ with nations. The British are, on the whole, more reticent, the Americans more outspoken, the French exist among their own excited ideas.

In conversation the women reveal distinctions beyond nationality. Some of them have succeeded flamboyantly in the commercial world — Erica Jong and Marilyn French, for example — where others, like Joan Barton, have succeeded only in their own way. With fame has come for some the constant calls for interviews, and the celebrated have learned to speak easily, even glibly, of the craft of writing and the struggle of women; they have said it all before many times. Yet in each repetition there is a freshness, a new word that hints at new ideas or a pause that reveals what has not so far been told. Other women have rarely been cornered to speak of themselves and they talk hesitatingly, groping for words to convey lives never in the limelight.

The women express themselves in a variety of forms: fiction, poetry, essays, memoirs, autobiography, journals, and filmscripts; their choices influence the content of their interviews. Some, like Robin Morgan, Germaine Greer, and Christiane Rochefort, see themselves as political writers and they speak on political matters; others, like May Sarton and Maya Angelou, stress the artist and bring the question of craft and form to the fore; others, like Margaret Drabble or Diane Johnson, are social novelists and they speak of fiction and society. For most of them, writing is their life's work; for some, such as Jeanne Moreau, it is only a part; for still others, it has never earned a living.

The purpose of the book is to juxtapose voices. Several themes run through the interviews with variations. A number of writers are sure there is a female language, for instance; others are certain there is no such thing; Luce Irigaray thinks there is no masculine one. Some regard themselves with Marilyn French as part of a female community, past and present, or, like Maya Angelou, as part of an Afro-American women's group; others, like Joan Barton, avoid the distinctions of gender. The substance of a woman's life is debated—children and art, or the possibility of combining motherhood with writing. For Erica Jong the reconciliation comes through a nanny; for Margaret Drabble the questions need no reconciling; for May Sarton motherhood and art cannot mix.

Many other themes run through the interviews, allowing the reader to make her own conversations, direct her own section of the party, and form a Bloomsbury of talk to her own liking. She should have an exhilarating time of it, for the voices, chiming, disagreeing, joyful, strident, or querulous, are always lively and engaged.

At the end of May Sarton's novel about an interview, *Mrs. Stevens Hears the Mermaids Singing,* the visitors take leave of the writer and exchange "a look of understanding and triumph." I hope that the interviews here will affect the reader in much the same way.

J.T.

Women
Writers
Talking

Lotte Jacobi

May Sarton

Interviewed by
Janet Todd

I met May Sarton on a clear fresh day in May in a car park in York, Maine. She was immediately welcoming and her warmth cancelled out the fatigue of my eight-hour drive from New York. We drove in her car down lanes of new leaves.

Her house was yellow and three-storied; the grass, colored with daffodils and red tulips, stretched down to the sea. Inside, the views of sun, sea, and flowers seemed part of the walls. It was a home, with a dog, a cat, flowers, knick-knacks, soft toys, and old furniture. A beautiful place. "Rented," she said quickly as I marvelled. "I could never afford to own anything like this."

After noisily greeting the dog, we sat in the light living room drinking tea and eating biscuits with orange-flavored butter. The books at eye level on the shelf were not May Sarton's own, handsomely bound below, but those of Elizabeth Bowen and Virginia Woolf, both friends from years before.

In *Mrs. Stevens Hears the Mermaids Singing* (1965) May Sarton tells of an interview in May with a famous woman poet of New England. The two younger interviewers come from New York to perform an "exemplary exercise in tact and persuasion," but the author nonetheless feels "badgered" at the idea of their arrival.

May Sarton is 69, a writer since the 1930s of novels, poems, diaries, and memoirs. She is famous, though not critically acclaimed; loved and consulted by readers for her exemplary life of solitude, open but unstressed lesbianism, and dedication to art. I too came in May from New York to Maine, and, before I knew the wonderful friendliness of May Sarton, I was made nervous by the analogy of *Mrs. Stevens*.

I questioned her about her identification with her creation. She laughed heartily. "And of course Mrs. Stevens lives by the sea as I do — but I'm not Mrs. Stevens. There are many things that are different. For example her parents are absolutely not my parents. Secondly I am a much more giving and warm person than she is, but for purposes of art I wanted to make her very much only the writer and the lover, these two which go together of course. One did not feel a person who was very welcoming to the world and I think I have made her more of an austere presence than I am on purpose. Of course I wrote it when I was fifty-five and I made her seventy. Now I'm nearly seventy I'd make her eighty I suppose."

And yet, I pursued, there is much of yourself in so many of your characters. Mrs Stevens certainly seems close in dedication to art. "In essence it is myself but characters in fiction can never be as complex as real people. You have to simplify and emphasize certain things at the expense of others. So that Mrs. Stevens is less and more than I am — more because more concentrated, a poet purely, and of course she didn't write fiction or journals or memoirs." She paused, remembering her life. "There's quite a large spectrum I've investigated through my writings."

May Sarton has written many times of the difficulties of reconciling life and art, of fulfilling oneself in reality and in writing. I asked her to talk on this and she replied volubly — clearly this was a topic still uppermost in her mind. "The conflict of life and poetry every writer has. It is an endless and agonizing conflict; I face it every single day at my desk. I haven't written a word of my own for art for months. I only answer letters. The life that pours in. People say, 'Why do you answer?' and I give them examples of the kinds of things people ask of me. I would be an absolute brute if I didn't reply. I'm doing it less now though." She was obviously on a hobbyhorse and she rode it at speed: "I feel more alive when I'm writing than I do at any other time — except when I'm making love. Two things when you forget time, when nothing exists except the moment — the moment of the writing, the moment of love. That perfect concentration is bliss."

> God of the empty room,
> Thy will be done. Thy will be done:
> Now shine the inward sun,
> The beating heart that glows
> Within the skeleton,
> The magic rose, the purer living gold,
> Shine now, grown old.
>
> [*SP*, p. 184][1]

And yet, I questioned, there is much prelude to working and love and may not the two be difficult to reconcile? May Sarton paused a while and then agreed, "Yes, you're right. Yes, I do feel there is perfection of life or art and I used to feel it even more. 'The intellect of man is forced to choose. . . .'" I felt this a romantic view and she took up the word: "I would say my whole work is based on the phrase 'the Romantic impulse, the Classic consideration' and I think the reason why there are so few first-class poets is that many people have intense feelings or first-class minds but to get the two together so that you will be willing to put a poem through sixty drafts, to be that self-critical, to keep breaking it down, that is what is rare. Right now most poetry is just self-indulgence. I don't see any fashioning—or almost none. The craft—as I've said more than once—is not something you paste on; it is organic, and you're discovering what you felt or meant to say by putting it into form. The struggle with the form is the struggle with yourself. Again we come to Yeats."

> Where waterfalls in shining folds
> Trouble the classic pools,
> And always formal green enfolds
> And frames the moving grays and golds—
> Who breathes on stone, who makes the rules?
>
> [*SP*, p. 27]

She needed no prompting to go on with this topic, one much explored in her work. "The other thing I feel is that the deeper you go the more universal what you touch is. What is in fashion now is often a personal reference which the reader cannot have any key to—the New

York school — you know, what happened on Second Avenue in March at that terrible moment. You have no idea what the terrible moment is and you couldn't care less. But it seems to me, if you really understand what's happened, the more universal it becomes. The poems I've written which I've feared no one could really understand are the poems that people respond to most. 'That's exactly what I felt and how did you know?' The strangest poem when it's completely evolved communicates."

> What of this personal all,
> The little world these hands have tried to fashion
> Using a single theme for their material,
> Always a human heart, a human passion?
>
> [*SP*, p. 187]

May Sarton has written more prose than poetry if one counts novels, memoirs, and journals and yet I suspected that she valued her poetry over her prose. She smiled at a question she had perhaps often been asked, and agreed. "If you're a poet at all, you must value your poetry above anything else. Because it's given. Like mathematics and music, I believe that poets are born, not made. And this sense of the music — which is of course very unfashionable now — you experience when very young. My first book of poems came out when I was twenty-five but I was publishing when I was seventeen." She laughed, remembering the delight of first acceptance. "*Poetry Magazine* took five sonnets — I was very thrilled, I remember, and rushed out and bought Katherine Mansfield's letters which had just come out. I'd never made any money before." She went on more thoughtfully, "If you were in solitary confinement, what would you do if you were a writer? I don't think I'd write a novel but I'm sure I'd write poetry. Because poetry is between you and God — I mean I'm not a believer in the obvious sense but it's something that comes from so deep in the subconscious you can't control it."

> Today, I have learned
> That to become
> A great, cracked,
> Wide-open door
> Into nowhere
> Is wisdom.
>
> [*HS*, p. 61]

"You can say, I'll write a novel next year, I have a good idea. But you can't say 'I'll write a poem next Wednesday because I have some free time, — you can't. Will doesn't operate. And this is why so many poets commit suicide I think or become alcoholic or take drugs — because that waiting for the muse is so agonizing if you have no other string to your bow. The more famous you are, the more terrible it must be if you dry up. Whereas I have the great advantage of being able to write novels — I hope to write one more — and I can go on with the journal forever which I think is a very minor part of my work, but it is something people seem to enjoy."

I asked her then about the relationship of art and life, the process of art feeding off life as a kind of cannibal. I wondered if she ever found herself experiencing for the sake of writing. She was emphatic in her reply. "No. If you do that, you're destroying your gift and you find you don't have it. It's got to come, you can't force it. You can't say 'I'm going to Japan because then I'll write a poem.' "

I felt there was still something here May Sarton had not addressed, that art evolves so often out of the unhappiness of life — especially love — and that this might conceivably make the misery welcome. She began to answer the question but then moved from it. "I've always believed love would be all right though it never has lasted; I did though live with Judy for fifteen years and was devoted to her, someone who has now become senile. I suppose the thing that makes the poetry is the first stages of a love affair where everything is being discovered and you are discovering yourself again under very naked and intense circumstances. Large parts are not there in just ordinary discourse, in gardening or whatever you do. It's the intensity."

> At first the whole world opens into sense:
> They learn their lives by looking at the wheat,
> And there let fall all that was shy and tense
> And be all they have seen.

[*SP*, p. 46]

"And another thing I believe is that intensity commands form. That is a statement I've made many times, and I believe it. I can write free-verse poems, but for me a poem is never completely satisfying unless it's in form and form is brought to me by intensity of feeling. Without it I can't write in form. That's the sadness for me — what's going to happen when I'm very old?" But, I worried, the intensity does cream off a little of the experience itself. "It gives you a chance of finding out what's happening to you," she replied. Yet, in that case, poetry would seem a safety valve. She agreed that it was. Poetry burgeons again at the end of the misery. "Yes," she replied thoughtfully, ". . .it's very mysterious."

The topic lapsed and we returned to the making of poems. "When one's not writing poems—and I'm not at the moment—you wonder how you ever did it. It's like another country you can't reach. That's what makes it so marvelous and is why anyone who writes poetry would put it first.

"People have often said that they like the novels more than the poems, but now I'm glad to say that I get more letters that say the opposite; the poems are what have really spoken to them most. Very simple people. I like it that my poems *do* reach."

I set my mind to artful work and craft,
I set my heart on friendship, hard and fast
Against the wild inflaming wink of chance
And all sensations opened in a glance.

[*SP*, p. 82]

"One of my problems is that my work is extremely clear and this is not fashionable. Clarity is earned. It looks simple but it hasn't been simple arriving at this simplicity. And this is where I haven't had a critical break. Partly because the influences on me were French. For example, Mauriac was my master for the novel—his economy and clarity; there's a great writer who appeals to every kind of person, far more perhaps than some of the famous women like Lessing, and other great writers today. I wanted a very clear style and I've felt that when people say about a writer, 'It's a wonderful style,' this is not positive. The reader should not be aware of the style, only fully experience what is being said. Afterwards if they are critics they should say to themselves, 'Why is this so compelling? Well, for these reasons . . .'"

I remembered May Sarton's partly European background and asked her if she felt she worked more within a French tradition than an English. She said she did not, but went on, "The strongest prose influence on me was French. In poetry, no. It is a damnable thing that in English it's so difficult to rhyme; it's much easier in French but the danger is of overrhyme and it looks too facile. So on the whole I'm very glad to be writing in English. I think the combination of Latin and Anglo-Saxon makes it a marvelous language for poetry, but in French you get too much of the Latin."

I asked her more specifically about poetic influences. "When I was young," she replied, "the people who influenced me most were Edna St. Vincent Millay — who was very much in fashion but I don't think a great poet — and H.D. who was then beginning with free verse to do something very exciting. Then I went back to the Elizabethans. Yeats was the strongest influence. Herbert came later in my life. He is one of the poets I live with and I love the form in his poems, which have been extremely nourishing to me. But Yeats is fascinating because of the change of styles — a person who could change to this marvelous clarity and hardness after that diffuse Romantic sensuality is thrilling to see. And he wrote so well into his old age. Which makes him a very happy person to have as a mentor.

"The saddest thing about American writing in general is that people peter out. So few great writers in America have kept on growing to the end. Faulkner, for instance, I don't think did and Millay didn't. Louise Bogan stopped writing almost entirely and she was an admirable poet, though she only had one subject."

I was especially impressed with May Sarton's use of the sonnet form and I asked her if it was an especial favorite. "I like the sonnet form," she responded, "but I've used it to an extent only four times in my life."

> Castrati have pure voices, as we know;
> But the mature, who mutilate by choice,
> Who cut the heart out so that they may grow,
> What sweetness flows from such a tortured voice?

> [*SP,* p. 57]

"Metaphor and music make the poem. The metaphor is given but then you have to explore it and in that is the excitement of the poem. Creating the music and then paring it down."

Painting features in many of May Sarton's works and I questioned her about the cross-fertilization between the arts. "Piero della Francesca was an enormous influence. He made me rethink my whole theory of art after I saw the Arezzo frescos, because I had to ask myself the question, 'Why is it so moving when what is involved is such a cold atmosphere?' There are tremendous distances between the people, immobility, huge silent space surrounding everything he did. It's in the poem."

O cruel cloudless space,
And pale bare ground where the poor infant lies!
Why do we feel restored
As in a sacramental place?
Here Mystery is artifice
And here a vision of such peace is stored,
Healing flows from it through our eyes. . .
Poised as a monument,
Thought rests, and in these balanced spaces
Images meditate;
Whatever Piero meant,
The strange impersonal does not relent:
Here is love, naked, lying in great state
On the bare ground, as in all human faces.

[*SP*, p. 17]

"I had to rethink a great deal. It didn't have as good an effect in the poem as it should have had, but I thought a lot about it, trying to create more silence and more spaces, a more austere atmosphere in which to communicate things that were not austere in themselves. Last year I wrote a poem about Poussin whose landscapes I love, and certain early landscapes of Corot before he got into his vague stage I think are absolutely beautiful. Painting has meant a great deal to me — and music, though I don't play an instrument. I just listen and enjoy."

I wondered if she saw the muse as passion, another person, or even herself. "The muse is a woman I'm in love with," she said. "Always. The muse in 'The Muse as Medusa' is a woman whom I saw only once alone, though it lasted for six months." But you are a part of it, I went on, she is your construct and, in a way, you yourself. "Yes, it is me," she admitted, "Medusa's face turns around and becomes your own face. That's the twist — Medusa forces one to face oneself."

I turn your face around! It is my face.
That frozen rage is what I must explore —
Oh secret, self-enclosed, and ravaged place!

[*SP*, p. 160]

"That's what being in love with women has done for me, I think. It's very often not consummated. It's something that goes on in the imagination to some extent — quite ludicrous really, and ridiculous."

She laughed at herself; then went on, "But there's no point in laughing about something that is so real and has made so much happen to me. I can see that from outside it must seem quite silly." She laughed again but with no self-pity.

> If I can let you go as trees let go
> Their leaves, so casually, one by one;
> If I can come to know what they do know,
> That fall is the release, the consummation,
> That fear of time and the uncertain fruit
> Would not distemper the great lucid skies
> This strangest autumn, mellow and acute.
>
> [*SP*, p. 51]

"I don't write poems long after the event. I write them at the time. It's like a seizure, you see. I did write the Piero poem long after seeing the Arezzo frescoes, but it had a deep meaning I had to find. Some images haunt me for years after — like the bulbs."

> These bulbs forgotten in a cellar,
> Pushing up through the dark their wan white shoots,
> Trying to live — their hopeless hope
> Has been with me like an illness. . .
>
> [*SP*, p. 70]

We turned then to other women poets and I asked her if she felt close to any in particular. "I admire Louise Bogan — I knew her well." She paused, remembering. "I was a bit in love with her I suppose, but it was never consummated. I was never close. There are a lot of letters. It is an interesting correspondence because there was a lot of tension and some argument. She was against *all* political poems and I agree that rhetorical poetry is bad, but a political poem *can* be good. 'Toussaint L'Ouverture' is marvelous and that's a political poem."

> Now let us honor with violin and flute
> A woman set so deeply in devotion
> That three times blasted to the root
> Still she grew green and poured strength out.
>
> [*SP*, p. 33]

What about recent feminist writers? Did she feel in tune with them? "I don't like most of the feminist poets or the lesbian poets who want to force everyone to be lesbians and hate men," May Sarton declared. "I'm not a joiner and I'm getting a lot of flack because I've said some things that suggest that I don't think being a lesbian is the happiest thing in the world. I wouldn't advise a young girl to go out and find another woman or say, 'For heaven's sake, why do you bother with men?' I would never say that to any human being, I can't imagine it. But these people are so militant."

May Sarton is open about being a lesbian but she is adamant about her poems being about human feelings rather than simply lesbian ones. "Take Olga Broumas's lesbian poetry which uses words like *clitoris*. I don't like that — I wouldn't like it if a man in love poetry was extremely physical and talked a great deal about his penis. I don't think it would communicate to me. My love poems are metaphysical, where hers are very physical."

I knew she liked Erica Jong but was not enthusiastic about her novels, and I asked if she felt it possible to like a person but not appreciate her work. "I like Erica Jong's poetry better than her novels," she replied. "Her poetry has a lot of life in it. It's very ebullient. Muriel Rukeyser was a very dear friend over a long period of years though we didn't see each other much in the last years. I never was a great admirer of her poetry which I think was too diffuse and oracular and somehow doesn't pack a wallop enough for me. But she was an admirable person. So I *can* make the distinction. But I may be wrong about her poetry — I should reread it. You batter out your own style against other people you see and Muriel was doing something very different from me, much more pretentious, not in a derogatory sense, but including a great deal more of the world. So in order to establish my identity against hers I had to dislike her poetry in a way. Now I don't think I'd feel that way so much. I do think she had greatness at her best. The 'Children's Elegy' is marvelous."

I moved the talk to May Sarton's own work, wondering whether she felt she inhabited her fictive world when she wrote. She agreed that she did, for she found it more real than the real world. But, when I asked her if she looked back on her works as if they were her past, she implied that she did not, that there was a break. "You know I'm awfully surprised when I reread anything of mine and dismayed because I feel I could never do that now. I feel very much weaker than my best work. Whenever I start a novel, I think I know nothing — and after all there are twelve or so novels—and I think, 'Well how do you get someone into the room' or 'what is dialogue all about?' I go through the whole process of discovering the form again and of how to do it. It's terrifying. I'm trying to do a novel now and I'm absolutely terrified. So when I go back, I'm sometimes pleasantly surprised, although I wouldn't do it that way now."

Yet, I noted, there are definite continuities of subjects in the fiction, for example the relationship of an older woman and a young man or woman. She agreed this was so. "All my best friends were much older and all the people I was in love with," she pointed out. Did the fiction sometimes come first? "Well maybe so. I did write a novel about a woman dying of cancer and then I got cancer. But it wasn't terminal. I did feel that here was life imitating art."

I found this an interesting point, worth pursuing. It seemed to me that May Sarton had in her novels long been preparing in fiction for her own famed old age as a wise woman. The theme was there when she was quite young—in *The Single Hound* (1938) and *The Shadow of a Man* (1950). She seemed surprised, then agreed. "Yes, that's right. I hadn't realized that. But there are other continuities. Being an only child and an exile and all the rest of it, I was in love with families. People like Carolyn Heilbrun blame me for this and think I'm much too romantic about family life and marriage. There is a great deal about marriage in my books, from young marriage all the way through to *Kinds of Love* (1970), where you get the old people who are learning to die together. I think there hasn't been enough written about marriage.

"The other thing is that very little has been written about friendship between women, not lesbianism, but friendship. In *Kinds of Love* the friendship between the city woman and the local person is important to me and, I think, successful in that book. There are other places, especially in a novel which I wish were better, but which I still like—*Birth of Grandfather* (1957). What interested me was the middle age of a marriage when people according to Jung begin to turn to their own sex, not sexually. The man is completely absorbed in the death of his friend and the wife turns to a woman confidante. Very little is written on this.

"Now what people want in fiction has to be so obvious and violent. It's all these nuances and delicacies of relationships which interest me, which I wish to write about, but it's not the fashion. Sexuality I'm very bad at doing. I don't want to do it and I don't like it in fiction. I don't think that physical descriptions of sex have to do with literature.

The only place where they fit is in the grotesque like Pantagruel. This may be a weakness of mine or to do with my generation. So much has happened in the last twenty years talking about sex. A young woman of twenty now could never be as ignorant as we were. So there are certain reticences that have to do with the generation. I've been very open about being a lesbian but I don't want to talk about it in sexual terms."

> This tapestry will unweave itself,
> Nor I spend what is left of me to tear
> Your bright thread out: let unfulfilled design
> Stand as your tragic epitaph, and mine.
>
> [*SP,* p. 56]

"I have always been fond of old people and I've always wanted to be old. But the trouble is it's not only a matter of being wise and above the melée but it's physical — I now have a sore knee which I wouldn't have had even a year ago. The fact that you're decaying gets to you. No one can freeze that. But here I have an advantage. When I think that Jean Dominique, the great woman who influenced me so much, Marie Closset, the poet in Belgium (she used the name Jean Dominique for her poetry), when she was sixty-eight behaved as if she were ninety and everyone surrounded her and coddled her; she was in cottonwool. When I first knew her she was sixty I suppose and an old woman. Now no one expects you to collapse, which is a good thing."

I remarked that death in her later books seemed less of an epiphany than a release, but she disagreed. "No there's an epiphany in *A Reckoning* (1978); the book is used in hospices and I get letters every week from people who say I've covered up all the horrors. But it's not true. My mother died of cancer and I watched it and in some ways the book was a way of exorcising my guilt because I wouldn't sit with her. I couldn't. I mention this in *Recovering* (1980) and I'm so glad — I've paid my debt and it means that some people will go and sit with their mothers who might not otherwise. That's not a reason for art. But all one can say I suppose is that everything is autobiographical but transposed and art comes in the transposition."

Some people were disturbed at the treatment of senility in *A Reckoning and As We Are Now* (1973). It almost seems as though senility, not sex, is the taboo of our times. "I think you're right," May Sarton agreed. "I felt this when I wrote about Judy. So many people face this and can't talk about it. It is terrifying. I now forget names and I wonder if I'm going to end like that — wondering where I am. This is Judy's state now. She doesn't even know me when I go to see her. I go very rarely because it's only a punishment.

"The fundamental thing which I knew when I was young and which I know now is that the person inside is exactly the same as they ever were."

> We sat smoking at a table by the river
> And then suddenly in the silence someone said
> "Look at the sunlight on the apple tree there shiver
> I shall remember that long after I am dead."

[*SP*, p. 48]

"It's only that something is disintegrating which is beyond your control. I am just as passionate about flowers as I was when I was five years old. Think of Bertrand Russell at ninety. The English seem to grow old very well."

I raised the issue of therapy, described in her more recent poems, and asked about her attitude to the analysis movement that seems to have swept America. "I have three times been helped by therapy. I think I would be against psychoanalysis, going for six years twice a week; the people I know who have been through it have not come out any better off. But therapy is just like an emergency operation. It can make you better able to deal with the reality situation. You need an objective view."

> Speak to me
> Of the communion of saints
> On earth.

[*SP*, p. 201]

"Writing as therapy makes me cross. I hate this teaching of journals. People don't know how hard it is to write a good journal and, mind you, I don't keep a journal except for publication. It's only at certain times when I felt it would help me to deal with a difficult situation — to be thinking about it and keeping a journal and, if it were so universal a thing as, say, the fear of death, then it's possible it would mean something to other people. I get a great many letters saying, 'This is what I have always felt and couldn't express; now you've said it I feel a great deal better.' I think a journal is extremely easy compared with a novel. I resent that the journals are so popular. It is a lesser form of art, but I don't minimize the fact that I'm pretty good at it. This is because I'm aware of the world outside — the flowers as well as the people."

> Fidelity to what? To a gnarled tree, a root
> To the necessity for growth and discipline.
>
> [*HS*, p. 56]

"It's not just someone sitting and looking at their navel and saying, 'I'm feeling worse today,' though that comes in of course. I hate Anais Nin's diaries because they're so narcissistic and she always has to be perfect. *The Journal of Solitude* (1973) appealed because I admitted I had anger and so on. Everything in the journals comes from some painful experience which I then analyze and put into philosophical terms. It's the combination of the concrete detail and thinking about feeling that is my strength.

"You must give yourself away if you're going to be a professional writer. It's the price. Look at someone like Philip Roth in *Portnoy's Complaint*; it's obvious that everything is himself though he's not saying 'I.' I had a letter from Willa Cather where she says that every one of her books is written out of a personal and usually painful experience — she who seems so classic and uninvolved."

> I am the unicorn and bow my head
> You are the lady woven into history . . .
> Our wine, Imagination, and our bread,
> And I the unicorn who bows his head.
>
> [*SP*, p. 16]

"I was very touched when the Methodist ministers asked me to come and be a *guru* for their summer session. The other two were holy people, and I said, 'Why do you want me? I'm not a Methodist.' They said, 'We want you to talk about vulnerability and self-healing. And read poems.'"

May Sarton has become in her late sixties a kind of seer or wise woman. She has done so in two main areas: lesbianism and solitude. I asked her how she responded to her position as model and how she thought it had come about. "I think I've been able to project a human being in its agonies and joys," she replied after a pause.

"I wish I could find a better word for *lesbian*. I liked Virginia Woolf's *sapphic* but I use *lesbian* because now everyone does. But it is a sexual word and people hearing it think immediately of intercourse between two women, whereas that's the last thing in a way that interests me — it's so much more than that.

"I was very upset by the *New York Times* review of *A Reckoning* — so much so I thought I'd never write another book. I felt that whatever I wrote now people would be looking for lesbianism. In *A Reckoning* it was not a lesbian relationship; yet I was accused of hiding something! But why would I hide it? If I had wanted to make it a lesbian relationship I would have done so. I have a friend whom I never see and who is married to an Englishman. If I were dying I would want her to come at the end and nobody else, but we were never lovers — this goes back to school and we have a psychic communication. She's a very upset, terribly neurotic, adorable woman but I would say 'I want to see Barbara before I die.'

"What was so enraging was to have that emotion labeled and also to take a poem that wasn't lesbian and label it so. The reviewer couldn't find a lesbian love poem. All my love poems are written to women but not in sexual terms. So she couldn't take an example from 'Divorce of Lovers' and say this is a lesbian love poem because it could be applied to any divorce."

> There is no poetry in lies
> But in crude honesty
> There is hope for poetry.
>
> [*HS*, p. 61]

"I'm very aware of being dangerous as a model for solitude. I didn't live alone until I was forty-five and even after that I had many love affairs. It's not a solitude of having closed the door on life. It's simply, partly, because I am a lesbian and I have not found after Judy anyone I could live with. I would gladly live with someone — but the trouble is that now I guess I wouldn't, because you get to be rather selfish when you live alone."

> I can tell you that solitude
> Is not all exaltation, inner space
> Where the soul breathes and work can be done.
> Solitude exposes the nerve,
> Raises up ghosts.
> The past, never at rest, flows through it.
>
> [*SP*, p. 83]

As a foreigner in America I was very interested in May Sarton's adjustment to the United States and her divided European-American heritage. I noted she felt less disquiet over this in later years. "I came to America when I bought my farm in Nelson when I was forty-five," she said. "Until then Europe had been home. I went to Europe every year until World War II and I just had to go back. It was the air, the old stones, something indefinable—the emotional loam is richer in Europe, relationships are deeper. There's less talk about them, less fuss made about lesbians or what not, but much more is accepted. I feel more at home. I can be more excitable, especially in French which is a volatile language and I'm a volatile person. Here in America I always feel that people are looking askance—there goes May in one of her fugues again."

To me her house was a mingling of Europe and America, a kind of escape from the peculiar harshness of each. May Sarton agreed it represented an escape. "Everything in my house is old, comes from my family, and has a meaning. It's not a matter of having the right things on the walls. It's all connected with my parents' life or with people who come to the house, all woven together. That's why this house is very alive."

> What has been plaited cannot be unplaited—
> Only the strands grow richer with each loss
> And memory makes kings and queens of us.
>
> [*SP,* p. 73]

I have always enjoyed May Sarton's memoirs—almost more than her other works. In them her parents and their generation seem so vital, so magic as the world must seem in childhood. I asked her about the Belgium and England of her earlier years and later youth. "My mother's family is from England and I was adopted so warmly there—by the Huxleys and Elizabeth Bowen. I don't admire Belgium; I hate the materialism—the food and all that. But the people I knew were not like that. When you say Belgium, what you think of is chocolate and pigs made of marzipan. But the landscape and the winds and the clouds skimming over the low lands is the thing that moves me to tears. And no other landscape does that to me. It's atavistic. We left when I was two, but when we went back in 1918 or 1919 and I was seven, the boat went up the river—I had no memory of it but I started to cry."

These images remain, these classic landscapes
That lie, immense and quiet behind eyes
Enlarged by love to think only in shapes
That compass time and frame the changing skies.
Triumph of arch, of spire, triumph of trees,
The pure perspective, the poignant formal scene.

[*SP,* p. 40]

"I've made roots here, but not with people."

Pain can make a whole winter bright,
Like fever, force us to live deep and hard,
Betrayal focus in a peculiar light
All we have ever dreamed or known or heard,
And from great shocks we do recover.

[*SP,* p. 92]

Note

1. The poems in the text are taken from *Selected Poems of May Sarton* (New York: Norton, 1978) and *Halfway to Silence* (New York: Norton, 1980). These collections are referred to in the text as *SP* and *HS*.

Erica Jong

Interviewed by
Wendy Martin

In Erica Jong's first novel, Fear of Flying, *which appeared in 1973 and became an international best-seller, the heroine, Isadora Wing, struggles with her conflicting needs for dependency and autonomy; the plot expressed the central problem in the lives of many readers. Commenting on the novel's extraordinary success, Jong observed that she had captured the* zeitgeist *of the decade. Indeed, Isadora Wing's efforts to transcend her fear of being alone and free reflects the lifestyle of many contemporary women.*

Jong began her writing career as a poet. Before publishing her first novel, she wrote two volumes of poetry, Fruits and Vegetables *(1971) and* Half-Lives *(1973). Several of her early poems focus on the special concerns of the woman poet. For example, in "The Commandments," Jong writes:*

> If a woman wants to be a poet,
> She should run backwards circling the volcano;
> She should feel for the moment along her faults;
> She should not get a Ph.D in seismography.[1]

A third collection of poems, Loveroot, *was published in 1975; the poems in this volume are often humorous and again express the preoccupations of the female artist. For example, "Menstruation in May" provides insouciant commentary on female sexuality and creativity:*

The word is flesh, I say
still unconvinced

The flesh is flesh
The word is on its own.[2]

Thoughts on the woman poet's relationship to her muse are found in "Insomnia and Poetry":

Sweet muse
With bitter milk,
I have lain
between your breasts,
put my ear
    to your sea-shell whispering navel,
& strained the salty marshes
of your sex
between my milk teeth.
There I've slept at last,
my teeming head
against your rocking thighs.[3]

"Dear Colette," one of the most effective poems in the volume, presents a vivid portrait of the French writer:

Dear Colette,
I only want to thank you.

for your eyes ringed
with bluest paint like bruises,
for your hair gathering sparks
like brush fire,
for your hands which never willingly
let go,
for your years, your child, your lovers,
all your books . . . [4]

Jong's second novel, How to Save Your Own Life, *was published in 1977; like* Fear of Flying, *it was widely read. This novel explores the issues of love and sexuality as well as the significance of commitment. Another collection of poems,* At the Edge of the Body, *appeared in 1979. One of the most lyrical poems in this volume, "People Who Live," is a meditation on death:*

> They know that the house of flesh
> is only a sandcastle
> built on the shore,
> that skin breaks
> under the waves
> like sand under the soles
> of the first walker on the beach
> when the tide recedes."[5]

Erica Jong's most recent novel, Fanny, Being the True History of the Adventures of Fanny Hackabout-Jones *(1980), is an epistolary novel in the style of Richardson and Fielding. This work has been highly praised by critics for its command of the history as well as the manners and morals of the eighteenth century. Like the heroes of episodic novels, Fanny leads a life of high adventure in which she meets witches, highwaymen, and pirates, as well as seducers and patrons. At the same time, the book is a mother's legacy to her daughter:*

> . . . I wisht to write a Book for you, which you might
> press unto your bosom as you roam'd the World,
> consult in Times of Need, and which I dreamt should
> bring you safely Home — to Merriman, your
> Birthright, and to me.[6]

Erica Jong was born in New York City and graduated from Barnard College and Columbia University. She now lives in Connecticut with Jonathan Fast and their daughter Molly. This interview contains a discussion of her life as a writer and as a mother and explores the conflicts and challenges of combining work and motherhood.

Wendy Martin: What authors have influenced you the most?
Erica Jong: It's so hard to answer that question. We tend to digest our influences, absorb them and bury them. When you are a young writer, at the beginning of your career, it's easier to determine the influences of other writers. For example, when I was in graduate school, I thought Nabokov was the cleverest writer in the world; now I find him rather arch and overclever and I tend to admire more the writers who have more heart and passion. One eats up influences in the course of one's career. Nabokov was a sad muse for me because he reinforced a tendency to be artificial, and

it was precisely artifice that I didn't need. In fact, it's precisely artifice that most writers don't need, especially those who come out of graduate school. I have had to rebel against my earlier influences. In poetry today, there is no woman writer who has not been liberated, whose work has not been opened up, by the so-called confessional poets like Lowell and Plath and Sexton — particularly the latter two who showed women that we could write honestly about being women, that we could write honestly about the madness of families. *Now* I think that Muriel Rukeyser was a better poet than either Plath or Sexton, and a grander poet in the tradition of Whitman. The people who influenced me as a young writer are not those I necessarily admire most now.

Wendy Martin: Would you say that you are more committed to poetry than fiction, or to both genres equally? Which do you prefer?

Erica Jong: Until the time I wrote *Fanny* (which is the first book in which I really combined the novelist with the poet — that is, the person who tells a story with the person who is besotted with language), until *Fanny*, I would have said that I was a poet who fell accidentally into writing novels and who accidentally became successful at it and was able to make a living at it. Until *Fanny*, I would have said I felt myself more truly a poet than a novelist, I felt that my true being was in poetry. Now I feel much more equally divided; I feel that I *am* a novelist, that I write novels not just to support my poetry habit, but because there is something about the *process* of writing a novel that is incredibly revealing about one's own motivations. It's a kind of meditation, a tremendous revelation of self. I don't think I could live without writing novels any more; it's become an inner need.

W.M.:   The novel, then, gives you the luxury of a large space in which to work?

E.J.:   The poem tends to be an epiphany, a kind of revelation; the novel deals with societies, families, the interweaving of lives, the way fate tricks people and reveals their lives quite differently than they had anticipated. The poem can't do that. The epic poem could do that, but we don't write epics any more.

W.M.:   There are many writers who started out in another art form. Henry James wanted to be a painter, I believe. Several writers have found to their surprise that they achieve a higher level of craftsmanship in drama rather than poetry, for example. So, as you write, you discover what your true skills are, or your preferences change.

E.J.:   But I really enjoy writing poetry and think I can do things in poetry that I can't do in fiction. I don't think it's necessary to choose a major; life is not a graduate school.

W.M.:   You used the word enjoy; you "enjoy writing poetry." Would you say that is true in writing your novels as well, that there is a sense of pleasure as you are actually writing and thinking through the plot and the character development?

E.J.:   It's infinitely pleasurable. There is nothing like being right in the middle of a book which has taken over your life. I don't think I ever enjoyed writing anything as much as I enjoyed writing *Fanny*. I was completely absorbed into a vanished world, or into creating a world that never existed. It was even more enjoyable than writing about the contemporary world. It was almost as if time were suspended for me. I can't say that everyday novel writing is pleasurable. Most mornings you get up and you go to your desk and struggle to get the pen to the paper. It's often difficult getting started in the morning; nine days out of ten, you feel that what you are doing is dull, but one day out of ten, you seem to be straddling the spheres and hurtling through space and everything seems easy and magical and wonderful. Nonetheless, even on the days when it is hard, it is such an absorbing way to spend one's life that I guess it is a happy thing to be doing.

W.M.:   Even with the anxieties that go along with the creation of the characters and the fear that your audience won't like it? How do you manage to balance those kinds of concerns?

E.J.:   I center myself into the writing of the novel; I try to suspend all thoughts of audience or critics. I try to pretend that I'm writing just for myself, for my own ears, and my own eyes. This was much easier to do when I wrote my first novel than it is now. When I wrote *Fear of Flying*, I could always say, it will never be published. I will go back and get my Ph.D. I just have to do this for myself because I don't want to be one of those people who never finishes a novel — like that awful character in one of Camus' books who is always *starting* a novel but can't get past the first sentence; I had to do it for myself.

W.M.:   Now that you know that you have an audience and you know that your work will be reviewed, are you able to circumvent whatever anxieties that causes by focusing on what interests you? What you would like to read about if you were the ideal reader? How do you keep yourself centered?

E.J.:   That is the hardest problem I face; it's the hardest problem that *any* well-known writer faces—especially in mid-career. That is precisely what's wrong with being very well known. I try to purify myself of all expectation when I write. I try to remember that one doesn't know one's audience; one discovers an audience. Maybe there are certain romance writers like Rosemary Rodgers or Barbara Cartland who can determine the demographics of their readers, but with other kinds of books, you never know the audience; it may be immense. *Fear of Flying* was thought to be a very uncommercial book when it was first published in hardcover. It was all I could do to get the publisher to do anything for it, to advertise it, to publicize it. They were very wrong. The paperback publisher believed that it could reach an enormous audience and promoted it as if it were very commercial—as indeed it proved to be. But all of that is hindsight; nobody knew that at the time of initial publication. I was always arguing with my hardcover publisher to take another ad.

W.M.:   So writing and publishing a novel is a process of discovery. You are never quite sure how it is all going to turn out, if any given novel is going to be well received, or even who is going to read it.

E.J.:   You don't really know. The only guarantee you have, and it's not an absolute one, is that as you develop a name, people want to read your next book. And even that doesn't always work. Well-known writers have sometimes published books that haven't sold.

W.M.:   Would you describe your study to me? Is your desk filled with a jungle of books and papers or is everything in neat, alphabetically arranged piles?

E.J.:   I work with piles of books, stacks of papers, but I can find everything. My desk is the size of a kitchen counter; it's L-shaped and on it there are books; galleys; poems in progress; a novel in progress, sometimes two; letters, often unanswered. It's not chaotic, however.

W.M.:   So there's a sense of lots of ongoing projects, and the desk accommodates all of them. Describe your average writing day. Do you have any rituals that you begin your writing day with? Any superstitious habits that you have? Do you keep a predictable schedule? Do your writing hours vary?

E.J.:   In the last few years I have tried to work normal hours; that is, from nine A.M. to two or three o'clock—perhaps with a short break for lunch to see my daughter Molly. I unplug the phone; but that hasn't always been the case with me. I have only tried to normalize my life since Molly was born and because Jon works those hours; it's nice to be able to goof off with Molly in the afternoons. Often, I still do my best writing at night. When I'm beginning a new work, or writing poems, I'll often get up at night to write from midnight to three. When a book is coming out and there are constant phone calls and demands, and when I have numerous public appearances to make, so that my writing schedule is really interrupted, I have to be ferocious and unplug the telephone. When things get really hectic, I work at night when everybody is asleep. *Fanny* was written from about nine to three every day. Toward the end of the novel I worked *all* the time; the book became absorbing. But generally I try to keep the old school hours.

W.M.:   Does it help to live away from Manhattan? Has your move to the country been beneficial in terms of giving you a little more time, or making you feel more relaxed? Do you think a more pastoral or natural setting is helpful? Or do you care?

E.J.:   I couldn't have written the last novel in New York. There is no way I could have written *Fanny* there.

W.M.:   Why not?

E.J.:   Time is too fragmented in New York. In order to write about the eighteenth century, I had to create a world in which people lolled about in great country houses and read two-thousand-page novels.

W.M.:   Then you needed open space to project your own imaginative interpretation of the period. The insistent modern rhythms of Manhattan would make it more difficult to sustain a vision of a different time. But trees, after all, are constant through time and enable you to make those imaginative leaps a little more easily.

E.J.:   I found that to be true even though Connecticut isn't really like England.

W.M.:   Do you think that living in the country will continue to be helpful? Is living in Connecticut an aesthetic choice or is it a practical choice?

E.J.:   I think my life is easier here. I can divide my days between writing days and days when I go to the city and do other things. I can't live in New York and have lunch with people and also write. I'm too gregarious; I like people; I like parties. When I live in the city, I never get any work done.

W.M.:   How has Molly affected your writing habits? Do you have to discipline yourself more carefully?

E.J.:   It has been such a transformation — the needs of the child change so much from infancy to toddlerhood to little girl-dom. It was a constant change for the first three years of her life. I think that I was very afraid that having a child would make it difficult for me to work. I was hell-bent on showing everyone that having a child wasn't going to impede my progress; in fact, showing the internalized mother in me that it wasn't going to impede my progress. But what I didn't count on was my own attachment to Molly. When you wait until your mid-thirties to have a child, your desire to be with the child becomes stronger. The other things that you might do with your time seem less important. I've allowed myself to slack off in my schedule recently because I want to be with her more. I went racing through *Fanny* while I was pregnant and then nursing the baby. I conceived Molly while I was in the middle of writing a book which was written in the form of a letter of a mother to her daughter. The pregnancy was the prophecy of the book confirmed.

W.M.:   Do you ever feel a conflict between your nurturing and achieving selves? Do you find that you are with Molly and thinking of the next chapter or that you are in your study thinking about the plot but wishing that you were with her?

E.J.:   There is a pull. I try to arrange it so that Molly goes off to the beach with her nanny when the weather is good or off to a playgroup or to nursery school or someplace where she has an activity during the hours I'm working; it's much better for her and much better for me. When she's off doing something appropriate for her age and I'm at home, I don't feel tugged.

W.M.:   You are able to claim the space for your work.

E.J.:   Because of Molly, we've now built another study that is completely separate from the house. Nevertheless, when I hear the car pull into the driveway when the nanny brings her home for lunch, I run downstairs to be with her. I *want* to be there; if it's a break in my concentration, so be it.

W.M.:   Would you want Molly to be a writer?

E.J.:   I don't know. I'd want her to be what she wants to be. I must say that the household I've created here is not very different from the household I grew up in. My mother and grandfather were both painters; they worked at home, and I grew up watching them paint. In many respects, that's what Jon and I have here. We both work at home and our child is being raised in that atmosphere. Maybe that is one of the things that makes a person able to function as a free-lance, creative worker. Jon grew up with a father who was a free-lance writer and a mother who was a painter; both of them worked at home.

W.M.:   So having parents as models for independent work who don't make the distinction between work at the office and at home was important to you. Many children never see their parents working and therefore work is a mystifying activity. Children who actually see the parent working have a great advantage; for them, work is not a magical event but is something that is done day in and day out.

E.J.:   I have made it a point to let Molly into my study and to take her on book tours when I can. I took her on the book tour for *Fanny* and she sat with me in B. Dalton all over the country while I signed books. She has been with me to a lot of my professional activities. I think it has been good for her.

W.M.:   When Molly grows up, she will undoubtedly realize that you were very widely read, and that some of your novels were quite controversial and that the erotic aspects were considered startling, even shocking to some. How do you feel about this? What do you think her response will be?

E.J.:   It's hard to say. Many writers' children avoid reading their parents work and don't want to think of their parents as novelists but as parents. One's family is really the worst audience for one's work always because they are too close to it and can't read it dispassionately. That goes for parents, siblings, and children as far as I can tell. And who knows what the world will be like then; maybe Molly will go through a prudish phase and resent me because she thinks I'm very notorious, maybe she'll go through a phase where she won't want to read my work at all. When she becomes an adult, I hope she'll be inspired by my own particular odyssey in the way that I've come to be inspired by my grandfather's odyssey, my mother's odyssey, my father's odyssey. However, I didn't appreciate them until my thirties; when I was younger I rebelled against them. Perhaps she'll repeat my pattern, and it may even be a healthy pattern.

W.M.:   What do you think about the reviews of your work that are critical of the explicit sexuality in your writing? Do you feel vulnerable? Do you feel that your erotic passages expose you to criticism and attacks?

E.J.:   It's not only the eroticism that exposes me to attacks; women writers have *always* been treated quite differently than men writers. If they write about sex, they are treated like sluts or tramps. It goes back to Aphra Benn and any women who were presumptuous enough to use that masculine object the pen — which was seen as representative of the penis — God only knows why. Women writers were always considered insufferable and presumptuous, and that hasn't really changed. The amazing thing is that ten years of feminism hasn't changed it either. We live in a very puritanical and very sexist country. Sometimes responses to my novels have been so abysmally stupid, so gossipy, so prurient, so ignorant, that I wouldn't dignify most of them with the word criticism. Abroad, I tend to get a much more intelligent press.

W.M.:   Even so, it must take extraordinary courage to write so openly and frankly about sexual subjects. Very few women have ever done it. Didn't you have some inner doubts that you had to overcome before you felt free to write about sex?

E.J.:   With every book that I write I have to go through that process again. Every time I start something new, I realize my fears and insecurities. I feel very vulnerable; that's why I've used the ploy of pretending that I'm not writing for publication but for myself. It's been very hard. Most women writers haven't written freely because of their need for approval. Most women artists want more approval than men, yet they get far less. That is the situation of the woman artist, it seems to me; as women, we are socialized to need approval, but we are often treated with great savagery. I feel frightened when it's time to publish a book. But during the time I'm writing, I try not to live in the future. I try to write as honestly as I can without concern about running the gauntlet of reviews.

W.M.:   When your work is described as popular, as appealing to a wide audience, what is your reaction?

E.J.:   It used to be defensive. When *Fear of Flying* was published, I was defensive about its popularity. I had won awards as a poet, had wanted to get a Ph.D. in English, and felt contempt for best-sellers as people do in that academic environment. But as the years went on, and I met my readers, I began to consider it a great *privilege* to be read. For example, when I met college students who had copies of my book that were dog-eared and underlined and stained with coffee, I was thrilled. It then seemed to me that the people who criticized me because I was popular were envious; they would have given their eyeteeth to be read. On one of my first book tours, I met blackjack dealers in Reno who never read a novel until *Fear of Flying*. The distinction between literary and popular is made by academics and it's a tragedy for literature in this country. The notion that novels that are popular cannot be good is quite idiotic, and it's killing the novel. If you go back to the major British novelists, they were all popular.

W.M.:   What do you think that the relationship of art and politics is? Is art political or is it beyond politics?

E.J.:   Art should not be political in the narrow sense; it would be a great mistake for a writer to serve a particular party line, to write for the Communist Party (as certain writers did in the thirties), or to write about the latest phase of feminism. For example, many women of the sixties and seventies turned out propagandistic novels — they were too worried about toeing the correct party line from a feminist point of view. In an integral way, one is political, but politics is expressed through individual experience, not through polemic. The novel *does* reflect political concerns — racism, sexism — but as the individual feels them, not in a doctrinaire way. A critic should never say, "I didn't like your novel because Isadora Wing doesn't leave her husband and go to a feminist commune" — that kind of criticism is absurd.

W.M.: Do you think that art changes life? Does art create social change? Can it? Should it?

E.J.: It can in a deep way, in a way that is not easily seen. I think that poets *are* the unacknowledged legislators; they *do* change society — not in a decade but over the centuries. You see this process clearly in the eighteenth century; there were tracts about the abolition of slavery, gradually the movement gained force, but it took a lot of time before there was any degree of consciousness of civil rights. Novels do augment this process and change what people think.

W.M.: What do you think the concerns of women novelists will be in the 1980s? If we can say that the exploration of self, autonomy, the meaning and reassessment of relationships were central to the sixties and seventies, are there parallel concerns for the eighties?

E.J.: A lot of the women novelists seem to be running scared right now. In America we treat social movements as if they were a branch of show business; right now, feminism is not considered good box office. Black liberation and Indian rights are no longer good box office. Instead of thinking of these movements as expressions of the need for social justice, we tend to ask, "Will it play?" I think a lot of women are running away from the confessional or autobiographical novel because it has been attacked as "narcissistic." There is a great casting about for the style of the eighties, but it hasn't been found yet. Off the top of my head, I think there will be a lot of books about motherhood written from the perspective of women who combine both work and childrearing. And a lot of novels about families — and what family really means.

W.M.: For many years, raising children was thought to be an inferior activity. Now women are looking at their experience and saying, "Yes, but this is what we do, and it's important."

E.J.: Many of the baby boom generation (like me) who postponed having babies until their thirties are looking at their experience in a different way than their mothers did. They are looking at the experience from the perspective of having had careers. Also we are seeing motherhood not as an either/or proposition. You have to reject motherhood if you see it as giving up your brain; but if you see it as a phase of life, it becomes intriguing. I think that's the way our generation is looking at it. And I expect that it will lead to new sorts of novels about the family, novels in which we make sense of this century and our families' odysseys through it, reappraised in the light of this century's coming to an end.

Notes

1. *Fruits and Vegetables* (New York: Holt, Rinehart and Winston, 1971), p. 43.
2. *Loveroot* (New York: Holt, Rinehart and Winston, 1975), p. 73.
3. Ibid., p. 100.
4. Ibid., p. 12.
5. *At the Edge of the Body* (New York: Holt, Rinehart and Winston, 1979), p. 92.
6. *Fanny, Being the True History of the Adventures of Fanny Hackabout-Jones* (New York: Holt, Rinehart and Winston, 1980), p. 495. [Hereafter identified as *Fanny* following excerpt in text.]

Grace Paley

Interviewed by
Ruth Perry

Grace Paley, writer, mother, peace activist, is the author of two collections of short stories: The Little Disturbances of Man: Stories of Women and Men at Love *(New York: Doubleday, 1959 [second publication New York: Viking, 1968]) and* Enormous Changes at the Last Minute *(New York: Farrar, Straus & Giroux, 1974), and numerous poems and short pieces. She is fifty-eight years old and married to Robert Nichols, also a writer. They live in New York City, where Grace Paley was born and raised. She teaches a course in fiction writing at Sarah Lawrence College.*

This interview began in Paley's long, cluttered apartment in the West Village and continued the next day, uptown at our mutual friend Sally Goodman's place, to provide against the steady stream of phone calls and visitors that flow through Grace's life. One of the interpolated visits the first day, which I have omitted here, was from Karen, one of Grace's friends, who was arrested at the Women's Pentagon Action on November 17, 1981, and who told us about her ten-day incarceration in Alderson prison.

Ruth Perry: How come you're never angry in your stories? I always admire your generosity, the fact that you never add to the stock of anger and hate in the world. The forbearance of the character Faith towards her friend Anne on the train ride home, in the story *Friends,* seems to me a good instance of that.

Grace Paley: I think what happens is humor sometimes takes the place of anger, and it may even subvert it. You know, in a way, sometimes there should be more anger, and there's humor instead.

Ruth Perry: What *do* you get angry at?

Grace Paley: Well, we did this antiwar action at the Pentagon, and we did it in four stages: Mourning, Rage, Empowering, Defiance. We began by walking through Arlington Cemetery, and when we came to the Pentagon, we walked in mourning, with a little bit of black on us here and there. And then we built this cemetery under the Pentagon for all our dead. I planted the Unknown Woman, and then there were these others. Karen Silkwood. The four little girls of Birmingham. There were many, forty or fifty of them. Someone made a marker for Jeannie Goldschmidt. All our dead. And then after that, from Mourning, they were going to go into Anger, and I didn't know how they were going to do it. But somebody walked the red puppet through, the giant red puppet from the Bread and Puppet Theater, made by Amy Trompeter, and *there* was anger. Everybody blew up. What I mean to say is, I was *very* angry. That's what I feel angry about. We just screamed at the building. People had been crying before, and now we were just bawling, just screaming at the building, telling it off, banging pots and pans, and hollering. People from the building peered out and then would go back and someone else would come out. And then after that was Empowering, when women really got all around the Pentagon, really did it, surrounded it. And then Defiance. Defiance. — We blocked the doors — then — the arrests. One hundred fifty people were arrested.

R.P.:   One hundred fifty. Did they pay bail?

G.P.:   No. Some of them didn't pay bail at all. You know Vera Williams? She's down in Alderson for thirty days. They put leg shackles on all the women. You know, you people from Massachusetts should send something to Tip O'Neill. Call those guys and say that you know those women on the peace action were sent down in leg chains on the very same day that the Ku Klux Klan men were acquitted of murder.

After being arrested in the November 17 Pentagon action for civil disobedience, Paley thought she might have to spend some time in jail.

R.P.:   Have you spent a lot of time in jail?

G.P.:   No. No, I haven't really. I've been arrested a number of times, I've spent a couple of nights here and there but only once did I spend a week. I've never spent more than a week. If I spent thirty days that would be a lot for me. Still — I believe in the stubbornness of civil disobedience and I'm not afraid of it.

I remember one May Day demonstration. In 1971. Still wartime. We were arrested and we were in this big, sort of football field. Barbara Deming and I were walking around, arm in arm. We had been arrested together. It was very cold. Everybody was finding someone to walk very close to. Later on, one person wasn't enough, we would try to get into groups that huddled: fifteen. But at that point, Barbara and I were walking arm in arm and it was a pretty messy place, because that was the year they arrested thirteen or fourteen thousand people, just picking them up off the street, and then they didn't know what the hell to do with them. At that point we were in a football field. Later, we were put inside a stadium. And so we were walking around, arm in arm, talking to each other, and then congresspeople came in to see what was going on, and Bella Abzug came over to talk to us. She and I had always had these disagreements about the electoral work and what you can call action, direct action, and we would talk to each other about this. So she came over and she looked at me and Barbara walking arm in arm. She asked how we were. She was a congresswoman at this time. She was worried about us. We said we were all right. And then she said, "Well, I guess you're where you want to be and I'm where I want to be." And we laughed, we all laughed together.

And I want to say about Bella that she was at this Women's Pentagon demonstration. She came, she walked with everybody, she didn't look for any limelight of any kind. She just sort of walked, and begged me not to get arrested. Again, she said she thought it was a waste of time. I could do more outside. But she really was just a part of the action. That's what we wanted all of our leaders to be, just a part of the women's action.

R.P.: Do you think that women's politics are different from standard politics, less hierarchical?

G.P.: I don't believe we could have done this in a mixed group, with men.

R.P.: Why not?

G.P.: Well, first of all, a lot of the ritual stuff, the ideas, came from women who had been thinking about this way of acting for a long time.

R.P.: Well, I can see wearing black and wailing as imitating eons of Mediterranean women.

G.P.: Yeah, but I mean the whole four-phased ritual. I'll tell you another thing that struck me. Lots of young kids, young women, were arrested, and they were not well treated. They were not miserably treated, but they were grabbed and pushed and pulled. I mean, those marshals are all big, and some of them are mean and some of them nice, but pulling and pushing, you know. And those kids were all crying. And I was thinking how wonderful. And I reminded them, I said, you know, if you had twenty guys like the kind you go out with, those of you who go out with guys, if you had any of those guys here, you know they would not be able to cry? They would be tense, they would be maybe tough, they would have had in fact all kinds of feelings. But they wouldn't be bawling in anger and pain and frustration like you kids are. So I think that that freedom to feel is one of the things that this demonstration was about. The marshals kept saying to us, "You going to let these girls keep crying? Aren't you going to tell them to quiet down? You're older, aren't you? Why don't you tell them to quiet down?" And I'd say, "Let them cry, let them cry."

I don't think that in a mixed group they would have been able to do it. There would have been a few guys who would have loved the business of the wailing, guys into co-counseling or something like that. But a lot of the men are not ready, would not have wanted to do that, or would not have liked it.

And I know from my own experiences in school with women and men that there's a whole stratum of women that won't speak up when men are present. Sometimes they're the women who are most men-dependent. It's not just that they're shy, and they may be the most pro-men — but whatever they really are, happens when the men aren't there. And they really need that. They still, right now, need that part for themselves, more so than the really politically developed feminists who can be pretty strong nowadays with a bunch of guys. Although, I've seen plenty of them, when their own man walks into the room, they die. No names.

R.P.:   Have you become freer yourself?

G.P.   Yeah, but I don't know what that has to do with it. I think that in almost any culture the older women really begin to have a certain power. So, I'm getting older, so I really feel freer than I ever felt. I probably will feel even more so. I think some of it comes from being part of a movement but some of it comes really from just getting older and also making my own living.

R.P.:   And yet there aren't many writers — I can only think of you — who have given us images of older, freer women.

G.P.:   Well, it's just because that's where I am and I seem to always be where I am. I mean, I write about other things too, but I look at my early stories of women who are suffering the loss of different guys, you know, and I see that people, young people, like them. They seem to refer to them.

R.P.:   You don't relate to those stories any more?

G.P.:   I relate to them a little bit, but I don't . . . I don't deeply.

R.P.:   How do you know when you have a story, the germ that you know is going to work out?

G.P.:   What happens with me and probably other writers as well —something really bugs me for a long, long time and I may write a page or two on it but I don't know what the hell to do next. *Something* is bugging me. That story that you mentioned before, *Friends*, that was after me a long, long time. I had written the first page maybe a year and a half before I wrote the rest of it. I wanted to write about this woman and I wanted to put it in terms of a visit. The visit is invented in the sense that I went to see her pretty much by myself, but I knew that groups of friends had gone to see her at different times. We were all pretty close. In fact, because of the story, one of the women who was with her now thinks that I was there with them, but I wasn't.

But I didn't know what to do with that beginning — it couldn't just be a story about her dying and our visit. I began with "To put us at our ease, to quiet our hearts as she lay dying, our dear friend Selena said, Life after all, has not been an unrelieved horror —you know, I *did* have many wonderful years with her." I wrote that paragraph partly because she really said it, and I never forgot that language. After that, it was really a big problem. Maybe a year later, you know, I was really doing other things. Finishing up some other stories. But I would write things, different parts, not so much about her but different conversations or different small sections. And when I really began to do Anne and her son and the conflicts among the women, I realized that it really wasn't just a story about Selena but it was a story about the end of relationships, or the dying of long friendship. (I hate that word relationship. I thought I'd never use it but I did. Now I don't have to be mad at other people who do it.) Something about, you know, deep, deep friendships and what they're based on and what happens to them. But, I mean, I didn't know that especially, until . . . in a way I had to make two stories before I could make one. That very often happens. You really don't have a story until you have two stories. It's those two stories working against each other and in connection with each other that make it happen. So I had to have those people visiting her and I had to figure out who they were, I had to make them up. They are pretty much, you know, based roughly on several women but they're reinvented in different ways.

R.P.:   That story ends by proclaiming your right to "report on these private deaths and the conditions of our lifelong attachments." Are the two stories that play off against each other always from private life in that way?

G.P.:   No. I have two stories in a story that I wrote about China. One was about an event that happened in China where people didn't want to be photographed and the other was an event that happened in this country on the lower east side where people didn't want to be photographed. That story about what happened in China, it interested me as a story to tell, you know, to gab about, to tell everyone who said, tell us about China. But it didn't interest me as a real hard-written story until I thought about the other story and decided to tell them together. One just didn't seem enough. It could have been a little article, a small journalistic thing. But it didn't really interest me until I began to realize what it was about and how it needed the other one.

R.P.:   What do you think has made women's private lives of interest? The movement? The women's movement?

G.P.:   Yeah, I think that's true.

R.P.:   Has the women's movement changed your sense of writing and relationships?

G.P.:   No. I mean, it informed me a lot because there's a lot of writing about this stuff. I can't say I had a high political consciousness when I began to write in the fifties. I was just part of what was happening. I myself couldn't have said, oh, I'm this feminist or I'm this or I'm that. The lives of these women, really apart from their men, just happened to interest me. Nobody is not part of their time. So I was part of what was really happening, and without knowing it—especially in the women's movement. The women's movement began to develop out of the left and a lot of things I did were supported by it. I think until then that women's daily lives, domestic lives were not considered interesting and their friendships were just considered, you know . . . gabby girlfriends.

R.P.:   Have you always had women friends?

G.P.:   Yes. I can't understand this baloney about women not having friends. In my mother's family they were aunts or they were half-aunts or they were cousins. They were related partly but a lot of them weren't related, you know. I have a little piece reprinted in one issue of *Feminist Studies. Esquire* wanted me to do something . . . they were doing a thing on that . . . "Mom and Apple Pie" . . . so I wrote a piece called "Other Mothers" and really it was about this whole bunch of aunts and the women in our streets who used to sit and talk to each other in the afternoons, and the aunts in my house and my grandmother. Although it's true my father was *the* figure in the house. As my sister said yesterday, "Poppa would say 'Where's the salt?' and both aunts, my mother, and my grandmother would leap up to get it first." But "Other Mothers" was about being raised by lots of women. My mother died when I was twenty-one or twenty-two, some bad time, but I had really parted from her earlier because she was very, very sick.

R.P.:   For how long was she very sick?

G.P.:   Oh, she began to get sick when I was about thirteen.

R.P.:   Was she at home sick? Or in the hospital sick?

G.P.:   Well, she was in the hospital some, but mostly she was home. She was there and I was home, too, and I was bad to her. She had good years in the middle of all that. My father was a doctor. She had cancer.

R.P.:   What do you mean bad to her?

G.P.:   I was bad at school, I ran around with boys—that was natural—a girl *could* get pregnant and then what? You know, nothing serious. But she knew she was going to die, really, and she trembled for me. She really knew she wouldn't live and she just couldn't bear the direction I was obviously going in.

R.P.:   Which was?

G.P.:   Badness. Trouble. I had an older sister, also, who was part of that "other mothers."

R.P.:   How much older?

G.P.:   Fourteen years.

R.P.:   Fourteen years older? Oh, she really is another mother.

G.P.:   Yeah. And she is now. Jeannie, my Jeannie. So that I have a lot of these close female relationships and I always had a best friend, a couple of friends. Although my special closeness to grown-up women really happened when I had kids.

R.P.:   That's all those wonderful playground stories.

G.P.:   Yeah.

R.P.:   Do you remember which were the first stories you wrote or the first story you published? Did those subjects differ from the subjects you later picked up?

G.P.:   I didn't write stories until I wrote those stories in *Little Disturbances.* I wrote poetry. I have found one or two stories that I did write *long* before — in my teens. The first story I wrote was a very tiny story about a boy who had to stop taking piano lessons with his teacher, a story Jess told me. I didn't know why I began it. All I could think of was that piano teacher. So it was really about this piano teacher who was losing a pupil. It was a very Joycean thing. It was four pages.

R.P.:   What do you mean Joycean?

G.P.:   It was just very spare already. Epiphanous. Then I wrote one more story sometime in there, again with a kid in it, about a Spanish superintendent's kid and the other kids on the block — written around the period of big garbage cans and coal heat. A kid by accident rolled a can off and killed somebody, and they were looking for him. It was very simple. Neither of them was too successful. And then the next stories I wrote were "The Contest" and "Goodbye and Good Luck" and the other stories in the first book [*The Little Disturbances of Man*]. Those I wrote in my thirties.

R.P.:   Then the incident in "A Conversation with my Father," that incident where your father says to you, "Can't you write stories like you used to? Like Chekhov?" That's all made up?

G.P.:   Yeah — the specific occasion's invented.

R.P.:   About writing?

G.P.:   He'd yell at me about it. He really kept me honest.

R.P.:   What do you mean by that?

G.P.:   I never even thought about it before. In some ways he was very good, but in some ways I could never have done anything until I got away from him. My father was wonderful. He was humorous, he was brilliant, he was sophisticated, but he really was . . . I wrote a poem one day in which my daughter says to me, "Ma, how come Grandpa didn't become great or famous. He seems like a famous man." And I say, "Well, he couldn't because really he was just a ghetto Jew." And my brother says, "What?" My sister says, "I don't believe that." And my son says, "Jew talk." I remember my first shocks in seeing him talking to Protestants or Catholics or whatever, somebody who wasn't Jewish. He really would go shy. I would be embarrassed a little, you know. He would have an aspect of deference. He didn't have it with, say, the Italian supers; he didn't have it with them. But there were certain "class" things that he revealed. He was after all considered a middle-class doctor — he did very well, he was much loved, and had a house in the country and a big car — but basically he was really a working-class man and he really never got over that kind of deference to Anglo-Saxonism. He worried a lot whether we would make fools of ourselves. But in order to really write, in order to be any kind of an artist, one of the things you have to be willing is to really be a total jackass and to really face that. So he inhibited my freedom to be a total jackass, you know? And he would say, you'll make a fool of yourself. My sister's under the impression he only said it to her, but I've assured her he said it to me many times. My mother was not too worried about that. She had more natural self-respect.

R.P.: How many children were there?

G.P.: Three. I was the youngest by a lot. He had been a poor boy when the other two were born. He was in his early twenties, going to medical school, working in a photography shop, bringing relatives over from Russia. He had been a poor, harassed young fellow from Chrystie Street when his two older children were born — children from his real working-class time. My mother was a retoucher. My brother and sister remember that she used to wear a black hood against the light retouching plates. But when I was born he was already a very successful doctor, and free to take some pleasure at least.

R.P.: And did he encourage your writing?

G.P.: Well, everybody did when I was little, sure. You know, they were very verbal people so they liked their little kid to be a writer.

R.P.: Was your father a literary man? In your stories he's always reading and quoting someone like Pushkin.

G.P.: He was a big reader. You know, from that time, that generation of immigrants that came in 1904-1905: they were all big readers. He learned English by reading Dickens — I mean, that's how he learned English. And he really had certain very elegant ways. He had the Russian lack of articles — even in his late 80s, he would forget an article; Russians do that. But he had very elegant ways of speaking or writing or talking. He wrote letters to me or to Nora — to my daughter — "Dearest Darling Daughter." He was a very fine writer. He wrote stories I tried to publish.

R.P.: And your mother?

G.P.: My mother didn't write to us much. I mean, she wrote me little letters, you know . . . and I'm sure that she was the one who made him write the letters — "You sit down and write to Grace," or something. You know? I have very few letters from her. But I never felt she did not love me. We just had too much conflict. You know, when someone worries about you all the time it gives you the feeling that you're going to end up god-knows-where. You try to step away from that anxiety.

R.P.: Was it mostly sexual anxiety on her part?

G.P.: Yes. A lot of it that I'd get pregnant or something.

R.P.: That is one of the main liabilities for women, no question about it.

G.P.: Well, she was very anxious about that and I, of course, I was outraged by it when I was sixteen, seventeen, and younger — fifteen.

R.P.: Were your parents political?

G.P.: Yes, they were Socialists. He had been in prison before he ever came here, in Siberia, and she had been sent into exile, to Germany.

R.P.: Why was he in Siberia?

G.P.: He was a Socialist. You didn't have to do much. And then the Czar had a son, so they were both released. Everybody under twenty-one was released.

R.P.: When you grew up, were there meetings at home? Did they write pamphlets on the kitchen table?

G.P.: No, my sister and brother grew up very unpolitical. They grew up with this immigrant man and woman who were bringing over relatives, who were expanding their financial horizons, who were trying to make money, who were trying to be successful, who were getting a good record player, and who were collecting first-class classical records, and who wanted their children to play the piano and tennis, both of which my sister and brother do to this day and they're in their seventies. They play the piano. In fact, my brother Vic just beat Bob and Duncan [Paley's husband and his son] at tennis and Vic's seventy-three. They wanted me to do these things but I didn't want to. They already had kids who were doing it. So I was harassed about it — and they [her sister and brother] became a doctor and a teacher. I also think my father and mother did not talk to them so much about their youth as to me, because then they were in *their* youth. I mean, they were in their twenties and thirties. I remember when I wanted to go to Europe or something and I said, "How come you never went back there?" And my mother said, "Europe, I never want to see it again. Why do you want to go to Europe? Are you crazy?"

R.P.: Where did you go to school? New York public schools all the way through?

G.P.: Sure.

R.P.: And did you go to Hunter?

G.P.: I went to Hunter College for one year and then I had to leave. Then about two years later I went to NYU for another year. And that was it altogether.

R.P.: How come? How come you quit?

G.P.: I would get up to the door of the school and I just couldn't go in.

R.P.: Because it was boring to you? Or didn't teach you what you wanted to know?

G.P.: I didn't think. I just couldn't bring myself to go in. I did take a writing class at NYU but I was married by then and Jess went overseas. I was about twenty-two and I took this writing class and the guy threw me out immediately. I started to write a story. It had some bad words in it, you know. He threw me out. I mean he said, "Get out." I wasn't even mad at him. I just thought: I guess I don't know how to do this, I guess I'd better stick to poetry. I knew all the poets — their poems — when I was quite young.

R.P.: Who were your favorites?

G.P.: I loved Robinson Jeffers. I loved Auden, I loved H.D.

R.P.: Did you read women writers because they were women writers?

G.P.: No. I thought about Woolf. Woolf meant something to me. *Mrs. Dalloway*, I remember, was the first thing I read. I loved the style; I was very interested in the style. And I was interested in Gertrude Stein. I loved the stories. They had drama in them. And I loved Jeffers and them all; I knew those poets, all of them. In high school — and I was young in high school, I was fifteen years when I graduated — I remember I had all the anthologies and I had just found these books that my aunt had given me. There was Christina Rossetti and Edna St. Vincent Millay, too. I knew them. I was in love a lot, so I really read what they had to say.

R.P.: And were you reading them just yourself? Or did you have buddies? Or teachers, even?

G.P.: In high school I remember I had a couple of friends, and I used to read poems. But I never talked in class. It was very hard — my school life became very hard early. In the middle of a class one of my friends went up to the teacher and said, very softly, "Grace knows all these poems by heart but she doesn't want to speak." Something nobody believed of me at this point. I really went through a long silence. Not an artistic silence, but a big mouth-silence.

R.P.: Did you have any teachers who meant something to you?

G.P.: Well, I had two high school teachers who found out I liked poems. I really loved those women. I talked to them. And also they shared my politics. A boyfriend of theirs had been killed in Spain; that was the time of the Civil War. I lived a lot of politics then, during high school.

R.P.: And that really came from your parents.

G.P.: Well, it came really from the romanticism I felt about them. I felt they were heroic, and I loved that stuff a lot. Of course by that time, they were very angry with me. I remember, as a child, in high school or even into junior high, we were wearing peace, something, armbands. This was in high school. The principal said, "As long as you wear those armbands, you can't come to class." Little by little different kids would take off their armbands, with chagrin, broken down. I knew that I would never, never, never take off that armband. It really was romantic, you know. And I remember my cousin came down the aisle of the auditorium of the school and said, "Gracie, you better come up, you better come up because you know your mother's sick, you know you're making her sicker. You're going to kill her, you know that?" So, you know, that was the general feeling.

R.P.:   Do you remember who you first showed your stuff to?

G.P.:   Well, I was writing, at that time, with an English accent. I was already kicked out of school, so I was about seventeen and was working in offices, because my parents wanted me to go to secretarial school. I was working in an office. And Auden came to this country and he was teaching at the New School. So I went and took the course. It was my life, my whole life in that Thursday night. I mean, it was on Thursday night. I came down to this fascinating place, and I sat in the back of this class with those other two hundred people, and he talked. I couldn't understand him. Not only was there this very strong accent, but he used to lisp a great deal. It was *impossible.* But I didn't miss a class. I really loved those poems, those early poems of his—and also Spender. That gang: Spender, Isherwood, MacNiece. So then he said, "Do you want me to look at your poems?" A couple of weeks later I went to see him and he said to me, "Do you usually use words like trousers?" —I had never said anything but pants in my whole life—"Yeah," I said, "I do . . . sometimes." "And what about this word?" he said. "Subaltern." You know, like a sublieutenant. This was the beginning of the war. "Subaltern." "Well, once in a while." That was my first experience. I was writing in English-English.

I tell that story to lots of classes, when we talk about imitation. You have to, you know. If you don't imitate anybody strong you are usually just imitating some dead center. But I did not show stuff to people. I mean, when I was a young kid, about fourteen, in the country, I had three or four girlfriends who used to sit upstairs in the attic and I'd read things I had written. But I have worked alone almost all of my writing life. I always tell people that it takes too long that way. There has to be privacy but there ought to be community.

R.P.:   When did you drop your English voice and start writing in this voice?

G.P.:   Let's say academic voice . . . When I wrote stories. When I wrote "The Contest," that's the first story I wrote. You know the expression "breakthrough" is funny, but it's really a break-through. Break through what? You know. Break through my own deafness. Break through my own literary falseness.

R.P.:   Did you know immediately that it was right?

G.P.:   Yeah. It all sounded like I'd heard it before. It was so familiar suddenly — I mean I didn't know it was good, I didn't think, "Oh, at last I'm good," I just thought, "How come all of a sudden I can do something?"

R.P.:   It was easier?

G.P.:   It wasn't just that. I really had gone to school to all my reading and writing for a long time, and really to short story writers, to poets, and to literature in general. So, I didn't have problems with cutting out a lot of stuff, you know, the business of shaping and form and cutting. It's as though I somehow knew how to do it.

R.P.:   That's the quality of your stuff. It's so incredibly dense.

G.P.:   I really had been living my life with a kind of literary ear. But the ear was far too literary. I mean it's no accident that I wrote in high-class English. Actually when I went home that night, I understood everything. My heart sort of failed me.

R.P.:   After Auden said that?

G.P.:   Yeah. But somehow or other in fiction I was able to really hear with this other ear — to use both. I mean the kind of traditional educated literary knowledge of this ear and *then* the ear that really had been just listening to people all the time, and used the language of place and time.

When you write poetry — this is a false definition, but you'll see what I mean when I say it — when people write poetry it's really talking to the world, especially in poetry of our time. It's got to change, but a lot of the poetry of our time says "I . . ."

R.P.:   Why has it got to change? Because it's so egocentric?

G.P.:   Yeah. Hopefully, more and more they write less and less like that. But that's one definition: poetry is addressing the world and fiction is getting the world to talk to you. When I was able to get into somebody else's voice, when I was able to speak in other people's voices, I found my own. Until then I did not have a voice that could tell a story.

R.P.:   Well, your stories certainly give the sense of an ongoing world.

Part of this is because characters from one reappear in another. What do you think accounts for that quality of denseness?

G.P.:   My feeling about trying to tell a lot. It has to be interesting to me too, you know. And I'm really not interested in writing things out and out and out. If I do, they're boring to me. It's not that I write so densely to begin with. In general, I write more and take stuff out; I realize I said too much. I think about connections.

R.P.:   That's part of that early poetry training . . .

G.P.:   I think it's the poetry. I think it's really going to school for that economy. At Sarah Lawrence, my students in fiction writing, I make them write poetry. They've got to write a couple of poems at the start.

R.P.:   Is it possible to teach people to write? Do those kids leave your class having learned something or other?

G.P.:   They must have learned something. I figure they learned as much as somebody leaving a biology class or a history class. If they're learners they'll learn. And if they're not learners they won't. I mean, that's true of any course that you take. The whole point about teaching is to keep them from following false gods of all kinds and so on, and to be honorable, and to love the language. I think all teaching is moral. I mean, where it's not, we really have — in the sciences where it's not moral, or in the social sciences where it's not moral — we have the great economists of the corporate-loving right and the inventors of neutron bombs and things like that. And also in literature you have a cold, conventional prose. It's only where you really feel a moral obligation towards literature and language that there's any hope.

Part of what you do as a teacher of writing is to weed out the kids who think they want to be writers, but really aren't interested in subject matter or aren't bugged by anything. You know, nobody needs them, nobody needs them to keep working. Lots of things for them to do. And there are sometimes kids who are not, you would say, not that gifted if you wanted to put it that way — but are really driven powerfully to speak, to write, and to investigate. In some ways they might be less brilliant than those other people. (I once talked about how one of my jobs was to keep a class of smart kids dumb.) But they so much want to understand. *They* are the kids who really are going to do the work.

R.P.:   One of the striking things about your stories is the sympathy with which you handle male characters. There is a great deal of empathy, for instance, when characterizing males in sexual attitudes, lust or tenderness. You must have had good male friends when you were young.

G.P.:   One of the things that made me write was that I was terribly upset about men. "The Contest" was the first thing I wrote. I was trying to think about what was going on between men and women, and the only way I could think about it was to write from [a man's] point of view. So I tried to get into this guy's head, and I wrote the story from his point of view, with him telling the story. I remember writing that first line — really it was the first line I wrote: "Up early or late, it never matters, the day gets away from me." I was trying to see women, in those stories, as men saw them, but I was trying not to see them the way I want to be seen, not to put it all in the best *or* worst light. I had been living in the army camps with Jess. It was wartime. And I loved being with the guys. I was just like any typical sort of tomboy young person; I loved being with the boys. The war was happening and it was happening to the men mostly. It was terrible. None of them wanted to go; I didn't know one boy who wanted to go. I worked as a secretary, an office worker, and I lived with the office workers. I didn't live with him, you know. I'd eat supper with him every night. I'd go on guard duty with him sometimes. It was a lot of fun — I mean I really had a good time. It wasn't until I was in my really late twenties and had these two little kids, and got over that little fence of thirty to the other side, that I really began to see they weren't so much my buddies as I thought. And it took me really a long time. And then I felt bad about it. I really did. And I began to try to figure out — to get in their heads, to try a little bit to see with their eyes. In fact there's a line in "Goodbye and Good Luck", which is the second story I wrote, where she tries to talk to him and she says to him, "A man's life is something I don't truly see." She says, in other words, "What do you want? What do you want here? What do you want to do? What do you have in mind?" She's asking him, you know. And she says "A man's life is something I don't truly see."

And at the same time I was getting closer and closer to women's lives through the kids. Specifically women without men. So those two things were happening.

R.P.:   What has been the relation of your writing to the rest of your life? To marriage and family, for instance. And has that changed in time? Does it fluctuate or has it got a steady place?

G.P.:   Well, I think at different times in my life it's probably been different things. I was a writer from a very early age. I feel that I would have done that no matter what else. Suppose I didn't have kids or anything like that, I might have written a longer book — that's the only thing that I can think.

When the boy I was married to went overseas, [writing] was

probably the most important thing in my life. I've looked at some of those poems of that very short period in my early twenties and I can see that I was making a good deal of progress. But when he came back, I have to say that *that* was the most important part of my life. He was very gloomy, and I was very concerned about him and what was happening to him. We were all into a lot of psychology at the time. It seems to me that, had we looked at it historically instead of so psychologically, there would have been better solutions. I wouldn't have regarded it as something personal. As against me. As against his mother. As against himself. I mean I would have seen he was a young soldier coming back from three years away from his life, and not knowing what to do next. Having a degree in physics and not being able to go on with it, having to make changes. Now it seems to me that anyone who has been in the army for three years and been subject to the authority of the army, that life, would be depressed and gloomy, would be suffering a lot. It would have helped to have seen the thing historically. This is an insight that I've had about that period in the last six months, remembering it back some thirty, thirty-five years ago. But although I never *myself* got tied up in a lot of psychological ideas, it was in the air at the time, and I was part of it, so I thought inside my time. And I generally never have gotten too much away from my own time.

I was also wild about the idea of having children. I loved the idea, and wanted to, as soon as possible. And after some years we did have kids and I enjoyed every bit of it, I must say. I never felt that writing and family life were mutually exclusive. Since I didn't go to school, I never got onto a time line. I didn't have a sense that at a certain age I should do this and at a certain age I should do that. You know?

I have a basic indolence about me which is essential to writing. It really is. Kids now call it space around you. It's thinking time, it's hanging-out time, it's daydreaming time. You know, it's lie-around-the-bed time, it's sitting-like-a-dope-in-your-chair time. And that seems to me essential to any work. Some people will do it just sitting at their desks looking serious, but I don't.

Right now, the problems with this political action of which I'm very much a part are complex, and require imagination. I have anxiety about that. Not guilt but anxiety, because I really feel the world's in the balance. I don't feel essential to the world, to the solution, but I just feel my normal citizenship in this—and the pity of it all. So I just find myself using my days and my mind in a different way.

The three things in my life have been writing, politics, and family. At different times each one has taken over, has been more strong. And when the kids were little, it was really family. I didn't do a lot of politics or stuff. Family of course means children, but it didn't mean my little nuclear family. It meant the life of families, schools, parks, the day-care centers. And that was the point at which I was most interested in those women and what was going on in the park. That was when I really began to think about our lives. I began to write poetry because I was being teased for thinking about all these things. But also that husband of mine at that time, Jess, who didn't like poetry much, would say, "Why don't you write a story sometime? I mean, you know, you have a sense of humor, and you like people and you talk about people all the time, you're always telling stories, why don't you write a story instead of these poems?"

So the family part of life is that without which I would not have had the other part of life. I think I would have eventually begun to use prose just to get the world to speak to me, just to get that to happen. But I probably would have written longer things because . . . that business of the children . . . I mean I don't like giving anything up for anything. I have a terrible greed. I don't like giving up writing for family. I don't like giving up family for writing. I don't like giving up politics to go to my family parties, and I don't like missing my granddaughter just because I have to finish a piece of some kind. I do it all by push; I don't work it out.

R.P.: You don't strike me as being ambitious. Is that right?

G.P.: Yes. I have very low ambition standards. I'm so pleased to have done as well as I've done. I'm amazed, I'm just delighted, it's extraordinary to me that people like those two books and read them, and that when I write something people want to see it. It's really amazing to me.

R.P.: Isn't that particularly female?

G.P.: Well, it may be particularly female, but not so many females feel like that, that I know. It's just that I give a lot of value to other things in my life. *That's it*, you know. Like, a lot of people nowadays don't want to have kids. I wanted to have them at the time more than anything. I would have given up anything — I mean when I had those children. I couldn't believe I'd had them, it was so miraculous to me. I still can't.

R.P.: Men of your age, of course, are more concerned with questions of career and ambition.

G.P.: Oh, they're dying, I mean they are *dying*. There isn't one of them

I know that isn't dying. Maybe I'd feel that way if my books weren't read or something. If I'd written a couple of books and nobody bought them. There's a lot of luck in my situation that I appreciate.

R.P.:   Why do you think you're so popular after twenty years?

G.P.:   It's cumulative you know. In the beginning the stories were not very much distributed. I'd get letters from women saying, "Thank you" and "I know how you feel." And then the stories would go out of print again. Certain editors would reprint the book—Aaron Asher has done that a couple of times. But I don't think it found its own audience for a long time. And then I think little by little it did. That's all.

And then the women's movement happened. And that has supported every woman, not just me. I mean it's brought Meridel LeSueur back to life and literature where she belonged. It's made her old age joyful even. There isn't a woman writer who . . . if they're not grateful to every woman in the world for hearing them, I don't know, they're nuts. We owe this moment in history a lot. We were part of it happening too. I don't think I would have happened if it wasn't on the way. The feeling of women for women was beginning to happen, not just for me, but for a lot of other people far away that I wasn't even seeing. If that hadn't begun to happen, I might have still been writing some academic poems.

R.P.:   Is there a particular age range, do you think, in your audience?

G.P.:   No, I wouldn't say so. It seems general somehow. Kids like it, although they are a different generation. I had a wonderful discussion at City College where a young black girl got up and said, "You know that woman you had in that story, that "Interest in Life", you know her?" I said, "Yeah." She said, "She didn't seem to learn. I mean the way she was waiting for that guy all the time. Did you think she was a hero or something?" I said, "No. I didn't think she was a hero, but she was a woman." The kid says, "Well, I think she was a dope." I said, "That's good. That means your life will be better."

R.P.:   Are you friends with other writers?

G.P.:   I had always shunned literary life. Just the same way that I was afraid of academic life and tried to stay away from it. But now I seem to know many writers. I've been active in PEN and I feel that community. There are people on my block who are writers I'm very fond of, and I'm very close to, friends like Barthelme and Sales and people like that. But I didn't want my everyday life to have anything to do with writers unless *they* were willing to have everyday lives, so to speak. If I can't be friends with them what's the point.

When I go to California, I spend time with Tillie [Olsen]. I mean time, like hours and hours; I stay at her house, we have taken long walks, you know. And I don't have really literary discussions with her. I don't have the knack. I mean we talk a little bit about it, but mostly we talk about women's lives, about different ideas. We have talked recently about language and Mary Daly. I guess that is literary. We've had long talks on that subject. But again I'm really more interested in political life than literary life. So Tillie and I talk about politics, women, the world. And we've done different things in our lives. She'll tell me about the thirties and forties which is terribly interesting to me. And Marge Piercy is very dear to me — a person who puts her life where her mouth is.

R.P.: Do you have any particular friends that you show your work to — stories as they come — besides Bob?

G.P.: Yeah, sometimes my friend Eva in the German department at school, or Sybil [another friend] or — you know. But I do read them to Bob, a lot of stories, when I'm working on them. If he's not in an impatient mood he'll pay attention. But he varies. Sometimes he's very incisive, really helpful, and sometimes some idea hits him and it's exasperating and I'll wish to God I had never said one single, solitary word to him. But that's his character, and I have to make those decisions when to read him stuff and when not to. Sometimes when I finish things, I bring them over to Don [Barthelme]. But that's when it's totally finished. I've sent stuff to Tillie [Olsen] sometimes — stories. I just got one of her infinitesimally printed postcards.

R.P.: Those postage stamp messages.

G.P.: Sometimes I'm so angry I don't read it for a couple of days.

R.P.: You think it's hostile, that teensie-weensie handwriting?

G.P.: It's not hostile, no. But when I write to her I write very big. I try to be an example; I write with enormous letters.

R.P.: What do you think it's about?

G.P.: She told me once that it was that she had very little paper.

R.P.: I've wondered that — if it was economy.

G.P.: I think there's much more to it than that. It could come from a wish to be really looked at seriously — like people who talk softly. You say to them, "Can't you speak louder?" And they say to you, "Why don't you listen?"

R.P.: It has always been a struggle for her to be heard, or just find the time to work. She always talks a lot about incursions on her time, interruptions.

G.P.: Yes, but she allows it. She may be resentful, but she's as bad as me. I know because I stayed with her a couple of times. I mean, anybody who gets phone calls like she does at 11:00 or 12:00 at night from somebody in some city who's in bad trouble and wants to talk to her and has her phone number . . . you know, she's around a lot. I think a lot of what she writes is really for others, she's speaking for other people, and she feels their pain keenly. People really think sometimes that she complains a lot, but she really is speaking for other people, because she herself, as I say, she knows what it means, she knows the cost. But for herself, she does allow it. She has allowed it. And she didn't in all cases have to allow it.

She feels my shortage of time terribly, for instance, and she's ten years older than I am. I'm almost fifty-eight, she's about sixty-seven. And she's put a lot of time into scholarship, which is a generous act. That has taken away from her own personal work. I made a political decision to do politics and she made a decision to do that. And who says we shouldn't? I mean, who the hell is in charge of saying that you shouldn't do that? Either you see life as a whole or you don't. It's a great big ball; everything's in it.

R.P.: Who else, of this whole batch of women writers that the Historical Moment has thrown up, do you like? Who do you read?

G.P.: I love Esther Broner, and I think she's really not known enough. That *Weave of Women* book, that's original. She really just came around from left field and took hold in a different way. It's really very interesting.

R.P.: Are you quicker to buy and read contemporary women writers than men writers? Do you have a special feeling about that?

G.P.: Well, I'm interested. But I have to say that there are certain writers that I can't like. You take something like *The Women's Room* or something like that. Now that book means an awful lot to a lot of women, it really means a lot to them. It's no shit, it's real. So I see it's very important in that way, but I have trouble reading it.

R.P.: Why?

G.P.: I can't get interested in it somehow. I bought it three times — maybe that's why its sales are so good — and tried to read it, but I just couldn't.

R.P.: I know that for myself the thing that I found hard to take is the spirit of victimization that runs through it, the way she gets off on sado-masochism.

G.P.: But the people who read it don't feel that, they feel strengthened by her saying all that. They're strengthened. They say, "Oh, this is how it is for me. This is how we were. This is true."

I'm always interested in what Marge [Piercy] does. I mean we have our differences about several things, and approaches to writing — what and who and how — but she's an amazing woman and a true writer, and she does a tremendous amount of work and is very particular about what she's doing. She's doing a certain kind of chronicling of our time. She has a book called *The High Cost of Living.* I think it's really a wonderful book. It's not well-known. And it's one of her shortest things. I think she thinks she just tossed it off.

Sometimes you come to literature that seems related to your own in some ways, but after you've been writing for a while. And then you feel terribly corroborated. Like Paul's [Goodman] stories, the ones I really love the most, I read them much later, but they made me feel very good about certain things I was doing. Or Babel. Isaac Babel. When I read him, also after many years, I said, "Wow! He had the same Mommy and Daddy I had!" You know? The other writer doesn't so much influence you as have the same historical life that you have, that you come from, the same language structures, talks English the same way — or Russian.

R.P.:   How about writers like Joyce Carol Oates or Didion or even Erica Jong?

G.P.:   Well, with Didion I really just feel moral, political, stylistic differences. People think she's such a great stylist, but I don't. I think she's sentimental. I mean, she doesn't overwrite. She doesn't do that at all. I will say that for her. But I don't like her attitude towards people, you know. I don't think she really illuminates them but darkens them so that we see them less by the time we're through. Maybe in the beginning we see them a little bit but by the end we really don't see them. And I don't think she wants us to. And I think that's a political thing.

R.P.:   How so?

G.P.:   The act of illumination is a political act. That is, the act of saying, "See, this has been in darkness. This life has been unseen, and unknown." Now, to make that decision and say, "I want to illuminate this life" — which is the act of bringing justice into the world a little bit — that's a decision you make. But if you say, "Here's a life that's lying there. Now I'd like to take a rock and slowly cover it," that's a political decision. I think people do that with language all the time. Sentimental language does that. So I think that there's a lot of that happening in her and I think that what you get at the end is sort of a rock, you know.

There's a cynicism in it. Who needs it? I mean sometimes you need it, but right now we don't need it.

R.P.:   Did you ever read *Fear of Flying?*

G.P.:   Well, that's another book that I really read part of several times and couldn't really finish. I thought it could have been done a lot faster and shorter. If she hadn't been so afraid of flying, she could have got there quicker. But again, that book was very important to a lot of women. I respect those facts, when people feel like that. I don't think it's just pure popularity; I don't think it's just that they were sold.

R.P.:   You mean hype and advertising?

G.P.:   I don't think it was just hype. I don't think the success of *The Women's Room* or *Fear of Flying* was just hype. I think maybe things they did after that could have been. I don't know but there could have been big advances which the publishers had to cover with a lot of hype. That's possible. But those books, those two books, really were very important for lots of women.

R.P.:   How do you account for the fact that there haven't been great women writers?

G.P.:   Oh, there really *have* been, haven't there? What do you mean? What's great? Great goes up and goes down. Shakespeare wasn't great for a period there. Then he got great, then he got greater, then he got greatless, then he got greater again. I think the main thing is that women have been bringing up children. They haven't had work of their own of any kind — I mean why should they, if they weren't great anythings, why would they be great writers? I mean they weren't great mercantilists either. They weren't great capitalists murdering the world. They were not in public life. And writing is an extremely public art. I just look at it from the other side. I say how amazing that Jane Austen wrote and was appreciated. There were plenty of women writing, different kinds of women, you know. George Eliot. How come they did it? How come Mrs. Gaskell really did it? How come Charlotte Perkins Gilman did it? How brave George Sand was! How come Kate Chopin did it? That's the way I look at it, in an entirely different way. The miracle is what women have done in this world. It's miraculous that they did the work they did on such a high level. Where did they do it? And wearing the clothes they were wearing? How could they even sit to do it? I mean they must have loosened something. But if they were in the family parlor, they couldn't loosen everything.

© *Susan Mullally Weil*

Maya Angelou

Interviewed by
Cheryl Wall

In 1969 Maya Angelou published I Know Why the Caged Bird Sings *(New York: Random House), a memoir of her girlhood in Stamps, Arkansas, and San Francisco, California. The book quickly became a contemporary classic. More fully than any writer before her, Angelou laid bare the pain of the black girl's coming of age. She counted the costs of being doubly disenfranchised in a society that denied black women's beauty and worth. Yet interlaced with the sadness was joy, conveyed in the spiritual peace and power of her grandmother and in the élan with which her mother lived her life. Ultimately,* Caged Bird *is a song of triumph: the young Maya's triumph over self-hatred, the triumph of the black communities that sustained themselves despite the white world's racism, and the triumph of a writer whose love and command of language are profound.*

Three subsequent volumes, Gather Together in My Name *(New York: Random House, 1974),* Singin', Swingin', and Gettin' Merry Like Christmas *(New York: Random House, 1976), and* The Heart of a Woman *(New York: Random House, 1981) document Angelou's womanhood. They record her successful careers as dancer, singer, actress, and civil rights administrator as well as her extensive travels in Africa and Europe. With the last book she has chronicled her life and times up until the early 1960s.*

Over the last decade she has published three books of poetry, Just Give Me a Cool Drink of Water 'fore I Diiie *(New York: Random House, 1971),* Oh Pray My Wings Are Gonna Fit Me Well *(New York: Random House, 1975), and* And Still I Rise *(New York: Random House, 1978). In addition she has written several movie and television scripts, including the adaptation of* Caged Bird.

Yet, it is on her four memoirs that her literary reputation mainly rests. In the following pages, Angelou discusses the art of autobiography —her sources and her method. Her claims for the originality of her form prove unexpectedly convincing. Hers is an audacious experiment. While the results have been uneven, the best of her books —like The Heart of a Woman *—blend the individual and the collective, the witty and the wise, in an inimitable style. Angelou subscribes fully to her own dictum: "A good autobiographer seems to write about herself and is in fact writing about the temper of the times."*

Assisted by Wendy Kuppermann, I interviewed Maya Angelou in New York in December, 1981. Angelou's calendar was characteristically full. She was to fly to Ghana the next day to arrange for a course, "African Culture and Its Impact on the West," she will offer next fall at Wake Forest University where she has accepted a professorship. Work in progress includes a book of narrative, free-verse poems that signal a new direction for her poetry. Although it will be a year or two before she starts writing the next one, she promises that more volumes of her memoir will be forthcoming.

Cheryl Wall: You have just published *The Heart of a Woman*, the fourth volume of an autobiography that began with *I Know Why the Caged Bird Sings* in 1969. Yet from passages in all four books, a reader may infer that Maya Angelou is a private person. If this inference is correct, how difficult has it been to relinquish that privacy in order to share your experiences with readers?

Maya Angelou: The difficulty is met early on by making a choice. I made a choice to become an autobiographer. You know the saying, "You make your bed and do whatever you want in it." I find autobiography as a form little used. I know no serious writer in the United States who has chosen to use autobiography as the vehicle for his or her most serious work. So as a form, it has few precedents. But I decided to use it. Now, I made that choice, I ain't got no choice. Unless I found it totally untenable —if it was running me totally mad or if I lost the magic —then that would be a different matter. I would start to look at fiction or go back to plays. But having said I'm going to write autobiography as literature and to write history as literature, then I have made that agreement with myself and my work and I can't be less than honest about it. So I have to tell private things, first to remember them and then to so enchant myself that I'm back there in that time.

Cheryl Wall: I love teaching *Caged Bird* because the voice of the child from the very beginning is so authentic. I understand that as a part of the

PBS television series, "Creativity," you returned to Stamps and once there, you said, "became twelve years old again." Did you revisit the scenes of your childhood before writing that book? How did you reawaken that part of your past?

Maya Angelou: It's a kind of enchantment. It's a scary one, whether it was in that book or in *Gather Together in My Name.* I go to work everyday about 6:30 in the morning. I keep a hotel room and I go to the same room each day, and it takes about a half hour to shuffle off the external coil and all that. Before I go — it's like a trip in a time machine — my concern, my hesitation in fact, is that I won't be able to come out. It is truly strange. But to write it so that the reader is there and *thinks* he's making it up, to make the reader believe that she is the one who is doing that, or is the one to whom it is being done, you have to be there in the place. Ohhh!

C.W.: Can you elaborate on the process? When you have finished for the day, is it easy then, or is it possible to put the past aside, to leave it in the hotel room?

M.A.: I always leave no earlier than 12:30, even when the work is going poorly; if the work is going well, I'll stay until 1:30. Then I leave the hotel and go shopping for my food. And *that's* real! And I'm six foot tall and my face is somewhat known. In a little town (and I always manage to live in small towns), people will have maybe the day before or week before seen me on the Merv Griffin show, but since I operate in the town I'm not a celebrity from whom people feel separate. So people see me and they say, "Hello, Miss Angelou. I saw you on the so and so." But they have also seen me in the gardening shop and in the old folks home and playing with children, so I'm kind of a celebrity with honor. But that means that when I come out of that hotel room and go to the market, suddenly my feet get the familiarity of the place. I'm encouraged back into the time in which I live. And it's real again.

Then I go home and have a drink or two or however many and prepare dinner. I love to cook. I am a cook. I write, cook, and drive. Those are my accomplishments.

S.W.: All of which you started early.

M.A.: That's true, too true. After I've put dinner on and showered, then I read the work. So by 4:30 or 5 o'clock in the afternoon, I read what I have written that day. I start then to cut extraneous "ands," "ifs," "toos," "fors," "buts," "howevers" — all those out! Any repetition of description, out. Just cut, cut, cut. And then I leave it and set the table and sit down to dinner. And about nine o'clock I pick up the work again, now with all those cuts, and look at it again and start making marginal notes. And I'm finished with the yellow pad. The next morning I take a fresh yellow pad and go out and start the thing all over again. And I do that five days a week.

In about a month, when I've got stacks of yellow pads, I will pull all the pages off and put them in order and I will take one day to read it all. Then I start to write again. As I write it the second time, I see how cavalier I have been with the language, with the craft, so I try to make that one really clean, hot, terse. And then when I've finished that, I go back to work. But at least in the period, I'm not doing that going down inside and it's a lot like a vacation in a way.

C.W.:   How long does the entire process take, for instance with this last book?

M.A.:   About a year and eight months.

C.W.:   Autobiographies by black women have been exceedingly rare, and to my knowledge, none of the few before yours has probed personal experience very deeply. Why and how did you select the form?

M.A.:   The form is intriguing. Maybe third, certainly half into *Caged Bird*, I realized that a good autobiographer (whatever that means and I don't know what that means *yet* —I'm learning the form. I am molding the form and the form is molding me. That's the truth of it.), a good autobiographer seems to write about herself and is in fact writing about the temper of the times. A good one is writing history from one person's viewpoint. So that a good one brings the reader into a historical event as if the reader was standing there, bridled the horse for Paul Revere, joined Dred Scott, actually was there. What I'm trying to do is very ambitious, because I am trying, I hope, to lay a foundation for a form. And I know it's ambitious, it's egomaniacal. I know all that, I don't mind. There it is. I mean, I do mind; I'd love to be nice and sweet and loved by everyone, but there it is.

There are writers now and coming who will develop that form. It is important to remember how new the novel as a form is. So somebody in the next twenty, thirty, five years, or next year will write autobiography going through the door I have opened, or cracked anyway, and really show us what that form can be. One has to see it as stemming from the slave narrative and developing into a new American literary form. It's ambitious, I told you, it's ambitious.

M.A.:   Oh, yes. Not just for my art, but for the pantheon of moral values: how to act, how to behave, how to interact. By the time I left

Momma, I knew what was right and what wasn't. I have a painting now by Phoebe Beasley called *Sister Fannie's Funeral*. It depicts women sitting on fold-up chairs, and it reminds me of all the women in my grandmother's prayer-meeting group. There's one empty chair that for me is Momma's. Whenever I have a debate within myself about right action, I just sit down and look at that and think now, what would Momma say? So, morals and generosity, good things, I believe I got at Momma's lap.

C.W.:   Your grandmother and her teachings seem always to have been an anchor. Many black children coming of age today don't have that link to their past; is there anything that can replace it?

M.A.:   Nothing. I see nothing. It's tragic. There is no substitute for parental and/or family love. And by love, I do not in any way mean indulgence. I mean love . . . that quality so strong it holds the earth on its axis. The child needs that carrying over of wisdom from the family to the child directly, and there is no substitute. Society cannot do it, despite the 1984 concepts of Big Brother and a larger society caring for a child and imbuing the child with values. One needs it from someone to whom one is physically attached.

C.W.:   That whole theme of the maternal figure is apparent in the work of many black women writers and white women as well. That leads me to wonder, is there a community of writers of which you feel a part —Afro-American writers, women writers, particular individual writers?

M.A.:   That's a question . . . I'm a member of the community of writers, serious writers; I suppose much like a drug addict is a member of a community. I know what it costs to write . . . as soon as that is so, one is part of that community.

I'm part of the Afro-American writing community, because that is so. I'm writing out of my own background, but it is also the background of Toni Morrison, Toni Cade Bambara, Nikki Giovanni, Carolyn Rodgers, Jayne Cortez. All the black women who are writing today and who have written in the past: we write out of the same pot.

C.W.:   I know that the title of *Caged Bird* is taken from a poem by Paul Laurence Dunbar. Does the new book's title allude to the poem by Georgia Douglas Johnson, the poet of the Harlem Renaissance?

M.A.:   It certainly does. "The heart of a woman goes forth with the dawn . . ." I love that woman. I have *Bronze* [Johnson's second book, published in 1922]. It's in my nightstand. I will not put it even in my own private bookcases, let alone in the library. It's in my nightstand and there it will stay.

C.W.: How long have you known of her work?

M.A.: Since I was a very young person. I love Anne Spencer too. So different . . . born a year apart . . . but so different.

C.W.: Many Afro-American writers cite music as a primary influence on their work. References to music recur in your prose and poetry. In fact, you begin *Singin', Swingin', and Gettin' Merry Like Christmas* with the statement: "Music was my refuge." Do you believe Afro-American music in particular has shaped your work as well as your life?

M.A.: So much. I listen for the rhythm in everything I write, in prose or poetry. And the rhythms I use are very much like the blues and the spirituals. So that more often than not they are in 3/4 or 4/4 time. For example: [she reads from *The Heart of a Woman*] "The drive to the airport was an adventure in motoring and a lesson in conversational dissembling" [p. 76]. "His clear tenor floated up over the heads of the already-irate passengers. The haunting beauty of the melody must have quelled some of the irritation, because no one asked Liam to shut up" [p. 77]. "It seemed to me that I washed, scrubbed, mopped, dusted and waxed thoroughly every other day. Vus was particular. He checked on my progress. Sometimes he would pull the sofa away from the wall to see if possibly . . ." [p. 141]. It is *always* there, wherever; it seems to me that there is the rhythm. And the melody of the piece, I work very hard for that melody.

    A young woman told me that I had it easy because I have the art which Graham Greene has of making writing, a complex thing, seem so simple. So I said yes, it's hard work, and she replied, yes, but you have the art. But [to paraphrase Hemingway] "easy reading is damned hard writing."

C.W.: Until I read *The Heart of a Woman*, I had not realized how very much involved you had been with the civil rights movement. In this book you really capture the incredible sense of momentum, the vitality, and the hope. How important were those experiences as catalysts for your art?

M.A.: I suppose it's so important for me in my life that it must come through in the work. Despite living in the middle of murk, I am an optimist. It is *contrived* optimism; it is not pollyanna. I have to really work very hard to find that flare of a kitchen match in a hurricane and claim it, shelter it, praise it. Very important. The challenge to hope in a hopeless time is a part of our history. And I take it for myself personally, for me, Maya. I believe somewhere just beyond my knowing now, there is knowing and I shall know. *This* I shall overcome. There is a light, no larger than a pinhead, but I shall know. When I say I take it personally, I take that tradition of hoping against hope, which is the tradition of black Americans, for myself.

C.W.: That may perhaps be defined as a spiritual quality. Do you see your writing as political as well as spiritual?

M.A.: Well, yes. In the large sense, in that everything is political. If something I write encourages one person to save her life, then that is a political act. I wrote *Gather Together in My Name* — the most painful book until *The Heart of a Woman*. In the book I had to admit, confess; I had to talk about prostitution, and it was painful. I talked to my son, my mother, my brother, and my husband, and they said, "Tell it." I called the book *Gather Together in My Name*, because so many people lie to young people. They say, "I have no skeletons in my closet. Why, when I was young I always obeyed." And they lie like everything. So I thought all those people could gather together in my name. I would tell it.

I had a lot of really ugly things happen as a result right after the book's publication. Then I arrived in Cleveland, Ohio, and I was doing a signing in a large department store. Maybe one hundred fifty people were in line. Suddenly I looked and there were black fingers and long fingernails that had curved over in the mandarin style. And I looked to follow those up and the woman had a wig down to here, a miniskirt, a fake-fur minicoat, which had been dirtied — it might have been white once — false eyelashes out to there. She was about eighteen, maybe twenty. She leaned over and said, "Lady, I wanna tell you something, you even give me goddamn hope." If she was the only person . . . The encouragement is: you may encounter defeats, but you must not be defeated.

C.W.: Apart from your grandmother, can you identify what gave you that belief?

M.A.: My mom, my mom is outrageous. And I'm a Christian or trying to be. I'm very religious. I try to live what I understand a Christian life to be. It's my nature to try to be larger than what I appear to be, and that's a religious yearning.

C.W.: Although all your books give insight into a quintessentially female experience, *The Heart of a Woman* seems to explore the most explicitly feminist themes. For example, your treatment of single motherhood and the portrayal of your marriage to a South African freedom fighter. Has the feminist movement influenced your reflections on your past?

M.A.:   No. I am a feminist, I am black, I am a human being. Now those three things are circumstances, as you look at the forces behind them, over which I have no control. I was born as a human being, born as a black, and born as a female. Other things I may deal with, my Americanness for example, or I may shift political loyalties. But, these three things I *am*. It is embarrassing, in fact insulting, for a woman to be asked if she's a feminist, or a human, if he's a humanist, or a black if he's black inside. It goes with the territory. It is embarrassing for a woman to hear another woman say, "I am not a feminist." What do you mean?! Who do you side with?

The book is about a woman's heart, about surviving and being done down, surviving and being done down. If I were a man, I hope I would have the presence of mind to write "The Heart of a Man" and the courage to do so. But I have to talk about what I see, what I see as a black woman. I have to speak with my own voice.

C.W.:   One of the most moving passages in *The Heart of a Woman* involves a conversation among women married to African freedom fighters. You and the other women — most of whom are African, one of whom is West Indian — forge a powerful common bond. Is there a broader lesson in that scene; are there bonds linking black women on several continents?

M.A.:   If you have the luck to encounter women who will tell. That experience had to do in particular with African women. In Egypt, through the poet Hanifa Fahty, I met a group of Egyptian women involved with the Arab Women's League. They were at once struggling against the larger oppressor, colonialism, and against a history of masculine oppression from their own men. I understood it. Unfortunately. I would like to say it's such a rare occurrence that it was exotic; unfortunately, I understood it clearly. It would be the same if I were in Vietnam and talked to the Vietnamese women. It is one of the internationally pervasive problems, and women today are choosing to take courage as their banner. Courage is the most important virtue because without it you can't practice any of the other virtues with consistency.

C.W.:   Do you see alliances being formed among women in various societies who are facing like problems?

M.A.:   I haven't seen them yet. It must happen. But you have to consider that certain movements are very new. One of the many American problems built into the fabric of the country, beyond the woven-in lie of "we hold these truths to be self-evident that all men are created equal," beyond the inherent lie that the people who were writing those statements owned other human beings, one of the serious problems has been looking at the idea of freedom as every human being's inherent right. Just by being born, you've got it. It is ridiculous as a concept. It is wishful, wistful, and foolish. Freedom and justice for a group of animals is a dream to work toward. It is not on every corner waiting to be picked up with the Sunday paper.

As a species we have not evolved much beyond the conceiving of the idea. Now that's fabulous, and for that we need to salute ourselves. But to say that we have conceived the idea and the next moment it is in our laps is ridiculous. We have to work diligently, courageously, without ceasing, to bring this thing into being. It is still in the mind. It will take us hundreds of years, if not thousands, to actually bring it so that we can see it. We need to tell our children that this quality which has been conceived of most recently by human beings is something wonderful to work for. And your children's children and your children's children's children and everybody will be working to pull this order out of disorder.

C.W.: The joy then is in the struggle.

M.A.: Yes, yes, then you begin to understand that you love the process. The process has as its final end the realization, but you fall in love with the process.

We are new as a species. We just got here yesterday. The reptiles were on this little ball of spit and sand 300 million years. We just grew an opposing thumb — I think it was last week — and grew it by trying to pick up something to beat somebody down.

The terrifying irony is that we live such a short time. And it takes so long for an idea to be realized. Can you imagine the first person who had these fingers and saw this little nub growing and said, "Got the nub, pretty soon we're going to be able to hold on to the whole hatchet?" Not to know that it was to be another three million years. You see?

Thomas Wolfe calls us "dupes of time and moths of gravity." We're like fireflies — lighted by an idea and hardly any time to work at it. Certainly no time if we don't realize it has to be worked for. At least in this brief span, we can try to come to grips with how large an idea it is and how much work it demands, and try to pass it on to one other person. That's more than some people can achieve in a lifetime.

Marilyn French

Interviewed by
Janet Todd

The room was elegant, expensive, overlooking Central Park; the interview formal, businesslike. It was my first meeting with Marilyn French and there was no intimacy or memories in our conversation.

I asked her about her first published book—on James Joyce's *Ulysses*—and why she chose to write on this topic. "It was my doctoral dissertation," she replied, "and it was a problem. I love Joyce, but if you're going to write a dissertation on something that's been written on a thousand times it's no fun; yet nobody had ever really been able to talk about what lies at the center of *Ulysses* or even seriously addressed the styles. It was interesting and something that I could get done in a year." She'd been planning another topic: images in sixteenth- and seventeenth-century literature, on which she is working now. She has just finished the first volume on Shakespeare. "It's taken me five years," she laughed, "so I'm very glad I didn't do that for a dissertation." Joyce, Marilyn French felt, had not influenced her thematically. "I was much too old when I read him seriously," she explained. "I'd already written five novels, finished two, although nothing was published. I think I learned things about writing from Joyce—about control of tone and so forth." She paused a moment. "But I think I'd already set out to learn that for myself long before as well. I got *more* knowledge from Joyce."

I wondered, however, whether she had not reacted *against* Joyce in one instance, since he seemed through guides to distance himself more and more from his characters, where she had moved nearer to hers between her two novels *The Women's Room* and *The Bleeding Heart*. No, she thought not, and she brought up the subject that intruded more than once into our conversation: the direct expression of emotion. "We live in a culture in which emotion is really looked down on," she pointed out. "If a work of art deals with human emotion as we feel it — which *Ulysses* does — it's going to be called sentimental and I think Joyce was extremely sentimental and knew it." Yet Joyce did not write a sentimental book — he was also very ironic. "If you look at *Dubliners*, his first book, it's cold eye and cold heart, except maybe a little bit in 'The Dead'; then his next book is all emotion — Stephen Daedalus — really a little bit much and I think he really was split between those things. Because he was so brilliant, he came up with an absolutely unique and brilliant form. But it has nothing to do with me — it's from a different world and a different gender. It's from a different attitude. I have serious respect for emotion."

Emotion came up again when we spoke of Marilyn French's best-known novel *The Women's Room,* which repeatedly details the extreme feelings of women. "I do think emotion is more accessible to women than men," she declared. "They're more aware of it. When men start to feel something, they immediately turn on the TV set and watch a ball game, go out and argue at a political meeting, get rid of their emotions there so they don't have to be aware they have them. I don't think men are less emotional than women. I think they're simply less aware of their emotion, and, when it does come out, it comes out in a very childish way — fourteen-year-old temper tantrums, or five-year-old jealousies." She waited a moment, then added emphatically, "I think women are terribly emotional. Emotion is as much a part of one's self as mind or body."

I admitted to being uncomfortable with the amount of feeling presented in *The Bleeding Heart*, where the main character Dolores manages to remain vulnerable and undeadened after a life of emoting and horrors. Marilyn French grew impatient. "That's just why she's in pain — because she isn't deadened. She wouldn't be a very interesting character if she was." She went on to note the similarity between *The Women's Room* and *The Bleeding Heart* in the progression from the statement of intense emotion to an investigation of its cause. She hadn't, she confessed, been aware of that progression in the first book, but in the second she was perfectly so. "A friend told me that when she first started to read the narrative sections [that took place] on the beach in *The Women's Room*, she thought that the amount of emotion, the sense of tragedy that this narrative had was way out of whack with what you knew. But by the time you'd finished reading the whole book, you realized that the emotions were nowhere near what they could have been."

I had read the reviews of Marilyn French's two novels. Most were favorable, but several had made very similar criticisms; that she loaded her books with extraneous detail which buried her themes and characters and, even more frequently, that she was too polemical, and — related to this — that her characters became exemplars, not living people. She seemed a little irritated by these charges. To the first she replied, "I don't think that this has been made as a negative criticism. I don't think the detail is ever extraneous. When that's been mentioned, it's been positive. I think that is how you create the texture of a day, a life, or an event. I don't think you do it by describing it in large historical terms. It seems to me that is the very technique of poetry."

The second criticism, she admitted, bothered her to the point that she thought about it; yet she felt it unjust. "When you're working against a current, against the very basic assumptions of the culture, if you don't get polemical, if you don't say what you have to say, no one is going to hear you. People can say, 'But that's damaging to your literature.' And maybe they're right but maybe they're not right. The one writer who means more to me than *any* other writer — and always has from the very first time I ever wrote a book a lot of years ago — was Dostoevsky. I recently reread *The Brothers Karamazov* and found he was writing on the other side of the same question I'm writing about. He's talking about patriarchy, he's talking about what does God mean and if a thing called God exists, why. And that huge district attorney's summing-up of the case against Mitya is essentially a defense of a primal being which is masculine, narrow-minded, insists on certain sexual and moral codes, and so forth. I never thought of that as polemical."

Perhaps it's English literature, especially the modern novel that has tended to avoid the polemical, I began. I meant this as English-language literature, but in her answer Marilyn French focused on the country. "English literature isn't polemical, especially the present day. The writers most popular in England today, like Drabble and Weldon, Bernice Rubens and Kingsley Amis, John Osborne and so forth . . ." She dismissed them expressively. "It's all very light. It's hesitant ever to be thought that it takes itself seriously." Certainly, I interrupted, it values the ironic mode. "Yes, ironic, a little distanced from things, never making large claims. That's not the tradition of English literature. Eliot, Dickens, Shakespeare . . ." As for her characters being exemplars, she considered that "most people do feel those characters and they live on the page. I think Mira of *The Women's Room* lives on the page — to the point where everyone thinks it's direct autobiography. What I say to them is 'Have you ever read an autobiography that was dead all the way through?' Because God knows there are lots of them. And the reason my books feel autobiographical and alive is that I'm a good writer, not because these things are real. I think the characters are very much alive."

We turned then to specific topics from Marilyn French's books. I felt she caught wonderfully the sense of loneliness in life, remembering the passage referring to Dolores's past in *The Bleeding Heart* — how she would "sigh her way to bed alone and be there feeling it, the pain that was with her always, so familiar and accustomed a guest that it could be ignored for long stretches. It shuffled around her house in bed-room slippers, and made its own tea."

"I don't see how you can really know who you are unless you allow yourself to be alone, which means feeling lonely on occasion. Loneliness is as much a part of life as togetherness . . . I think that, if you're alone and you've been with people and there's a lot of loneliness going on and they go home and the door shuts, the sense of loneliness at that moment is really overwhelming; but within an hour you're perfectly contented. I think you could have exactly the same sense of loneliness if there was a body in the bed."

Which brought us to sexuality, so much a male topic in literature. I asked her how she managed to write about sex, since sexual vocabulary is overwhelmingly male. (One critic unkindly said that her sex scenes are copies from old semipornographic models.) "It's difficult to write a sex scene, period," she replied. "I think there's really only one in *The Women's Room* and in *The Bleeding Heart* there aren't many." She hesitated. "There are, but I use metaphors from other areas rather than bodily terms to describe the sex. I thought about it — I mean I had to think about how to depict female experience itself, which has traditionally been rendered by men as a surrender to, a vanquishing, a giving into, a being taken, and so forth. But I think that's not necessarily how women feel. I try to find the right language when there isn't any other. A lot of things in our experience have no words."

From sexuality we moved to marriage, which, *The Bleeding Heart* suggests, is an outdated and hopeless institution. Marilyn French thought it just a word. "You enter a marriage with the expectations of your period. Some people are entering marriage nowadays with a different set of expectations from people of my generation. I think for us, it's finished. I know one or two marriages of people in my generation that don't have the usual power relation underlying them, but I don't know many, and most of the people I know of my age are not married and never will marry again — in fact find it difficult to find men because the men of our age are all so hollow and mechanical, emotional zombies. But I think there are some, a handful of younger men, who are a little bit better." I mentioned the view of traditional marriage in *The Bleeding Heart*, emblematized by Edith, wrecked and immobile, with no legs. This, for Marilyn French, was indeed marriage.

I raised the problem of children in an age of separations. In French's books, they appear blighted by their parents' breakings. Marilyn French disagreed with this, feeling that the blight comes not from the breaking of a marriage but from the marriage itself. "It's not the fact of the divorce but all that leads up to it," she went on, "the quarreling, the hatred that suddenly fills the house that is so bad for the children. But even when parents stay together, people are so terribly crippled by their childhoods, people whose parents didn't get divorced, it didn't make any difference; what was done to them as children was so horrendously cruel and you don't really ever get over it." There is then nothing traumatic about having only one parent? "No, I think that when you don't have to have these miserable marriages, people might have a little better chance for personal fulfillment and may not be so miserable, and if they're not so miserable, they're not going to be quite so miserable to their children."

I wanted to go back to her earlier point about the absence of language for women's experiences, and I asked her if she felt prose had a gender, whether there was such a thing as a female style. "There must be because when I get mail — and I get an awful lot of fan mail — I know within two sentences whether a man or a woman wrote it and I'm *always* right. In fact one time I got a letter which started out in the usual pompous way that male letters begin and I thought, this has to be a man, and I looked at the name and it was a woman's name. I thought, wow, this is unusual and I went back and read the letter and, though he had a woman's name — maybe it was Evelyn or something like that — he said 'I am a man' at some point in the letter, so that I knew and, indeed, I was right. But in prose I think it would be hard to tell. The only way you could really say that is if you could get sentences that no one knew and laid them out to test people — which you can't do because people who know literature would know where they came from."

French women critics never tire of pointing out that up to now women have had to write male writing and that they have had a subservient relationship to language itself. Marilyn French took this point, agreeing that the English sentence, like the French or German, is masculine. "That is, the structure is subject, verb, object — he fucks her. You have a doer and a done-to. I think language will change. For instance in seventeeth-century English prose or twentieth-century poetry, particularly of people like Yeats, you find a lot of verbals. The subject is not necessarily clear and there is no object. There is a doing. I find it in Sir Thomas Browne and even in Bacon. I think that the syntax of sentences will change in time, as women have more influence not only on what gets done in the world, but what gets felt and thought. Meantime, I do not myself choose to experiment with other forms of prose because, frankly, I want to be understood and, if I have to use a male sentence to do it, I will do it."

If one can see gender cutting through language and syntax, can one, I wondered, see it affecting tradition? Is there a female tradition of the type American feminist critics have tried to isolate? Marilyn French thought not and found it a dangerous idea. "Whenever one isolates a tradition," she explained, "I start to worry, because a tradition is a hierarchy, a passing on, a continuity of a particular line. So if you're F. R. Leavis and you say 'This is the Great Tradition in English literature,' you have to leave out some of the most interesting things that were done in English literature in order to say it. I find that a terrible thing to do — as though Blake or Sterne were somehow extraneous to other things. I don't think they are.

"I think that the woman writer who wants to write about women's experience in some typical way almost has to break with the tradition of the past. The great novelists of the past dealt with women who were unmarried, who were about to make the one choice they were allowed to make in their whole lives: whom to marry. The novel ends with them marrying or perhaps marrying anew as with Dorothea Brooke. A woman must be sexually chaste no matter what she thinks or does. She can rebel, but only so far. Male supremacy is it. And even if you're someone like Charlotte Brontë who, as Virginia Woolf says, breaks into her novel to complain (I've no problems with that in the way Woolf did — it's clearly related to the rest of her novel because what does Jane Eyre do to

Rochester at the end in order to be an equal? She has to blind and cripple him), she's writing about male supremacy. I think if you want to write about women now, you have to break forcefully these conventions. You can't just ignore them or go round them — you really have to break with them directly. So you're breaking with the past, period."

If, then, she felt no community with past writers, did she feel part of a community of contemporary ones? "Not of female *writers* particularly. I have been part of a female community *always* — ever since I was an adult. I didn't like girls when I was a girl. I thought they were silly: they talked about nail polish and dresses and I was reading Schopenhauer. There was just no communication. There was only a little communication with boys in those days but there was some. You could at least sing Mozart together. But when I became a woman I had absolutely a community of women and have never been without one — since in fact some of my present friends are the friends I had then. As I've gotten older and met different kinds of women it does happen that a lot of my friends write. They aren't necessarily novelists. Since *The Women's Room* was published, I've come to know other female writers, whom I like very much, but life is at a different point now and I don't have the time to spend hours and hours — and neither do they — getting to know someone; so they're not as close to me as my other friends are."

I asked her if she'd always had the urge to write and, if she had, whether this grew out of some childhood loneliness or unhappiness. She thought this a negative way of looking at it. "I was lonely and unhappy but I think most children are and I don't think I read or wrote because I was lonely. I did other things. I played the piano, I drew. I could have spent all my time doing these things and not reading and writing." I was interested in her childhood unhappiness. "My parents are still married and they're both very sweet people. They didn't abuse me. It was a sad childhood but it wasn't horrible. It was sad because my mother was so moody and she was so unhappy because she hated her life. She didn't take it out on me, but you come home and this woman is there and she's put away the washboard and put the clothes on the line and she's got a mind but she doesn't even know it. She was unhappy, that's all. And that's not good."

With her independent views, I wondered how Marilyn French had got into the academic routine and come to take a Ph.D. "I'd always wanted to. I started on a master's when I was first married, but then I got pregnant. I stayed home with the children and I wrote novels and short stories and so forth. And after about ten years I was pretty lonely and very unsuccessful and I thought, I've got to get out, I've got to talk to other people with my own interests. And I'm not going to make it as a writer — I don't know what's wrong, but I'm not. So I went back. I'd always been good at academics and one-half of my desire had been to teach — the other half was to write."

Now that fame had come, did she feel at all unworthy of it? "No, I think I felt very bad at one point — which was, after twenty years of writing and publishing one book and teaching and being very good at what I did, I was out of work. I didn't think *The Women's Room* was going to get taken and I was feeling pretty despairing. But once it did, everything was all right again."

How about the jealousy that fame brings? Did she feel any from other women? "Not from my friends. I suppose there might be some, but if there is I don't get friendly with those people. I have a very rich life. I have a lot of good friends. In fact if I meet new people, it's hard to squeeze them into my life. There's so little time. And fame does make new relationships more difficult — you can't credit them."

You seem a secure person now, I interrupted. "I liked what the French said when I was there — that I was serene, that I have a kind of equanimity because I've been through an awful lot in my life and I know I've survived."

I questioned her then about her present work. "I have a book on Shakespeare coming out in March. In the following year there will be a book of essays in which my ideas will be laid out. I go about the country giving speeches a lot and women want the ten commandments of feminism. Not only don't I have them but if I had them I wouldn't give them to them. It's horrible — you may as well join the Communist party or the Catholic Church. But it is a thoughtful summary of what I see and I attempt to offer whatever vision I have. And then after that, there'll be another novel."

Marilyn French is clearly a feminist writer. She judges herself so and reviewers use the phrase to praise or belittle depending on stance. I wanted therefore to ask her about feminism and its meaning to her. I began with the TV film of *The Women's Room*, which, instead of ending with a rape, a death, and the main character at a community college drinking brandy, sailed out on the high winds of a feminist speech. "I think the people involved in making the film tried very hard to get as much of the truth of the book into it as is permitted on American television. The networks did not want a rape; they did not want a death at the end; they did not want a downbeat ending — in fact they wanted Mira and Ben to marry at the end. What they did present is Eleanor Holmes Norton's words — in my book!"

In *The Bleeding Heart*, Marilyn French wrote of England, and I asked her about the very different feminist consciousness there. "I find almost no feminist consciousness," she replied emphatically. "I find a class structure which separates one group of women from others. I find that the group of women who are doing the writing — for magazines, newspapers, and television — are enormously competitive with each other. I find them all deferential to men. I find them very, *very* threatened by feminism. I think this is largely the class system. I mean if you've got a group of women who are able to get to Oxford and Cambridge and are able to get jobs because they've connections and they know people and because they're in that upper elite, then you're going to have a hard time having them sympathize or identify with the women on the other level."

When I pointed out that Americans too seem to distinguish between university feminism and activist feminism, she went on, "In the first place, the country's so much huger and there's so much more upward mobility — people from lower classes getting to positions of power. And there isn't the same kind of entrenched power structure. I'm not saying there isn't a tiny little elite class in America because there is, but people slip out of it and in all the time. It's a bigger, less stable country and because of that this situation is less severe. Which is not to say that I don't know any women in England who are feminists but the few I meet are very embattled, very untrusting, likely to be separatist — which is also true in Italy, Spain, and Germany. The most intense feminists are militant, socialist, separatist. If they're socialist they're working with the Marxists or they're separatist because they're dealing with a fascist tradition. And they know they have to raise the same kind of vigor and hatred against what they're encountering. It's a direct response to the entrenched governmental politics. Franco may be dead, but all the people who put him in office and the people who own the money are not. Hitler may be gone but Germany is the same and Italy is the same. So the feminism of a country has far more to do with the immediate situation of that country than it has with worldwide feminism, which is why feminists have such a hard time getting together across international barriers."

Despite Marilyn French's last statements, I sensed a certainty in belief and purpose. Do you never fear the results of feminism, I asked, never feel that it is cold out there and that it might have been warmer if more suffocating indoors?

"It's very cold out there. It's war out there. When I go round the country I have to fight my way. In England too. Continually. And I get tired of it. I hate it. But I have a kind of certitude. That may be seen as ridiculous. But I don't see it as ridiculous. I think certain values are absolutely right. I think that my philosophy, which doesn't appear as much in the novels as it will in the nonfiction things, is right. There's no deciding to go back to some other way. What other way? I've always been this way — I've been this way since I was a child. To think that you have a handle on truth, to think that you have certitude about something is, of course, ludicrous. But I'm not claiming to have the truth about what human life means or where it began or where it ends up. I do claim to have a truth about how it should be led. It's a limited truth but it's absolute for me.

"To me feminism is not just about women," Marilyn French went on, "it's about moral values, identified with women, though I don't think women have a gene for them. In this world at this moment, technology and the power people are becoming fewer and fewer and more and more powerful, so that you have essentially three huge centers of power which are capable of wiping out the world. Countries dedicatd to profit are less and less concerned with the human life they destroy, about the nature they destroy. I don't see how you can be alive at a time like this and not devote your energies to countering that and it seems that feminism is the most cohesive and comprehensive philosophy opposing it. One could become an ecologist or an antinuclear person, all of which I'm sympathetic with — but feminism embraces all of it."

And you never doubt. "Oh no, I never doubt."

Alison Lurie

Interviewed by
Dorothy Mermin

Alison Lurie has written six novels and numerous articles, reviews, books, and prefaces on a variety of subjects, most notably children's literature, fairy tales, and the interpretation of clothes. Her novels give a vivid and detailed picture of women's lives in the last three decades, recording as they happened the changes brought about by feminism and the other social and intellectual movements of the 1960s and 1970s. Her first book, Love and Friendship *(1962), tells of Emmy, rich, handsome, and good, who grows restive at the men's college in New England where her husband comes to teach, loses her reverence for the college's male bonding rituals and intellectual mystique, has an affair, contemplates divorce, but stays with her husband in the end — partly from loyalty and partly, it seems, because she has no plausible alternative. It is a funny, good-humored book: the rural pleasures of adultery give the lovers poison ivy and lead the deceived husband, who never finds out what his wife has been doing, into farcical displays of misdirected suspicion. Emmy rocks the boat a little, but she doesn't sink it.* Love and Friendship *establishes as Lurie's main subject the social history of our times as it appears in changing modes of marriage and adultery.*

But her novels also deal with more abstract themes. Her characters represent modes of thinking as well as feeling and behaving. Men think in the terms of their professions, as literary critics, historians, psychologists, sociologists, political scientists, or whatever — terms that generally turn out to be inadequate to the complexities of their lives. The Nowhere City *(1965), as cheerful as* Love and Friendship *but with a wider scope, takes a young couple rather like Emmy and her husband to Los Angeles, where they meet up with a variety of more or less nutty people: beatniks, starlets, psychiatrists married to starlets, social scientists, and others equally peculiar. The wife is miserable at first but proves adaptable; freed from her sinus troubles, sexual inhibitions, and inherited furniture, she goes native and decides to stay in Los Angeles when her husband, a historian who is bewildered and appalled by the ahistorical character of erotic and professional behavior in a city that lives only in the present, flees back to the east.* Imaginary Friends *(1967) tells of a small group of uneducated, unsophisticated people (led by two women) who think they're receiving messages from outer space, and the sociologists (two men) who set out to study the group's dynamics and slowly become drawn into it. In* Real People *(1969) a writer examines her life and her work and the conditions of art.*

The War Between the Tates *(1974) returns to the forms, themes, and milieu of the first books, but with an increased range of theme and feeling. The characters are now middle-aged, struggling to come to terms with the new era of Vietnam, drugs, mysticism, the sexual revolution, and feminism. The men leave their wives, their children grow into horrible adolescents, "nasty, brutish and tall," and the women get jobs. What the Tates discover about each other and themselves is more painful than anything in Lurie's earlier novels; if they come back together at the end of the book it will be so that they can "forget for a few moments that they were once exceptionally handsome, intelligent, righteous and successful young people; they will forget that they are ugly, foolish, guilty and dying." The next and latest novel,* Only Children *(1979), breaks the chronological sequence to describe children growing up in the 1930s and show how the people in the other books became what they are: how so many of the men became narrow, pompous, ambitious, and mean, and the women dwindled into wives.*

All these books are finely crafted and highly finished, with elaborate and satisfyingly worked out plots, inventive comic set pieces, and accurate observation of the small events and things of daily life. The writing is clean, precise, and elegant. While characters and places reappear from book to book, the formal structures vary. Imaginary Friends *has a male narrator (who appears in other books too),* Real People *is in the form of a diary,* Only Children *gives a child's point of view, and in the other books the narrator's voice is witty and unobtrusive.*

Dorothy Mermin: Do you think of yourself as a feminist novelist?
Alison Lurie: Well, more or less. I don't think of myself as someone who is primarily a feminist, but as more of a novelist. But I think that all my books are in some degree feminist.
Dorothy Mermin: Do you think they've become more feminist?
Alison Lurie: I don't think so, except that the last one is more feminist in

the sense that it's more about the choice women make as children as to what kind of women they are going to be. I saw this as a more central problem than I did in any of the other books.

D.M.: What writers do you think influenced you? Everyone says Jane Austen first, of course.

A.L.: People say that because of the title of my first book, which was the same as the title of one of her juvenilia. But I think it is certainly true that Jane Austen influenced me, and next to Jane Austen, of older writers, I would certainly say Dickens. Just because you can't imitate someone successfully or fully doesn't mean that they're not an influence on you. They may move you in a direction you need to go even if you can't get as far as they did . . . Dickens influenced me, I think, in allowing myself to enjoy certain kinds of silliness that people demonstrate, and to carry invention a little further than I was able to do when I first started writing, allowing strange things to happen, and not having to write only the generalized, the absolutely believable. Allowing myself to write about starlets, and beatniks, and floods, and people who believe in flying saucers, all that kind of thing, that I perhaps haven't seen firsthand but can imagine . . . George Eliot is very impressive, and some of the things she does, I like to try to do: the way she uses metaphors to tell you things that she doesn't quite want to say, almost poetically. Among modern writers, probably Christopher Isherwood most of all.

D.M.: People like Elizabeth Bowen and Elizabeth Taylor?

A.L.: I like them, but I wanted to move away from that sort of dreamy, subjective type of writing. It's not what I do best. I don't think I do it as well as the people who do it well. It's not the way my mind naturally works, though I've tried to imitate that way of thinking in certain of my books because I know it's a way that a lot of people's minds work, women and men both; but I don't do it naturally. I don't think that way naturally.

D.M.: So you don't think of yourself as working in a female line, a female tradition?

A.L.: Yes, I certainly do. I think it's a mistake to believe that there's one female line which is intensely personal, subjective, intuitive, emotional. That's not the only female line. There's also a line in Fanny Burney and Jane Austen that's just as true as the other. I think it's a mistake for women writers to feel that they've got to be subjective and dreamy and intuitive all the time. —There are some women whose minds honestly work that way. I've known them. And there are some men whose minds honestly work that way too. I don't think it's sex-linked. On the other hand, there have been forces trying to push women into feeling that they're all like this and they should be like this. Even someone like Virginia Woolf was able to do both voices: she wasn't just subjective. If you read her essays, she's very much in the other tradition.

D.M.:   Do you find that there's a community of women writers now, as there seems to have been in the nineteenth century?

A.L.:   I think women writers have always been friends with other women writers, if they are lucky enough to meet them. If you shut yourself up in a house in Amherst, of course, you don't meet *any* writers; but all the women writers I know have friends who are women writers. (But that may just be because I know them — it's a skewed sample.) . . . In this country, Diane Johnson, Mary Lee Settle. There are people I see, but I don't exchange work with them . . . In England, Margaret Drabble, and there are people whose names you wouldn't know, like Diana Melly, who's published two good novels.

D.M.:   Then do you think there's a specifically female subject matter?

A.L.:   Well, I think there *is* a female subject matter, but that's a historical accident. Women didn't have much to write about except domestic affairs and emotional attachments. They weren't allowed out where other things were going on. There's a female subject matter just as there's a Chinese subject matter, or an Indian subject matter, or whatever, because you have to write about what you know. I think that women's novels will be very different now that women are out in the world much more.

D.M.:   But in your novels you always portray the world in which men work as comic and flat and full of self-deception. The women seem to inhabit a richer, more interesting world.

A.L.:   Well, there are various ways of looking at it. For one thing, it's extremely hard to write about work successfully, especially about nonphysical work. You can write about hard physical labor as Eugene O'Neill or Hardy did, but it's awfully hard to write about the kind of work that a teacher or professional man or a business man does. Well, it's not so bad with business — Sinclair Lewis manages with Babbitt — isn't he a real estate agent? But what does a professor do? What does a lawyer do? Doctors are a little easier. So that's one answer: that it's hard to write about the working world. The other answer is that most of the working men I've seen have been professors, and maybe there's something just a little silly about professors anyhow.

D.M.:   The professors in your books seem rather like literary critics, people who put down novelists and writers.

A.L.:   I think there's a natural antagonism between the world of art and the world of scholarship.

Lurie's books also encompass a world of magic and witchcraft. First there's Miranda in Love and Friendship, *a young instructor's wife who is neither rich nor beautiful, tends to think in terms of magic, and indulges in mild forms of witchcraft when her life becomes particularly difficult. It is her way of asserting power. "'We all want to be guilty,'" she says at the end of the book when everyone seems to be nobly accepting responsibility for whatever's gone wrong, "'because guilt is power. It's the proof that one's magic works.'" Magical thinking is pervasive and contagious.* Imaginary Friends *depicts a collision between women who think they are in contact with preternatural forces and social scientists who are apparently controlled, rational, and superior. But when the beings from outer space do not arrive as expected, the young heroine goes happily off to college and exerts her persuasive powers in the campus revolution, while the men retire defeated: one back to the university, the other to a madhouse. Magic is the power of the powerless, the counterpart of science which scientists do not acknowledge.*

Lurie has made a particular study of children's literature and folklore, subjects in which she teaches courses at Cornell. She is coeditor of the Garland series of reprints of children's classics and has put together a book of "forgotten" fairy tales with strong, brave, capable, and resourceful female protagonists (Clever Gretchen, *1980). Most fairy tales, she says in the preface, are good feminist literature: "the original tellers were mainly women . . . working women . . . [who] lived active, interesting lives" —but men obscured this when they made their selections for the famous compilations. In children's literature in general she finds a view of the world that goes against patriarchal culture: "Many of the famous children's classics . . . are, or were when they first appeared, deeply subversive. That is, they dealt with matters that were denied in adult life, and/or literature, or they mocked ideals and institutions that were commonly regarded with solemn approval."* Only Children *draws on both these traditions: seeing things largely from a child's point of view, according to which most adult behavior is incomprehensible or monstrous, or both, it shows how two little girls experience their own lives in terms of fairy princes and princesses, and the book itself turns into something like a fairy tale at the end.*

A.L.:   Witchcraft is an old interest of mine. It's something that I've always been rather keen on, and it keeps coming up. I'm interested in it, not so much as a believer. It works, but it doesn't work in the strict magical way. Magic does work. But it works psychologically rather than supernaturally. It's certainly a very significant part of life, more than we mostly think. That is one reason I wanted to teach the folklore course: I wanted to see if I could make a bunch of people aware of how much of their lives is shot through with magical thinking.

D.M.: French feminism is interested in witches. That's what women did when they were most repressed—female power expressed itself as witchcraft.

A.L.: There's also the view, though, that witchcraft was projected onto women who seemed to be getting too big for their britches, without their ever having said "Gee, I think I'm a witch this week."

D.M.: Yes, the comparison has been made between the woman who came before the Inquisition as a witch, and the Victorian woman who was studied as a hysteric by male doctors. Female speech and expression were interpreted by one of these terms.

A.L.: If people you're competitive with have power, there are various ways of getting back at them. One is to say that they are wicked, and one is to say that they are crazy, and best of all is if you can say they are both wicked and crazy.

D.M.: Do you connect witchcraft with feminism?

A.L.: Well, in all these ways. If you don't have power, you'll take power any way you can. People who cut themselves off from this side of life are very susceptible to it. I could spook many professors much more easily than I could spook someone who's aware of the power of the irrational. People who cut themselves off from the magical, folklore side of life are very much endangered by it. You can get at them easily, and so why not?

D.M.: In your novels it appears that being a writer is incompatible with being a woman, a wife, and a mother. The novelist in *Love and Friendship* is a homosexual . . .

A.L.: But that's not because it's incompatible with being a woman. That's because of two things. I wanted a commentator on the action who couldn't actually be drawn into it. And since the action had to do with romantic love and family life I needed people who were cut off from this. One possibility was people who were much older, but I didn't think I could do that too well; not having been much older at the time, I thought I might get it wrong. And when I was at Amherst, Jimmy Merrill was there, and I became friends with him, and I was interested in the way he looked at the academic world, which he was just visiting for a year, as against the way we all looked at it when we were living in it permanently. The letters in the book are very largely based on letters he wrote. I don't mean to say that I used the same phrases, but the tone is his tone in letters to me later.

D.M.:   You seem to be interested in the question of whether you can observe things without getting drawn into them. It always seems to be men who think that they won't get drawn in; the women seem to *be* in.

A.L.:   The population of my books isn't exactly fair — or maybe that's not true of all the books — but in the first couple of books the men are in professions where they have to specialize. In order to succeed in a profession, at least at that time, it was believed that you had to close almost all the doors so that you could go further down the hallway, and so they're cut off from a lot of life. The women have been thwarted in their ambition by the then male chauvinist piggy situation, and therefore they have had to generalize. I don't think we are seeing that so much now. I think we are seeing women who are specializing and men who are generalizing, but there was much more separation in those days, in the fifties and sixties, the period I was writing about in those early books.

D.M.:   It struck me that all your books are about women freeing themselves from male dominance.

A.L.:   That's very possible. — No, I don't think that's quite true. That's true of the first book and of the second to some extent, but it's also about so many other things. It's not true of *Imaginary Friends* because there the dominance is more the dominance of the aunt over the niece.

D.M.:   But then what's finally left is the sociologist, McMann, who's gone crazy and thinks he's king of everything; but in fact he's locked up and it's really the aunt who's in power.

A.L.:   Yes, but she's in control of a very reduced, nothing sort of group. Her day of glory is over just as much as his. I don't think it's true of that book, though I can see it to some extent in the others.

D.M.:   Your women seem to start off imagining themselves in terms defined socially by men and discover in the course of the book how inadequate those definitions are.

A.L.:   I think that's true of all of us. Well, not now, things may be so different now. But after all, society hasn't really done a flip-flop. We're still living in a society dominated by men. All you need to do is look around any room you're in — like the one where the English department meets.

D.M.:   What do you think of some of the ideas about male dominance of language that have been raised by French feminist criticism? Is language patriarchal? Are women trapped in a language they didn't make? Women should be writing of the witches' heath, and from below and beyond culture, and from childhood, and about their bodies.

A.L.:   I know that line of thought. I have a friend in London named Emma Tennant who is very much influenced by these things. Her novels are full of it, they are full of witches and all. You've got to write about what it comes to you to write.

D.M.:   Cixous talks about a gestation drive. There's a drive to have babies — as opposed to a Freudian view that the baby is the substitute for the phallus.

A.L.:   I have never believed that. It's ridiculous. I really think the whole thing about penis envy is complete nonsense, and it's just made up by men who are suffering from womb envy. I think it's phony, really.

D.M.:   Cixous is saying that there's a connection between the desire to have a child and the desire to write.

A.L.:   Oh, sure, I think that they are very similar, because what you want to do is to create something which in some way will be connected with you and will exist in the future when you're gone. I think writing books and having babies are psychologically very similar: not the process of doing it so much, but one is the physical analogue of the other. It takes a long time, it comes out, it's not exactly what you had in mind, some people like it, some people hate it, it'll grow away from you, and as time passes you feel further and further separated from it. Sure. I think most women at some time in their life would like to have a baby. For some women, the bad side of it is so heavy that they don't do it. But there are certainly nice things about it, that even they probably want. Well, almost everybody can have a baby; not everybody can write a book. Especially in a world where women are not producing anything that's going to last, because they are keeping house, there must be a tremendous urge to leave something behind, to create something that isn't going to be eaten or have mud tracked over it. But I suppose in the past you would get the same satisfaction from making a patchwork quilt or sewing a sampler. You want to leave something, you don't want to be completely swallowed up in the process of time.

D.M.:   Would this be the same for men as for women, or, if anything, stronger for men?

A.L.:   I think equally strong for men. It's possible that one reason women allowed themselves to be kept down so long was that they were able to achieve something just by having kids — whereas men, not having that, had a motive to struggle harder.

D.M.:   Couldn't that circle round to implying that if Emily Dickinson had had a good sex life she wouldn't have written all those poems?

A.L.:   No, of course not. She would have written different poems, maybe, but she certainly would have written. The idea that sex is a substitute for writing is ridiculous.

D.M.:   Is writing a substitute for sex?

A.L.:   That's ridiculous too, as I said in one of the books. I know people who think that it is, but they are all men. I know several men who think that semen is ink and that, as Philip Roth said, it all comes out of the same tap and therefore if you're screwing too much you won't write anything. That's a complete delusion, but it's like magic. The whole thing is magic. If you believe it, of course it's instantly true, and permanently true.

D.M.:   Cixous says that women write with white ink, with milk — or would, or could. That would work round to the same thing, I suppose; you could run out of it.

A.L.:   In my observation semen is not black. — That's mixing it up, because if you write with milk then you're nourishing somebody that you've produced. I think *criticism* is more like milk. Maybe.

D.M.:   Can or should the writer be bisexual, with a sexuality that is not exclusive but includes both sexes? Another way of coming at that question is, can you tell the difference between male and female writing?

A.L.:   Well, you can tell the difference between me Tarzan you Jane writing, and me Elizabeth Bowen you Ernest Hemingway. I don't know, I think there are stereotyped ideas about women writers, but I don't think you can always tell or even tell most of the time. I think it's obviously true that some men seem more masculine according to our stereotype of what is masculine than others do, and some women more feminine — but whether this is biological or psychological or sociological, I just don't know. I certainly don't belong to the school that thinks that all women should try sleeping with other women because it will be good for them . . . It's something worth writing about, because I've had friends who say to me — in fact, I can think of a couple who've said to me — "I really like women much better than men and I wish I could find them physically attractive, but I just don't; what I find physically attractive is men." They feel regret because of this. The fact that men turn them on they regard as a regressive drag on the expansion of their consciousness.

The question of a woman writer's subject matter is central in Real People. *Janet, the narrator, thinks that she hasn't written really well because "she left too much out." "She didn't want to depress her readers; she didn't want to make herself uncomfortable. She didn't want to expose her family, her friends, or (above all) herself; she didn't want them to be laughed at, or pitied or condemned — not even when they were in fact ridiculous, pitiable and wrong." Janet's work is not like her creator's — she writes dreamy, sensitive, subjective stories in the Elizabeth Bowen line — but her final assertion on the job of the writer could well be Lurie's own: "If nothing will finally survive of life besides what artists report of it, we have no right to report what we know to be lies."*

D.M.:   Haven't women been afraid to write because they were afraid of exposing themselves?

A.L.:   When I think of women's writing — they are exposing themselves right and left. That seems to be one of the current themes of women's writings.

D.M.:   Janet in *Real People* is afraid she'll embarrass her family, and the book ends with the question both of self-exposure and of exposing.

A.L.:   She's got a problem, but that's not the problem of *all* writers. That's the problem of someone who wants it both ways. You usually don't get it both ways. She wants the reputation of being a nice suburban woman. I exaggerated her position by giving her the stuffiest background that I could imagine for her, that I could possibly create, in order to exaggerate something that we all go through anyhow. . . . It's not a question of exposing yourself, but of exposing your opinions. I'm not suggesting that she's got to run around with her inmost thoughts hanging out, but simply that she's got to write in such a way that she doesn't preserve the accepted pieties of the life she's living in. It's possible to be extremely honest without being confessional.

D.M.:   One of the things women writers are said to be doing now in a new way is celebrating female sexuality.

A.L.:   I think that's true, but it's only part of the larger discovery that people can celebrate sexuality anyhow. In the past, whether you were male or female you had to do it metaphorically. I don't think that's something that women are doing now, more than men, but perhaps it seems that they pay more attention to it because women were supposed to be so refined and not supposed to think or speak, let alone write, about sexuality; so when women started doing it, in some circles it seemed more shocking. . . . Strangely enough—you wouldn't think so—but my first novel was burned in a couple of small towns in the midwest. People found copies in the library and it was one of those periods when they were destroying books, and a couple of contemporary books were burned and my first novel was among them. It seems very tame now, but at the time apparently it was shocking. . . . It was a great surprise to me, because I don't write pornographically at all.

D.M.:   It's not pornographic, but it seems to be about women having sexual feelings and enjoying sexuality the way men do in men's books—not particularly romantically, and not because they want to get married at the end of it, but just to have it.

A.L.:   That's true, but for them I think it was just the fact that it was about adultery. They didn't want the brats to go into the library and be able to read about adultery, in case perhaps it might start happening in their town.

D.M.:   We've been getting close to the question of polemical feminist writing. What do you think of polemical novels, like Marilyn French's?

A.L.:   If you're angry, you write an angry book. I don't think there's that much difference between feminist anger and economic anger or political anger. If lousy things have happened to you, naturally you are going to be furious. Some of us have had more lousy things happen to us than others.

D.M.:   Are female comic novelists in a different relation to feminism, with different problems? If you laugh at things people can say that you're just trivial-minded.

A.L.:   I hear that all the time. On the other hand, I think that's just as good a way to get at things, to laugh at them, as to shout at them. If something annoys you, you get at it in the way you best can.

D.M.:   Your books laugh at the world you and I live in—the academic world—and people's defense is to say it isn't the subject matter that's trivial, but the eye that sees it.

A.L.:   Oh, sure, I'm used to that. But any satirical novelist is going to have this; that's people's defense against taking it seriously—whereas if you write a noncomic novel, then the defense is to make fun of you: "Oh, she's getting so weepy and breathing so hard," they'll say, "taking herself so seriously"—like they do about Marilyn French, or the sort of thing that was said about Virginia Woolf at one time. If they don't like you, they'll find something to say. . . . But there's a problem. Suppose you want to write a feminist novel today, and you don't want to convince only the converted. You want to convince people who are not seriously feminists, and you'd even like some men to read it. Well, if you write *The Women's Room* you're not going to get very many nonconverted readers, I wouldn't think. —That's probably not a very good example. —Maybe you have a better chance if you write a book that is amusing and you sort of sneak around behind them.

D.M.:   Do you think of *The War Between the Tates* as polemical? That reached a huge audience, presumably.

A.L.:   No, I think *The War Between the Tates* became popular because it could be read as a conservative book. I think that's why it became a best-seller, partly. By accident, due partly to the fact that I write slowly, by the time that book came out we had turned the corner of the sixties and early seventies and people wanted to see all the sixties things made fun of, and astrology, political action, feminism, everything was in it. I think the book became popular for that reason, even though it wasn't intended that way. . . . Feminists hate that book, because it contains a group of people called the Hens. *Ms.* [magazine] wrote a very destructive review of it. I thought of it as being feminist, but it isn't feminist enough to please the feminists because it doesn't end up suggesting what women are supposed to do. It has a scene where women destroy a man, but that didn't seem to please them somehow because that isn't the way we're supposed to destroy men —we're supposed to do it in a more highbrow way.

D.M.:   One tends to think of satirical novels in terms of male images of aggression and acts of power.

A.L.:   I don't believe that satire is male, or power is male, or aggression is male, necessarily.

D.M.:   The witch is a figure of aggression, and in the introduction to *Clever Gretchen* you talk about children's books as subversive, and that one can think of fairy tales as subversive. And you remember how Mary Russell Mitford's friend described Jane Austen: that she was silent, like a poker —but a poker of whom everybody was afraid. Can one think of your novels as the novels of the wife, the woman in the male community who is reporting it?

A.L.:   Yes; but you know a lot of writers, both male and female, have decided that they were observers rather than participants. It's a style either sex can adopt, and that I think most writers have to adopt, because otherwise they're too involved to see what they are writing about, really.

Lurie herself mostly writes about the personal and professional lives of university people. Her books are "about" intellectual attitudes or social themes, but the ideas are set in ordinary domestic life —the casual, contingent, diurnal round of houses, shopping, cooking, parties, children, husbands, and (breaking the routine in the only way most women can) lovers. Her books convey the texture of housewives' lives in the kitchen and the bedroom, with friends or with children, and in the alien, slightly comic world of men. And the novels are written from within this domesticated life as well as about it. The settings of most of them are the places where Lurie lived when her husband (a professor of English, from whom she is now separated) had jobs there: Amherst, Massachusetts; Los Angeles; and Ithaca, New York. Janet in Real People *notes in her diary that all the men at the artists' colony speak of her life as a housewife "as if it were a rather eccentric hobby for a writer. Since it interferes with my work, why don't I give it up? They don't see . . . that it's the essential substance of my work." The same is true of Lurie's novels, though they include much more than Janet's stories do. In both their domestic themes and their dissections of academic attitudes they take much of their "essential substance" from the ordinary life of a professor's wife.*

A.L.:   I was always a literary little girl; I learned to read early and read a great deal as a child. It was my view at about the age of six or seven, encouraged by my doting parents, that I was going to be a writer or an artist of some kind. I think I was more encouraged in this because I obviously wasn't good at very many other things. I always assumed that I would be some kind of writer. That was my role. I'm one of those people who was always being patted on the back and told, "What a nice little poem." That was my identity, really. The only time I considered giving it up was when I wasn't published for ten years. Then I began to receive a lot of encouragement to give it up. I gave it up for about a year; I had a year in which I had two kids in diapers and I really didn't have the energy to write very much. So I considered giving it up, but it was so boring not writing that I went back to it.

D.M.:   How did you write, when you had little kids? Did you write like Jane Austen, in the living room?

A.L.:   No. Jane Austen didn't have toddlers, you have to remember, when she wrote in the living room. Did you ever try to write in the living room with toddlers? . . . They take hold of the pieces of paper. —I always had playpen pals. I always cultivated the society of women with small children, and I impressed on them how important it was to exchange small children. So I would always have a friend and try to set up an arrangement whereby every day I would take her child or she would take my children for a couple of hours.

D.M.:   Were a couple of hours every other day enough?

A.L.:   Well, then I could also work at night. The bad times are before your kids are old enough to go to nursery school. That's very serious. For instance, when I first got here I had two kids at school and one at home. I had a friend named Dino Read, and she wanted to draw and I wanted to write, so every day we would exchange children, and that meant that three mornings a week I got to write and she got to draw. . . . There was only one kid at home, and when he was three he could go to nursery school three mornings a week, and then we exchanged children on the other mornings. So then we would have three or four mornings. I tell you, it is not so easy, but you can do it. It just slows you down. . . . Well, then, gradually, once I published a book — which was after I got here — I had a little money, so then I got a cleaning lady to come in one morning a week. And then when I made more money, I rented a room to write in.

D.M.:   Is being a woman writer difficult in special ways apart from the question of toddlers and children? Is it more difficult for a woman to be a writer than for a man?

A.L.:   Practically, I think it is easier to be a woman writer, once you don't have toddlers. It depends of course on whether you're working or not, because if you are working it's hard to be a writer whatever your sex, if you have a nine to five job or anything of the sort. If you are a woman whose children are in school at least part of the day, it's easier to be a writer than it is if you're a man working full time. It depends so much on the kind of job you have. Women still traditionally have jobs which don't demand more than forty hours a week of commitment. But a man can decide that he isn't going to get ahead in his career, he is just going to practice it in order to support his writing habit. So it's maybe not all that different. — I think psychologically it's a great advantage to be a woman. There are too many male writers now that are in this awful bind: they haven't anything to write about after their first novel. It's like this, if you've noticed: there's a very bright guy, and he grows up, and he takes writing courses in college, and then he gets an M.F.A. or a Ph.D. degree, and the more he writes, the more everybody says, "wonderful," and he writes a novel about his childhood or his adolescence — or maybe two novels, one about his childhood and one about his adolescence. His childhood and his adolescence are real and unique. Say he's the son of a professor at Cornell, or of a person who runs a motel in Cortland, or whatever; there is a world he knows, there is some series of experiences that he has had that are unique, so he writes about this. And he writes well, and the novel is published and widely acclaimed. Then he gets a job teaching somewhere. And that's all he does for the rest of his life. I know some wonderful American writers, including some famous names I wouldn't want to mention because their feelings would be hurt, who've done nothing in their lives except teach and sleep with different women. So their books get kind of boring; they have nothing to write about. (You can't write any more about the university and being graduate students; it's been done so often and so well.) But women are forced to live more in the real world. Of course now we're going to have a bunch of girls who are in this same bind.

D.M.: That partly answers another question: has it gotten easier for women to be writers?

A.L.: It's easier to *say* that you want to be a writer, just as it's easier to say that you want to be a doctor, or a lawyer, or a dancer, or anything that you might want to be. In fact, nowadays there are girls who complain that all they want to do is to have kids and bring them up, and there's pressure on them to say what their career is going to be. But it isn't any easier to *become* a writer than it ever was. It's hard to learn how to do it, and it's much harder to get published nowadays than it used to be.

D.M.: Janet in *Real People* says that women aren't taken seriously as writers. Is it harder for a woman to be taken seriously?

A.L.: I think it is, but maybe it's changing. For instance, I think that it wouldn't have taken me so long to get a job at Cornell if I had been a man. I think if I had been a man who had just happened to be living in Ithaca, maybe married to some lady professor (if you can imagine that, in that climate), I wouldn't have had to publish four novels before I could get a job as a part-time lecturer.

D.M.: How long did it take you to get a job as a part-time lecturer?

A.L.: Fifteen years. But I didn't start asking for a job for the first five years because I still had small kids. So, ten years really. They weren't hiring women to teach creative writing at that time, and I didn't have the qualifications to teach freshman English.

D.M.: All you'd done was write all those books.

A.L.: Right.

Alison Lurie lives in Ithaca, New York. She is professor of English at Cornell University, where she teaches courses in creative writing, children's literature, and folklore, and is at work on a new novel.

Bettye Lane

Robin Morgan

Interviewed by
Helen Cooper

Robin Morgan was born in 1941 in Lake Worth, Florida, grew up in Mount Vernon, New York, and at eleven moved to Manhattan. There she continued the TV, film, and theater work, into which she had been entered as a small child by her mother and aunt. While that work was lucrative, writing was an early passion. In her late teens, while attending classes at Columbia University, she extricated herself from her acting career and seriously committed herself to writing poetry. A little later she met the poet, Kenneth Pitchford, whom she subsequently married and with whom she had a son, Blake Ariel, in 1969.

During the 1960s both Morgan and Pitchford were engaged in civil rights and antiwar activism. This, combined with her understanding that even in such groups women were usually relegated to envelope sticking, tea making, and serving as on-the-pill easy sexual partners, led to her early activism from the mid-1960s onwards in the most recent wave of the feminist movement. Her picketing of the Miss America Pageant in Atlantic City in 1968 and her organization of and participation in many radical feminist groups and activities in the late 1960s and early 1970s were counterbalanced, as her activism has always been, by writing. She compiled and edited Sisterhood Is Powerful (1970), the first anthology of the contemporary women's movement. "Letter to a Sister Underground" and "Monster" from her first poetry collection, Monster (1972),[1] were early attempts in poetry to articulate an increasingly conscious female vision. An inveterate and dedicated organizer, marcher, consciousness raiser, speaker, and researcher, Morgan has been involved in heightening awareness about crimes against women: battery, rape, violent pornography, child

97

pornography, genital mutilation of women, and political torture. She has also been a contributing editor of Ms. *magazine, and has published a second book of poems;* Lady of the Beasts *(New York: Random House, 1976) and a prose work,* Going Too Far: The Personal Chronicle of a Feminist *(New York: Random House, 1977). A third book of poetry,* Depth Perception: New Poems and a Masque *(New York: Doubleday/Anchor), was published in May 1982, and her second prose book,* The Anatomy of Freedom: A Quantum Metaphysics of Sex *in November 1982. In addition she has given lectures, seminars, and poetry readings throughout the country.*

Morgan's political activism and her writing are harmoniously integrated in vision, if often competitive for her time and energies. The struggle between the solitary and the communal, the female and the male, between art and politics informs Morgan's work, in which her fundamental concern is the connection between women. Her poems record a commitment to exploring and naming the female, the male, and their relation to the universe from a staunchly female viewpoint. Incorporating images from biology, anthropology, mysticism, alchemy, herbal lore, the tarot, mythology, art, politics, kitchenware, and the nitty-gritty of Manhattan apartment life, Morgan echoes E.M. Forster's dictum "Only connect" —with the proviso that this be done with the female naming her terms, as the male has always named his.

This interview was conducted in March 1981. Since then Robin Morgan has added two important poems, "Depth Perception" and "The Hallowing of Hell," to her most recent book, Depth Perception. *The interview does not, therefore, cover the ideas and poetics of these two recent works, although they address themselves to issues that arose during the discussion.*

Helen Cooper: Which woman writer influenced you most?
Robin Morgan: I really can't pick one: Amy Lowell, Christina Rossetti, Charlotte Mew, Dickinson, Plath, "the Matchless Orinda" Katherine Philips (a seventeenth-century English poet), younger American feminist poets who are doing their work and who give me strength to do mine. Certainly Audre Lorde, Josephine Miles, Yvonne, and oh, Barrett Browning of course—her political poems and *Aurora Leigh* because she had the courage to write it when she did. In terms of subject matter I really can't think of that many direct influences. Certainly your hard-core card-carrying feminist subject matter overlaps an element in my work which has always been there, prefeminism, and still is there strongly, a metaphysical element which comes from Donne. So there is this strange mixture. I began writing poetry very much in a sort of academic model and worked hard at learning my craft.

Helen Cooper: Who were you reading then?
Robin Morgan: I was reading a lot of Yeats. I certainly did my turn with
Eliot, Pound, and Williams, with the modernists, and found
them — Eliot especially — certainly moving in some ways, but ultimately
alien. It wasn't until I had a political context in which to view why they
seemed so odd in their alienation that I understood that modernism as a
cause célèbre was really a mask for male supremacy in the poetic
establishment in this country. But Yeats was a very important influence
because he combined the political and mystical albeit he was not quite a
feminist.
H.C.:   In what way do you feel you appropriated Donne or Yeats to a
female vision?
R.M.:   I think the audacity of metaphor, the metaphysical spine to
Donne's poems had a conscious and unconscious influence just because I
saw it could be done. Certainly there have been women poets who have
taken such work and made it their own, but for me it was just that Donne
and Yeats came at a very formative moment. In my first book, *Monster*,
there's a real shift from formal traditional modes to an "unconscious
consciousness" about myself as a woman and what that means. "Satellite"
and "The Improvisors" for example, both in *Monster*, were written before I
had any notion of feminism, but they're absolutely feminist poems — like
uncut diamonds. I just didn't know I knew. "Satellite" begins "I wonder
if I hate him yet." And then there are the images:

> space, water, time, my breasts and blood divide us:
>   dishes ticking, clocks to be laundered,
> even his eyes that know these things divide us.
>
>   "We are equal," he says and says. I will write
> my poems in indelible ink on the laundry then
>   while lost buttons roll where green-marbled meat
>   molds books unfinished, unvacuumed ovaries, self-pity.
>   Women ought to be born one-breasted or male
> or mindless. "We are equal," he says. We find me wanting.
>
>   [*M*, p. 7]

H.C.:   Where would you counterbalance that incipient feminism with
male influence in the poem?
R.M.:   Well, the structure of the poem is in slant rhymes. It's in a very
specific traditional mode, albeit my version of that mode: so many lines to

a stanza, so many feet to a line. It's a tight academic poem. What was shocking about that poem was those ridiculous metaphors. You just didn't have lost buttons and ovaries and dishes and laundry in a poem then, and in a sense I disguised them in a surrealist structure, so that they almost appeared like a Dali painting. Later on though, even in "Monster," they come out much more blatantly, without apology, as in "The City of God" in *Lady of the Beasts*. When I broke the traditional content, then the lines got longer, the poems got longer. It's like coming out of bound feet or corsets.

H.C.:   It's taking up space.

R.M.:   Precisely. One is spreading out, elbowing, breathing deeper, and saying no more cramped and ladylike precision. And then it takes a while (like a thesis-antithesis-synthesis dialectic) before one begins to reconstruct precision without its being "ladylike." Because in fact they are not synonymous. And I think that towards the end of *Lady of the Beasts* that begins to happen, and I hope it has happened in the poems since. Lately I've been writing more sonnets, and some sestinas and villanelles, traditional forms. I'm not the only feminist poet doing that, Marilyn Hacker does it quite brilliantly.

H.C.:   Right.

R.M.:   But something's happening with those forms in terms of the content that's very different. I even started to do that in *Monster*, although not with feminist politics. I was a civil rights and New Left activist. "Dachau" is a villanelle, and I deliberately chose the most elegant French form and juxtaposed it with subject matter about concentration camps, racism, bombings, genocide. I was looking for the tension created between the two. The political content was not feminist. I was still in that period where you identified yourself with every other oppressed group because you haven't faced up to the fact that you are one yourself.

But we've strayed from your original question. Now I remember the name of the other poet who influenced me—Alice Meynell. In Meynell, there's an audacity, a totally original voice. I know at the point when I first read her, it was like discovering an incredibly fresh strong female sensibility that in no way was compromised and did not compromise the aesthetics of the poem. And at that point it was still fairly rare even to discover that. You either had Louise Bogan, Denise Levertov, Elizabeth Bishop, or Marianne Moore—distinguished, important, fine poets, who were not necessarily speaking from a woman's experience. Even Adrienne Rich was like that until feminism took over her life: and that's a transformation which has really happened to no other poet of her generation, and I embrace her courage.

H.C.:   Yes. You've said that when you were in your teens you were reading Donne and Yeats. At what point were you first aware of women poets?

R.M.:   My mother loved Barrett. But she loved her for most of the wrong reasons. She loved the sonnets and she knew some of them by heart and they were among the earliest poems that I ever remember encountering. So Barrett loomed large as a female poet and then certainly Dickinson. But it took a long while to be able to affirm either one of them. This was long before there were scholars who had penetrated the Victorian haze about them as "lady poets," and so they were being affirmed only as tokens and in the old ways. After I began sending out poems and going to poetry workshops and gatherings, I discovered what an abysmal cliché the woman poet was. Even though she'd never had a chance to authentically exist, she managed still to go immediately from nonexistent to laughable: lady poets with three names, Elizabeth Barrett Ha-Ha, all women poets wrote about flowers and lay on chaises longues being neurasthenic. What one immediately wants to do then for survival is to say, not me, and be acceptable.

H.C.:   Can you point to any poems in *Monster* where you feel that kind of anxious voice speaking? Where you are in some way trying to be a male poet?

R.M.:   There were poems like that, but at the time I assembled the book I was a feminist and was bloody well not going to include them. I remember a series of poems shortly after I married Kenneth that I addressed to my mother. One ended, "I have met the enemy and I am his." And it was a great affirmation. There was a poem in the voice of Persephone saying to Demeter: Don't come looking for me, I'm really very happy here, and you may think it's hell, but to me it's heaven. So that there was that whole affirmation of entering the male world. The Vietnam War was still going on when I published the book and so I felt it would be revisionist in a sense not to include those poems that were very strong political poems even if they had less feminist consciousness. Although, in fact, "Four Visions on Vietnam" is a mixture of a nascent, fragile feminist consciousness with heavy leftist analysis.

H.C.:   I'd like to talk now about poetic standards. In "Letter to a Sister Underground" in *Monster* you reject poems of "the well-wrought kind" and endorse instead "a prosy poem" which "sprawls" across the page:

Dear Jane:

It's funny, now, to write like this:
a letter I don't even dare shape like one
(not that you'll probably ever read it, which may be
the reason it can now be written);
sprawled in a prosy poem
unlike the poems you often asked to see
but which I somehow never brought around.
Well, it's a poem, or non-poem, because
I don't write what I once called poems anymore —
the well-wrought kind that you and I
might once have critically discussed over a gentle lunch
where we were both in former incarnations
"bright young editors."
Instead, I write, or try to, between actions
(which hardly leaves much time but that's okay)
things about women, my sisters and myself
in the hope that some small ticking insight
from the page, which is the one place I don't lie,
ignites a fuse of righteous bitterness
in a woman (my sister or myself)
that can flash into an action no one — least of all me —
could have foreseen erupting.

[*M*, p. 58]

But then in your play "Art and Feminism: A One Act Whimsical Amusement on All That Matters" from *Going Too Far* you imply a rejection of such sprawling prosy poems as a viable aesthetic:

Calliope: For myself, I confess that I am becoming impatient with Daughters who appear to feel that any set of words blatted out on a page with the right-hand margins unjustified is a poem. Do you think that I am becoming a crotchety old grump?

Euterpe: No, you are an admirable old grump, Calliope. You're right, of course. "Having a lot to express" is all very well, but if one is indifferent to color and line then one should refrain from making that expression on canvas, and if one is indifferent to language, to the richness of vowels and the wit of consonants, indifferent to rhythm and echo and music and rhyme and simile and metaphor, then one had best refrain from making that expression on the page. Or *do* so, by all means, but have the civility not to call it art.

[*GTF*, p. 276]

Where do you stand now on this issue of poetic standards?

R.M.:   Well, when you throw out patriarchal standards it doesn't mean you throw out standards. I think now that both those passages you quoted are extreme positions. "Letter to a Sister Underground" is very much a thesis. (Although it in turn is an antithesis to the kinds of poems I wrote before, that I describe as "well-wrought.") It was important that I write and think like that at the time, in order to break through to my own voice. I think there are parts of that poem, to my secret delight, where I let some metaphorical richness creep through and those are probably the best parts of the poem. But it was important that one could break through to say (since we were being told whenever a woman wrote about her own subject matter she was being polemical), with feet being planted firm on the ground and nailing the words to the door like Luther: Then this is polemic; those are your terms, but this is my truth. The danger in the thinking was that it was simply myopic. A woman writing about her own subject matter doesn't necessarily mean that the poem can't be, per se, well-wrought. Although I agree with the passage from *Going Too Far*, there is an antithetical judgmental quality about it that could stand a bit more compassion. So that now I could say a third thing, which is that although everything that is blatted out into a page may not be a poem, polemically I certainly affirm every woman's right to do that. Whether it is catharsis, whether it is for her sanity, whether it is in journals. Even though when I look at that and apply to it the standards of art, I may very well say it is filled with cliché, or lack of discipline, or it doesn't have any wordplay, or any of those things that transform a cry of pain or rage or anger or celebration into a work of art.

H.C.:   That leads me into thinking about language. At the end of "Monster" you say:

And you, men. Lovers, brothers, fathers, sons.
I have loved you and love you still, if for no other reason
than that you came wailing from the monster
while the monster hunched in pain to give you the power
to break her spell.

> Well, we must break it ourselves, at last.
> And I will speak less and less and less to you
> and more and more in crazy gibberish you cannot understand:
> witches' incantations, poetry, old women's mutterings,
> schizophrenic code, accents, keening, firebombs,
> poison, knives, bullets, and whatever else will invent
> this freedom.
>
> [*M*, p. 85]

I take this to be a statement about a poet who is consciously not addressing herself to a male audience.

R.M.:   Yes, it is an attempt to get out of the phenomenon that Virginia Woolf referred to, where even when you think you're free of begging you find yourself writing for the male eavesdropper in the next room, for his approval. It is what Honor Moore calls the "male approval desire syndrome." That passage shows a desire to break free of that. It came out of a place in myself that exploded, a place I didn't even know was bleeding till I looked.

H.C.:   That stanza has always seemed very strong to me.

R.M.:   It's strong because it has concrete metaphor. I'm not denying it's also because of the political message, but it's the way the message is stated that is strong.

H.C.:   Yes. Then in 1976 in *Going Too Far* in an introduction to a journal entry you wrote about a troubled time in your relationship with Kenneth in 1966 you say:

> But the underlying theme, of course, was our love for each other, spoken in two enforcedly different languages, a woman's and a man's. There was yet no technique of translation available to us. . . . There were days of talking after, of sorting things out, still without the aid of translation (which would not be available for three more years), but with renewed will.
>
> [*GTF*, p. 46–47]

What was the technique of translation available between the two "different languages, a woman's and a man's" in "three more years"?

R.M.:   It was feminism. Since both of us were very political beings and still are, and had been active together in the New Left, the antiwar movement, the civil rights movement etc., there was a frame of reference. It wasn't just "my problem." Suddenly there began to be a context of communication between women. One discovered in consciousness-raising groups, My God, you too have faked an orgasm, you too have this weird little eccentricity about housework. Those two words, "you too," with a question mark and exclamation point were the most commonly heard in those rooms. One came back to struggle with a man with a frame of reference: I am not crazy, I am not alone, this is not only personal, it is political, the personal *is* the political.

H.C.: How did this affect your language in poetry?

R.M.: In that context of *Going Too Far* I'm talking about the language with which we were trying to communicate in daily life and in our writing. Kenneth and I would argue back and forth in poems as early as 1965. But to some extent I'm talking about a question of metaphor. Plath, in a last interview, spoke very movingly about this. She had felt she couldn't use the word "toothbrush" in a poem and why couldn't she? And I think it's Joan Larkin who has a funny, witty poem, maybe a sonnet, about trying to use the word "vagina" in a poem and why does it seem funny, impossible, improbable, ridiculous, awkward when in fact "phallus" and "penis" and "rod" and "cock" — all the euphemisms and Latinisms and slang — are perfectly fine in the tradition of American and English poetry. So we have found "penis" in poetry by men but not "vagina" and *never* "clitoris" until the last few years in feminist poetry. Some words were unspeakable and some subjects were unwritable. There was no way you could actually talk about changing a baby without seeming to be just a light-verse poet. Then there are also your basic great themes. It is perfectly all right for Oedipus to become larger than mythic proportions, and the subject of innumerable poems, either directly or through Freudian analysis of the man's search for his father, his manhood, his ambivalence about his mother, his lust for his mother. But if you have a woman searching for her origins it's somehow trivial. To shift that is an enormous job which I think we have begun to do, and we have made very strong headway. It is remarkable, however, how many people in the poetry establishment have managed to avoid feeling the ripples.

H.C.: I've always thought there are two kinds of language in your poems. One is the language with which you make connection with a female network. You use it in "Monster," in "The Mother" and "The Sister" section of "The Network of the Imaginary Mother" in *Lady of the Beasts*, and "Documentary," "Heirloom," and "Piecing" in your latest collection, *Depth Perception*. These poems reflect that breakthrough in language you talked about earlier. At the end of "Monster" in that passage

I read earlier about woman's language, and in *Lady of the Beasts*, I recognize that you are making connections with a women's network, articulating things which haven't been said and relationships that haven't been explored before with women. But I also felt that in poems about men or a man, there was a way in which I couldn't understand as well. This was not because the poems were addressed to a man per se, but because they seemed to be in a different language. When you start addressing a man, or trying to work out a relationship with a man, there seems to be a greater anxiety. Partly, of course, this can be because of writing about a particular relationship whose privacy shouldn't be intruded upon. But it contrasts with the strength and security and realism in your writing about women.

R.M.:   The world of women is relatively free of fear. I don't mean to say that women aren't afraid of one another in subtle and blatant ways, but at least when one is working aesthetically in that arena, it is devoid of fear. In fact, the peer pressure, God love it, is not only to say the unspeakable, but is: "So? So? What new unspeakable can you say now?" And that's a very interesting kind of peer pressure.

H.C.:   Yes. Now in "The Network of the Imaginary Mother" the sections are entitled "The Mother," "The Consort," "The Sister," "The Child," and "The Self." You use everyday language except for "consort." So instead of "husband" or "lover" or "spouse" the word for the male becomes mythic, formal, other than everyday as though maybe there is an anxiety present about how to do this naming.

R.M.:   That is definitely one element in it. I think there was another element more conscious at least. I was striving for the archetypal; and in myths about women, either patriarchal myths where we have to peel the layers off in order to see what is really there, or myths that we've unearthed that were in fact prepatriarchal, you have mother-daughter, sisters, mother-child (whether son or daughter) a whole lot. What you do not have is equal male-female relationships. Either the male is in power and the female is consort or, if you go back far enough into goddess myths, the goddess when she relates to the male relates to him as a consort, sometimes a son-consort, or brother-consort, but consort. And in the patriarchal world today he is the superior with all the power; and in the feminist world he is the enemy — or he is very rarely the brother or son. And when you get into sexual relationships again, he's not the equal. If he is there at all and the relationship has lasted, he is usually struggling so hard he has wound up in some sort of consort situation, even though there may be guilt attendant on that and rage and a whole lot of other knotted up things. But despite that conscious reasoning I would not at all quibble with your own analysis that there is no language right now for trying to name the male as equal because he isn't.

H.C.: Yes, and perhaps this manifests itself in your language as a lack of concreteness. The struggle with the male is there in poem after poem, year after year, but we never really know exactly what the nature of the struggle is, the details of it. We know more about it from the letters to Kenneth you published in *Going Too Far*, but when it gets transmuted or transformed into poetry it becomes more abstract. Whereas we do have much more of a concrete sense of the struggle between the mother and daughter in "The Mother": it is about the hatred of the female body learned from the mother, and how the daughter works out of that. Or in "Heirloom" there is a very concrete delineation of the struggle with the mother in which the daughter poet finally conceded the mother's right to imagination also without feeling threatened.

R.M.: It's in "Matrilineal Descent" in *Monster* too.

H.C.: Now in *Going Too Far* (and also earlier today) you mentioned the influence of metaphysical thought on your work. I perceive this mainly when you are trying to delineate a relationship with the male sex: it becomes plugged into a cosmic, a universal, and in the process it becomes mythic. It gets talked about in terms of energy. You use metaphors from physics, from botany . . .

R.M.: Yes.

H.C.: . . . from rocks, not nearly so much from domesticity. Now it's true you do sometimes use domestic words to describe the male, and you sometimes use metaphysical words in poems about women and about yourself. But it seems to me that this tendency indicates some avoidance, some difficulty.

R.M.: Yes. Okay. Terrific. I can't wait to answer. I have only recently become conscious of this. Only in the past year, and only with very recent poems. First of all, what I tend to think of as among the best metaphysical work that I've done is totally in a woman's ambience: in "The Self" section of "The Network of the Imaginary Mother" and in the very last section of "The City of God" addressing the female god in the self.

H.C.: And in "Ceremony."

R.M.: Yes, even in "Ceremony," which is a shorter, lesser poem, but it's definitely there. And I think the place where I'm most successful without it getting abstractified vis-à-vis the male is in "Voices from Six Tapestries" in *Lady of the Beasts*. There I was trying to have a multileveled metaphysical ambience working throughout the whole poem, and that was permitted by a kind of elevated language that the entire structure of the tapestries invited, without, I hope, falling into the abyss of preciousness. But it is also true, and Kenneth has pointed out, not without at times some justifiable bitterness, that he is almost always "transformed" in my poems. Whereas he has written love poetry to me which ranges from very concrete poetry about the folds of my labia all the way to seeing me as the high priestess on the Tarot deck or in an incarnation of the Goddess, and every other point along the spectrum, he appears most frequently in my poems as a dolphin, as a unicorn, as a spider, as a lion.

H.C.:   Or Osiris.

R.M.:   Or Osiris, that's right. But there has not been any comparable celebration of the male body in my poems. When I get concrete about him in poems, it is usually in anger poems and that is where the domestic imagery begins to come in again. But it doesn't even come in there early on. So you have "War Games (a mescaline quartet)" in *Monster*, a poem about the incredible violation that I am feeling, which is such a dense poem you really have to work hard to find out what's going on there. It is layered with a pallet knife. It is only very recently that I have found a way, to my absolute surprise, to write concretely (even then it is not as concrete as others would like) about the male. But that's also not, frankly, been one of my preoccupations, seeking that subject matter. Nonetheless you are quite right. It has been true for a long while that the abstraction is almost a form of evasion. It is not that one is seeking more elegant language there, but that somehow one is being driven to it. There is also a rebellion going on against a whole parenthetical period in which women poets, in trying to be "one of the boys," wrote about a man's cock and his terrific balls and the wonderful ridges on his chest—as well as some anger poems. And that was also imitation of the male. It was not the way that women might really write about men.

H.C.:   It is a quite new subject.

R.M.:   And it may not be the time yet. To try to speak of commitment, love, vulnerability in an affirmative tone and about a male—there is no language for that yet. It is very possibly because the relationships themselves are so raw; so newly emerging; so two-steps-forward, one-step-back. They don't exist, they're in the process of being invented.

H.C.:   It seems to me there is a third position. You say there is a language for talking in anger, and you have found a language for affirmation, be it dolphin, unicorn, or Osiris . . .

R.M.:   Yes, it seems I have to go out of the human species.

H.C.:   . . . what we haven't got or what these poems are struggling with is a language which speaks to the ambivalence.

R.M.:   Yes, that's quite true. You have to understand that there is a safe place which is the feminist ethos and there is an unsafe place which is the patriarchal world. And in the feminist ethos celebration of him feels crazy and you are *told* that it's crazy. So that until fairly recently the most that I have been able to get into the work was an approximation of that tension. It's still extremely rough: it evades here and deflects there. But there's another element about going outside the species which *was* conscious, and it's a valid one and one I stand by. It just isn't the whole truth. It seems to me that in this historical moment there is really such a vast gap between women and men, such an enormous wound, that our first priority as women has been trying to articulate ourselves and each other. And to try and love or relate to, let alone write about, the male is to take a leap into exogamy. When a people are only endogamous all sorts of problems begin, and exogamy is a very healthy thing in evolution. So then what was a conscious thought was that I might as well really be exogamous in terms of metaphor. I might as well think about dolphins, about eagles. And then you see there's a connection at a metaphysical level — the type of thing that happens at the end of "Voices from Six Tapestries" — where you're operating on the level where all sentient life begins to be one organism, and where you want those connections *so* intensely and desire them *so* continuously, that that's what the poem begins to be about. I affirm that level with every fiber of my being. But I want to be on that level and write out of that level, intentionally and affirmatively. I don't want to be there because I've escaped there for fear of saying something else out here. So I'm not saying anything that different from what you're saying. It's just that the task for me now as a metaphysical feminist poet is to affirm those connections, the cellular connections throughout life — without fudging this area.

H.C.:   That reminds me of George Eliot in *Middlemarch*, where the web imagery reflects Eliot's feeling of the absolute connection of all things. I'd like to look at three passages in connection with this issue. In "The Consort" you say:

> There is a place beyond our struggle
> where I will take us —
> beyond the archetypal, the animal,
> even the human,

beyond all we have been so far.
It will exist, see, I am creating it now.
You are utterly given over unto me.
And I will make of you the beloved.
I will call sacred antlers up from your brow
and place pipes against your lips.
Your haunches are mine, your sly buttocks,
your body disarrayed of all but my arms' garlands,
your brain encelled with my brain, double lotus.

[*LB,* p. 72]

R.M.:   Yes, I was proud of myself for getting those concrete haunches
and buttocks in there. Even though they are a little parenthetical, I was
touching base!
H.C.:

Before your Osirian trance will I unveil myself.
You shall be again the luminous bridegroom
all my suffering foresaw —
upon whose groin I placed my palm
to consecrate the light that streamed
from all your prophecies.

[*LB,* p. 72]

Now, at the very end of "Voices from Six Tapestries" the Lady is
addressing the Unicorn, imagining a time when they will not be "hunted
or adored":

And there, like a leap of thought or matter
toward the other's grace, we are transformed,
merged across species —
              female and male, myth and human,
beast, bird, leaf, fruit, flower,
music and blood and visions
all facets of one jewel, faultless,
within whose rainbow galleries we pulse as prisms, . . .

[*LB,* p. 130]

R.M.:   *That* one I really affirm, although over the fudging of the issue at
the end of "The Consort" I certainly agree with you. I think of the poem I

wrote about Kenneth's having been beaten up, "The Annunciation" in *Monster*, which is very specific. But it's interesting that I can name on the fingers of both hands those that are specific, and there are not many.

H.C.:   Yes. Now, in "The Mother" section of "The Network of the Imaginary Mother" you think back to a past where you

> . . . wept with lust for deliverance into spirit,
> light, soul, intellect.
> This blood was not of my making.
> These breasts were not of my willing.
>
> [*LB,* p. 64]

Here "lust for deliverance into spirit" delineates escape.

R.M.:   Yes.

H.C.:   And the effort is to ground yourself in the flesh, in the body.

R.M.:   Yes, and there's an open statement of that at the end of "The Self" section of "Network":

> Let me sit at the center of myself
> and see with all my eyes,
> speak with both my mouths,
> feel with all my setae,
> know my own sharp pleasure,
> learning at last and blessedly and utterly:
> The life comes first. There is no spirit without the form.
>
> [*LB,* p. 84]

H.C.:   Now it seems to me that idea of wanting "deliverance into spirit/light, soul, intellect" echoes in "The Consort."

R.M.:   Yes.

H.C.:   But there seems to be a change in "The Fall of a Sparrow" from your new book *Depth Perception*:

> 5
>
> Duel in the sun or the shadow,
> it ends the same.
> She rides on her revenge for days
> to his desert hideaway. She fires
> the signal shot. He shouts a welcome.
> She aims at him, shoots, hits. He falls.
> She screams his name and drops her weapons.

He struggles upright, aims, shoots her, and hits.
She falls. He screams her name.
How shocked each lover is to hit the mark aimed for.
How they crawl toward one another between
bullets, how they weep and curse and call
each other liars, how they bleed their parts
according to the rules.

I've heard your promises before, she rails.
How could you do this to me, he recites.
I'm dying, he calls, see, I'm a shadow now, come to me, hurry.
You lie, she sings, it's in your nature,
I was a fool. She claws the rockface, scaling
her own jagged hunger. Red lacy cuffs unfeather
from both her wrists. She climbs,
she reaches him, leaf dizzying upward in her
inner hurricane's blind eye.
"I love you," he sobs. At last and means it.
Kisses her and dies. One gesture
later — her hand poised on his head in blessing —
then she is dead as well.
High on their ledge above sunset and cliché
their bodies cling. Oh beauteous enemy.
Oh murderous grace, inevitable.

6

Until now, I'd have ended there. And been grateful.
(Transcendence, even "not at last but
at the very last" still worth damnation.)
But this once I find myself
turn, imagining how to imagine
a way to descend and still live. . . .

[*DP,* p. 96–7.]

The rhetoric of that reunion up on the rockface is very similar to the vision of transcendence in those earlier passages.

R.M.:   It is.

H.C.:   And when you say "Until now, I'd have ended there. . . . / But this once I find myself / turn," that is a real turning point, a refusal to escape.

R.M.:   Yes. And when I went on to that next section of "The Fall of a Sparrow," I did so with extremely sweaty palms and a nervous stomach. I think it was a watershed poem for me. When I had finished writing "Monster," which came in one sitting, I was shaking from head to foot, and I knew something had happened to me that I didn't particularly expect even when I had invited it. And I knew that something in my work would not be the same again. And I had a similar feeling about "The City of God" and about "The Network of the Imaginary Mother" — particularly the first section, "The Mother." And I kept having flashes of a similar feeling during "Voices from Six Tapestries." But it took me two years to write "Tapestries" and it was such a long process of revising and immersion in the esoteric secrets of the different herbs and it was such a rich poem that it was a very different thing. But I had intimations of this when I began "The Fall of a Sparrow" and when I sustained those intimations through to the end of the poem, I was deeply shocked. Glad, but very surprised.

H.C.:   What shocked you? Where had you gone on to by writing that?

R.M.:   Well, it was like stepping off the edge in some strange way. As I say in the poem:

> Surely, this time, I am done with professions of love
> between taking aim, surely done with
> the beauty of sin, dying, death. Oh let me be
> done with all revolutions that long for
> catastrophe, done with this crawling
> along the rockface, with training
> my heart to live in love, killing for it,
> coming undone.
>
> [*DP*, p. 97]

There are glimmerings of this earlier in prose at the end of *Going Too Far*. In "Metaphysical Feminism" there is a section called "Another Parable." This is about the eternal male being in love with Thanatos, with Death, in an agony of existence and blaming the female for his existence. And the eternal female being (as she says laughably) somebody who is ridiculously, hopelessly, forever saying, "I never met a universe I didn't like." But she always feels slightly embarrassed by it. Ironically, it was inspired by "King Zero," a work of Kenneth's. The parable is prose so in some strange way it is more grounded, but I had not made that statement as baldly in a poem until "The Fall of a Sparrow." It's a barometer poem, from which there's no returning. There are lapses, but there's no returning.

H.C.:   Part of that feeling has to do with these lines:

> Surely this time I will gather my wits, doggerel,
> props, and exit this tragedy, knowing that some will say
> this proves I lack tragic sense —but knowing the oldest
> of tragediennes is always some terrified clown
> circling a doom she insists is comedic,
> and knowing as well how preposterous
> I must look now, and how commonplace:
> blind, bloody, convulsively alert, face streaked
> with autumn, ridiculously
> twittering I can do it rhyme and reason
> I can do it, see?

> [*DP*, p. 97]

I want to place this in terms of the cycle of your three poetry books. *Monster* is very confrontative, rhetorical, angry, focused on something-out-there. *Lady of the Beasts* has a more unified aesthetic purpose and fulfills the promise at the end of *Monster* of speaking in a woman's language. There is a real sense of trying to establish that female network. You still look out to a male world but in that kind of uneasy metaphysical way we've been talking about. And I think that's partly true even of "Voices from Six Tapestries," as though all that dense research, all that detail, is also a way of still feeling uneasy about a certain subject matter. What I feel about *Depth Perception* with the "face streaked with autumn" is a coming into middle age.

R.M.:   I do hope so.

H.C.:   It produces more of a meditative calm. Some of these poems catch that younger voice going all over the place, and try to calm it down. Do you feel that way?

R.M.:   Yes. I hope there's a greater maturity in the poems. And I feel that in some of them there really is. It is meditative. I don't sense it as compromise or "settling." It seems to me that the voice is more confident of itself and willing in fact to settle less for other than it deserves.

H.C.:   Okay. Let me tie this in with another whole strand of thought. In *Going Too Far* you refer to "steps in the journey of a woman whose peculiar private grief includes having found herself, as an artist, seized by her time and typecast into a political figure" (*GTF,* p. 293). It seems you felt in some way you would be castigated if ever you allowed yourself to be first and foremost an artist.

R.M.: Less and less as I grow older.

H.C.: A very striking piece in *Depth Perception* which addresses this and which represents a real change from your earlier work is "Piecing":

> Once I thought this work could be less solitary.
> Many of us, I imagined, would range ourselves
> along the edges of some pattern we would all agree on
> well beforehand, talking quietly while we worked
> each with her unique stitch inward to the same shared center.
>
> This can still be done, of course, but some designs
> emerge before they can be planned, much less agreed on,
> demand an entire life's work, and are best viewed upon completion.
> And then, so many designers bore too easily
> to work the same theme over and over, with only
> the slightest gradual adjustments, like subtly changing
> your thread from brown to gray.
>
> [*DP,* p. 4]

This indicates an acceptance of the solitary and rigorous work of the artist. How did you get to this state?

R.M.: Painfully. There was no magic moment. It was a long process, some of which is articulated in the play "Art and Feminism: A One Act Whimsical Amusement on All That Matters" in *Going Too Far.* It's what we were saying earlier: if you throw out patriarchal standards, that doesn't mean you throw out standards. I began to understand that it didn't necessarily serve one's people, in my case women, to be less of oneself than one could be. There was that period in the sixties of intellectual downward mobility and that was rather dreary and I certainly got caught in that for a while. But I did get out of that. Nonetheless the subtler thing that you're talking about did persist. And it does no good, it embitters the artist, thereby making her much less of a useful productive political person. In addition, it does an enormous disservice to one's people to be producing less real art than one might for oneself *and* them. The best politics is honesty, and the best art is also honest. That's not enough in either case; both have to be put through a crucible of discipline and form and craft. But once there begin to be prevarication and mendacity around the edges, that's when in art you get your charlatans and in politics you get your fascists. On the other hand, the political existence of the feminist movement freed my own real voice as a poet. Otherwise I might have continued writing nice neat "academic poems" about other oppressed peoples, or maybe not even that. So it freed my voice, and I owe it a debt. I feel that, ethically, as a debt. Recently, I've been asked, are you taking yourself more seriously as an artist and therefore mellowing as a political figure? On the contrary, I feel that to take myself more seriously as an artist is to deepen myself as a political figure. I remember once after a reading when an individual woman had requested that I read "Monster." I had done a long reading and I was sick and tired of reading "Monster" and I said laughingly back to her, "Oh listen, sister, this is getting to be like, 'Hey, Judy, sing "Over the Rainbow." ' But I'm not Judy Garland and I don't really want to read 'Monster' anymore. If you insist, I will read another poem, but it will be another *new* poem and I'd be glad to do that, but I don't want to read 'Monster.' " And I remember that all the women in the entire room began stomping their feet and chanting, "We want 'Monster,' we want 'Monster.' " And the mixture of emotions to that in the individual artist is quite strange. You get the feeling that it's all they ever want to hear from you again, you might as well end it now, because you'll never top it again unless you try to imitate it and you know already that that's death for the artist. And you also don't want to play Dylan Thomas games of becoming a reader who is less a poet but more of a reading personality on the stage. So it gets very painful. I was enormously flattered and moved and *terrified* by that room. And I didn't read "Monster." I tried to explain all of those feelings right out and there were many women who understood and who came up afterwards and said so, and there were others who did not. There were still others who three years later wrote to me and said, "I've come a few turns on my own feminist spiral now and I realize what you were trying to say and the complexity of our evolution." But that process goes on. There were women who were very upset by *Lady of the Beasts*, by the complexity of the poems, and by the very thing that you characterized — a beginning affirmation of oneself as an artist, a complexity of forms, a richer language, a less polemical approach. God knows what will be thought of *Depth Perception*. But all I know is that those are my truths. I am a poet. I am also a woman and I am also a feminist. What is required of the artist is the courage to continue speaking her own truths, but they are a lot of women's. Even if they weren't, I would still have to speak them. I hate the split-off of politics and art, but the politics *are* very much in the new poems; they're just subtler, more complex, as my own life is.

H.C.:   My final question comes from "Piecing":

> So I discover how
> I am rejoicing slowly into a woman
> who grows older daring to write
> the same poem over and over, not merely
> rearranged, revisits, reworded, but one poem
> hundreds of times anew.

[*DP,* p. 3]

What is that "one poem," Robin?

R.M.:   This has been a peculiar year for me and I know less after 1980 what that poem is than I did before. I think up until 1981 that one poem is like the *Three Marias* quote in *New Portuguese Letters* that I use as an epigraph in *Going Too Far*: "How can we love? How can we not love?" It is about trying to exist with the invisibility, the nonexistence, and the rage about that, that men as a group and even the individual man that one loves represent to one, have done to one. And at the same time to love across and *through* that. Beginning with the self, and then extending to other women, and then to men. How to make that rage transformative and not just destructive. How to love in a world where love has not really existed. How not to commit suicide—either specifically or in any metaphorical way—by going under, giving up, giving in, giving out; that survival is not sufficient, that rage is not sufficient. They're poems about trying to love, they're all love poems—including sentient life and loving the universe. It's a search for grace. And the one poem written over and over again, I think even more concretely, has been a search for grace within a particular relationship, a particular marriage. Albeit a search informed by and equipped with feminist consciousness and all the attendant pain *and* all the attendant strength. *Now* I don't know whether I write the same poem over and over. Something quite extraordinary, even beginning with "The Fall of a Sparrow," happened to my work and I've had the feeling from very recent raw poems that there is something substantively changed, and I don't quite yet know what it is. It's a strange new confidence that I feel in myself as an artist, a maturity upon being forty, a coming to terms with the ambivalences about a certain kind of political activism. Some kinds of activism are always to be affirmed, but there are other kinds where one is *highly* dispensable. Whereas at my typewriter, writing my poems, I am not dispensable. I am the only human being alive who can do that, in the particular way that has my fingerprints on it. It is the thing I was born for, and I don't want to die without having done it.

© *Martha Kaplan*

Diane Johnson

Interviewed by
Janet Todd

Diane Johnson: "I was born in a small place in Illinois, along the Mississippi, a bookish childhood spending Saturdays in the Carnegie library, keeping a diary, writing stories. My stories were always like in school; when I was about ten or so I wrote a novel, a sort of mystery influenced chiefly by, it appears reading it today, the *Bobbsey Twins*, or *Five Little Peppers*. But I never had the idea to become a writer. In our town nobody had any idea that writers were anyone alive, living somewhere. They were abstractions, mostly born in the nineteenth century. Most of what I read, apart from children's books, were Victorian writers, because that was what was in the library and at home. I read all of Dumas *père*; but when I worked my way along to *fils*, the librarian wouldn't let me have *Camille*. Or *Madame Bovary*, when I was reading "The World's Great Novels," a list I found somewhere. I didn't know about modern poetry; though my father quoted extensively from James Russell Lowell and Longfellow. When I went to college, at seventeen, [in] my first class [I] read Mailer and Dos Passos. I was amazed and excited.

"Then I left college when I was nineteen, to get married, which was the fashion then; and I spent a few years having babies. I tried novel writing at home when they had their naps. I had moved with my husband, a medical student, to California, and we spent one year in Utah, during his internship. I took courses and finished my college degree there, and had two babies that year [1956] and eventually wrote a novel, *Loving Hands at Home*, about a Mormon family, somewhat based on experiences of a friend, and somewhat based on my own discontented housewife state at the time. Well, *Loving Hands* was my second novel; I wrote another first, *Fair Game*, published in 1965. I should add that somewhere along in here I had realized, or had inferred from the example of a friend, Alison Lurie, that a writer was something you could be — could be seriously and get published. But I had a hard time learning to take my own work seriously. I worked hard, of course, but could not believe it could be of consequence to anyone else.

"As somebody who married young and had a number of children, I think I confronted female problems early and in an immediate way, and came to terms with them rather quickly (devised defensive strategies) compared to other women now in their forties who more trustfully believed in Woman's True Happiness, etc., and are only now finding themselves without vocations. So I'm grateful for whatever circumstances prodded me in the direction of discovering mine. Maybe I would have found it whenever and whatever, but one can never be sure."

Diane Johnson's recent novels have a Southern Californian setting. Some critics have taken this location as part of their meaning, but perhaps California is a metaphor for anywhere in America or the future of any country. Certainly her world is not full of Hollywood starlets, but of rather plain heroines and neglected pizza-filled children, the stuff of all Western towns. I asked her about the Californian background, especially in *Burning* (1971).

"My first three novels take place in Southern California, the latest two in Northern California, because I write about where I live, for convenience. I have always felt that California is, if not anywhere in America, the future of America, and so setting stories here is valid as well as convenient. I've had a hard time with critics about this, for at first they tended to dismiss California as only about kooks, not about America. I notice that they react more strongly to Los Angeles; Sacramento or 'Orris,' being less highly colored, escaped the stigma of 'place' novels."

Yet if Diane Johnson's world is not necessarily the real California, it still seems essentially the fictive one, the non-Californian's image, a crazy society of fads in therapy and drugs. I wondered whether these fads, in her view, indicated some religious lack or were simply the result of too great affluence and license. She was not sure how to answer this, but supposed that they did come from a breakdown in belief, as well as from affluence. "More and more I feel that they arise from some tradition deeply other than mine, which I simply don't get, that there is some temperamental skepticism or midwestern something that makes me find all this deeply strange, that's all. And I have noticed that these therapies don't seem to work. I could expand on this. It seems to me that the message of traditional religions of all kinds, which have in fact given peace and happiness, has usually been to encourage unself-consciousness. The self is submerged in mystical reflection, or collective action, and even the Western tradition, which we think of as individualistic, contains these elements which we think of more typically as Eastern. Protestantism in the last two centuries has led some people into some doubt — self-searching, self-conscious forms of spiritual life; but the ideal of unself-conscious service and devotion has been there. Anyhow — it is presumably unself-consciousness that gives peace and happiness, the putative goals of all these therapies. A condition of the therapies, however, is total self-consciousness. The objectification of the self into an other whose progression [one] watches, whose needs one inquires into. The central question is 'Who am I?' or, how do they put it, 'I want to find out who I am,' which is the absolutely last question one can profitably ask and expect to find a happy or peaceful answer."

After *Burning*, Diane Johnson's next book was *Lesser Lives, The True History of the First Mrs. Meredith* (1972). It created some controversy as an example of creative or semifictionalized biography, for in it Johnson filled out facts and letters with speculation. I asked her if she could justify this approach to history or whether she regarded herself as a creative writer taking a plot from history. She seemed a little annoyed by the question.

"The rules I made up for *Lesser Lives* were pretty scrupulous. Whenever I hazarded a speculation, I labeled it as such. I didn't make anything up that wasn't set off as speculation. All biography is interpretation, after all, and when lives are not fully documented, more interpretation is required, that's all. I remember Mark Schorer telling me that he'd decided not to write a biography of, I think it was Wallace Stevens — there was simply too much material. But I do think that being a novelist, whose business it is, that is, to describe and imagine, has an advantage in describing and being intuitive about a biographical subject—an advantage, I mean, over someone who is simply a sleuth of facts. The only scruple one must have is to be perfectly plain about what is conjecture."

The main character of *Lesser Lives* is Mary Ellen Peacock, daughter of Thomas Love Peacock and first wife of the novelist George Meredith. In literary and historical discussions of the period she is merely a footnote to the famous men, but Diane Johnson has given her centrality. The result is a put-down of the usually central men, especially Meredith. I felt that Johnson had a personal animosity to a man who unkindly treated a woman with whom she had come to sympathize; the perceptive quotations from Meredith she used in the book often appeared at odds with her interpretation of his behavior.

"I did find myself becoming a little down on George Meredith," Johnson admitted. "The evidence is that he was horrid to his wives, his children—but at the same time I respect and admire his work, especially his attitudes to women and pioneering attitudes to sexuality in women, and so on. He was a kind of early Lawrence, really—visionary and ahead of his time. His wisdom arose from hard experience, and he was honest enough to identify in his work the male attitudes he deplored because he found them in himself. For him it was not so easy in real life, evidently, to behave other than as an Egoist; but none of us behave as we wish we would. I sympathize with him really; but my aim in *Lesser Lives* was to present the other side of a man who, after all, has had a lot of sympathetic biographical treatment."

There is something fascinating and disturbing about the tone and style of *Lesser Lives*. In her speculations, for example, Diane Johnson conveys the character, the times, and sometimes her own mockery. "We can only guess whether it was with happy heedlessness or with a self-justified feeling of bitter rectitude that Mary Ellen removed her camisole, chemise, corset, six petticoats, stockings and garters to make love to Henry." When I questioned whether such historical mockery was fair, Diane Johnson replied that she did not quite understand the question. "I think I was only dismayed by the idea of all the clothes you had to wear in those days. V.S. Pritchett in a review took exception to the same quotation and pointed out that Madame Bovary was a real whiz at getting out of all those garments." The simple, childlike style which I felt often got to the heart of the matter but which sometimes obscured was likewise justified: "My style is pretty unconscious. I guess I felt it was suitable to the subject. Kind of an oracular tone, commenting over the distance of years? I didn't mean ever to obscure. But I didn't mean to analyze too elaborately—I wanted drama rather than a rational analysis of women's plight or anything like that. In the notes the tone is more scholarly — there is a lot of scholarship, new unknown things about Meredith, that I felt I should annotate, but I didn't want footnotes, etc., distracting from the text too much."

The Shadow Knows (1974) is very different in subject from *Lesser Lives*, and yet it too deals with shadowy figures on the margins. It is the first-person story of one woman and her paranoia/persecution/obsessions — it's unclear which. I returned to my speculation about California, querying whether this shadowiness was for Diane Johnson a female or a human condition or one specific to a housewife in California in the 1970s. "All three," she responded. "It was meant to be about persons on the fringe; they happen to be women; and what happens to them is meant to be particular to America in the seventies, rather than to California. It's meant to be the fringes of places where blacks and whites both live." The ending leaves ambiguous whether or not the central character N. had reason for her overwhelming fear. If all happened as she claimed — and it seems to have done so — then her horror was founded. This was a surprise to me, for I had, I suppose, taken the horror N. feared as more figurative than the ending allowed. "I had meant her to be a reliable narrator," Johnson pointed out, "and the events more or less real, and the fear certainly real. Most of the things in the book really happened — that favorite claim of authors — and are not even that unusual, so critical reaction, which was often to doubt or assume that the narrator was unbalanced in some way, surprised me a little."

The title came from the tag line of a radio melodrama: "Who knows what evil lurks in the hearts of men? The Shadow Knows!" — and the book was about facing that evil. I felt N. had learned little and that in her world there was nothing significant to learn, that her final acceptance of the worst was just one in a series of little epiphanies. I asked Johnson if she thought this a fair reading of the novel. "The ending was figurative; when the worst happens and you have nothing much left to fear, you feel better, something like that. The facing of evil, or some recognition of complicity in it. What was there for N. to learn, really? It wasn't in fact her story — it was the story of the other women. Osella and Ev."

"If someone is trying to kill you, do you maybe deserve it?" asks N.; the question suggests a wonderfully tentative certainty, a general guilt, and I wanted to know what Johnson felt was the source of that guilt. But she pulled away from the point, noting how hard it was to talk about her books in this way. "Not that they can't be reduced to theme," she admitted, "I suppose they can, but I don't think of them like that when I'm writing them. That's for literary critics. I do literary criticism too, of course, and am aware of it as a separate procedure. But it's hard to do it on yourself. But as to this question, I heard a police chief on the radio the other night saying that people commonly wonder if they did something to bring on bad things that happen to them; and since there is a lot of crime, a lot of people go through the stage of wondering. I suppose the source of this in our culture is religious; bad visitations can be interpreted as punishment."

In my reading of *The Shadow Knows*, N. seems to imagine characters in advance of their actual appearance in the novel — the inspector, the great lover. There is a kind of movement from imagination to reality that is a comment on the power of imagination. Diane Johnson agreed and added that there was also a need or tendency to imagine authority figures.

"But I was also playing with the genre of detective fiction, in which the detective/authority figure (and N. is familiar with the genre) is also somehow in touch with the criminal intuitively; there is some connection."

The two black women in *The Shadow Knows*, Ev and Osella, seem at home in the horrific world of N. This may be part of N.'s racial fear or perhaps their violence, provoked or not, makes them part of the evil society in a way N. is not. Johnson intended their separation from N. who does not really live in their shakier world. "This is just sociological observation; in their world there is more risk, more violence. They are victims, of course, and they take more peril for granted. Peril and violence astonish the middle-class N." The mad and huge Osella is in many ways the madwoman in the attic for N., and I asked Diane Johnson if she had a literary continuity in mind when she created her. She replied that she did. "Osella is the double, the huge, unleashed person. I had a similar person in my life, and in fact she was born on the same day as I and was, like me, left-handed. But I thought that would be too much. So often in fiction you have to leave out real things which would be too much."

There seems some criticism in *The Shadow Knows*, as in the earlier *Burning*, of the self-indulgent, self-actualizing therapy philosophies America has so wholeheartedly embraced. N. herself criticizes her friend Bess for the lack of restraint and control in herself and her child. And yet she still feels her own emotions must always be right: "If you can't trust in your own instincts about things, in your own feeling of rightness, in the things that you know, in your deepest intuitions — then where are you?" I worried about the still current emphasis on the self, self-actualization, and the primacy of one's own feelings. Diane Johnson shared the worry but felt that N. was not talking about self-actualization or the primacy of her feelings, but rather about having common sense, about depending on your own rather than on the instincts of a *guru* or doctor. "She is extending the criticism of therapy, etc. She doesn't mean to be anti-intellectual, feeling over thought, but believes in knowing what you think and feel without someone else having to tell you what you think and feel."

I have found Diane Johnson very perceptive about the comforts of pessimism. "There is a badness to things that satisfies your soul, confirming that you were right about what you thought was what," she has written. I asked her whether this could translate into a personal philosophy. "I suppose so. I suppose I am a pessimistic person who has been lucky in my own life, putting me in an odd dilemma, which I apologize for in fiction."

Johnson's last book, *Lying Low* (1978), again takes up the feeling of persecution so clear in *The Shadow Knows* but it gives the chief characters a reason — Marybeth her activist past and Ouida her missing passport. Nonetheless the effect is again of persecution beyond provocation. Did Diane Johnson feel this was a human condition or an aspect of the political situation in the United States? "N., I would emphasize, has reasons for her feelings of persecution too — the various bad things that happen actually happen. But, as you say, the idea of persecution beyond provocation is there too, and meant to be an aspect of America more than of the human condition. It seems worse in the United States than, say, Europe. I suppose it seems worse in Argentina than in the U.S. Politics and social facts."

Most of the book deals with incomprehension and confusion, as did *The Shadow Knows* — for example, Theo, the older woman, feels that young people fail to understand her criticism of liberation when in fact they feared she knew of their violent plan. Language here seemed an ambiguous and uncertain means of communication. "I am always struck, when eavesdropping for instance, with how two people carry on two parallel conversations, rather than an interlocking one. People don't say what they mean or feel; and no one understands them anyway. Ouida, in *Lying Low*, is meant to exaggerate this by not quite understanding all English words. But of course language is the main thing we have, which is why it's so fascinating."

Diane Johnson's books are much concerned with age — Theo is in her sixties yet seems in some ways younger than the disillusioned young people. Sometimes it appears that there is a necessary difference between the consciousness of young and old, but at other times there is clearly an embarrassing and surprising continuity. Diane Johnson related *Lying Low* to her own experience: "In that book I got to be the age myself where a person of my age would no longer do for a romantic heroine — so I tried imaginatively leaping ahead a couple of decades to see if I could do that. And Theo is more innocent than the disillusioned young — she's meant to represent those rather sweet and naive old liberals who still think that the Spanish Civil War was the main political event of the century. I think people's consciousness, especially their political perceptions, tend to be arrested with the great event they themselves were most closely connected with, and this lends them an unworldliness about other political events. Theo about Vietnam protest, Ouida about everything American. So there are necessary gaps. At the same time there is a continuity, I believe, about emotions and hopes, and I don't find this embarrassing, or at least not yet. I suppose, someday as a very antique old thing trying to think young, I will embarrass others."

There seems an odd contrast in *Lying Low* between the English-style eccentric old people and the violent young and between turbulent America and Chuck's cultured Europe. It seems the choice is in some ways culture or violence. The only person we get close to who has no sustaining culture or art is Marybeth, for whom the youth culture of violence failed. "I suppose that it does seem to me as an American that our choice is between culture and violence. We have tried to say that our culture is violence, that's how we are; but I think this is an evasion, an attempt to substitute something for what we think is nothing. We doubt that there is an American culture, that is. If we believed in American culture, or in a heritage from other cultures, we would be more conservative of it, and I think would control or disapprove violence. This all seems sort of abstract, but I guess it's the question. Theo and her brother in *Lying Low* have an affinity for the continuity of the culture of art in Europe and the U.S.; Chuck wishes to get culture; Marybeth will have to learn it, presumably."

Death haunts all Johnson's books — *Burning* ends in cataclysm and so does *Lying Low* (Theo is killed, the house vandalized, and Marybeth and Ouida neutralized); *The Shadow Knows* closes with the sudden death of Ev. Death seems violent and feared and yet, when it comes, it is sad rather than horrifying. I asked Diane Johnson if she felt death in America had been so marginalized and avoided that it became the shadow lurking? "I tell my students in writing class not to kill people off, that it's too simple a climax, too often cheap drama, unearned. Yet I do it myself. I try to watch it though, and not kill off characters as a simple way of getting rid of them. I always mind it in others, gratuitous fictional deaths. I always minded the ending of Mary McCarthy's *A Charmed Life*, for instance, except for the ending such a fine book. Or there are other examples. In life, I hate thinking about death at all. In fiction there's no question that it has its uses. Some of the deaths in my books, though, are literal events, taken from newspapers. I forget the figure now, but the year when I was writing about Theo's death in a prison breakout attempt, there were a huge number, a really large number of Americans killed in prison breakouts. Quite a few people just murdered in laundry rooms of cheap housing projects. I've never written about illness, about death from within, as it were. Yes, I do think we marginalize death, as you put it, or else — I don't know. I don't seem to draw any conclusions from it."

> She knew it was silly, crying for hens and for the little families of doves. It was not for hens exactly that she cried, but for whole orders of bald edible creatures that had been optimistically furred or feathered against danger, whose little artifices did not suffice, meager-brained, but trying to get along, against whom death would come slashing when it was not expected.
>
> —*Lying Low* (New York: Knopf, 1978.)

I found this a wonderful passage of the sadness of mortality and the vulnerability of most people and other creatures. Diane Johnson accepted my reading of the passage, which, she said was just as she intended and felt it.

The quotation also provoked a discussion of Johnson's style, for I found it an example of the tone of most of her books — mocking, loving, simple-seeming. I asked her to comment on this style, its development and the influences on it. "I think it is just my style and probably the way I talk," she replied. "I try to write as clearly, as exactly as I can what I think. I often wish I could write figuratively, and sometimes expend a conscious effort toward that. Someone once told me I use too many semicolons, and I try to watch those. I often think I should take more pains with style, but when I'm writing, there seem to be so many other things to watch out for too. Who influences style? I suppose the books you read as a child, in my case English Victorians and nineteenth-century American writers like Twain. When I began to choose for myself and could see the ones I admired most — Flaubert, Kafka, Virginia Woolf, V.S. Pritchett — I could see that they had things in common, but all seemed far from me, alas. But these are the people I read for stylistic inspiration, as it happens. I used to look at certain passages in Hartley's *The Go-Between*, and Pritchett's *A Cab at the Door*. I think my style is changing some, and growing more flexible and less conventional. But not much."

The tone sometimes reminded me of Iris Murdoch, sometimes of Joan Didion, and occasionally of Fay Weldon. "I admire Murdoch and Didion. I'm not familiar with Fay Weldon's work, except for one book, whose title I forget, which I thought very funny and wonderful. Some people living in the country, baking a lot of bread, with a lot of English-style domestic chaos.

"I also love the work of several friends — Alison Lurie and Alice Adams, and Elizabeth Hardwick. Admire Rosellen Brown's work, Margaret Drabble. Beryl Bainbridge is wonderful. I've just been reading all of her. Iris Murdoch and Joan Didion as mentioned above, of course. I'm sure I'm forgetting people. Nadine Gordimer is most impressive. I admire Grace Paley tremendously, and really haven't taken Jong seriously."

I wondered what Johnson thought of the autobiographical literature of Kate Millett and the heavily polemical writing of Marilyn French. "I read Kate Millett's *Sexual Politics*, and admired and liked it tremendously, but I haven't read her two subsequent books, and I haven't read any of Marilyn French. One page or so of her first book. It just wasn't the sort of book I would read. I think autobiographical writing is okay on principle, why not? But it should be good, well written, like Tillie Olsen's — autobiographical, good, and well written. Polemics are okay too, I guess, but the same rules apply."

I tried to provoke her into further criticisms, but she was not to be budged. "If I start something and dislike it intensely, I don't read it. I don't feel any special obligation to suffer. I don't like long self-indulgent formless works by anyone, and I don't like family chronicles — all these works about people's grandmothers that seem to be coming along. But this is doubtless a matter of taste.

"When I was growing up, after the usual children's books—except Louisa Alcott whom I did not like—I liked adventure writers: Dumas *père,* Sabatini, Joseph Henry Dana. When a little older, Jane Austen and Thackeray and Trollope. Trash historical novels. I loved *Moby Dick,* and Twain, and Henry James. I read all of James when I was quite young. And Hardy.

"Sometimes I wonder if I am that sinister thing, the male-identified woman. I would be the right generation for it. I don't think I am, really, but I do know that I don't entirely agree, from my own experience, with critical contentions about the forlorn estrangement of the female artist from the creative tradition because all the previous writers were men. It was a long time, for me, before I realized my femininity, or femaleness; as a girl I read "boys' " books and it never occurred to me that I couldn't sign on to a whaler or go before the mast or whatever. I mean that I could participate imaginatively in adventures had by males. By the time I realized that my situation was different, I had already profited, I hope, from the things that great books have to give no matter by whom they were written. And then one found that the great women writers were not such wonderful comforting models, at least George Eliot was not."

I asked her then whether she thought women wrote differently from men and had different subjects? "I think that women have different subjects," she responded. "Set their novels in houses, center them in families, things that correspond to the facts of female life. I don't think that they write any differently, though. I mean there are good ones and bad ones, as among men. Poseurs of both sexes, only the poses are different. I don't see how one can say that a sentence is male. Anymore than handwriting, which also can't be distinguished by sex."

"I regard myself as a feminist, as any nice woman would be. I don't see how another attitude is possible to any serious person. I don't regard myself as a feminist writer, though. To be any kind of writer with an 'ism' would make it harder to be an artist, and art is hard enough. Of course my books have women in them, and women's problems because those are the ones I know about. I resent, as many women writers surely have, the current view that seems to hold that men write 'literature' but women write 'feminist' literature, or women's literature, just because the former have, likely, male, the latter female protagonists; and if a book by a man has a female protagonist it is still excused. I think that feminists perpetuate this odd convention (which seems always to have existed, but not so much, perhaps, in the nineteenth century), by emphasizing the differences and the polemical issues. A house can be as apt a metaphor for life as a ship is; there are military tales; a woman's story about courage or valor would have to have a different setting. But I don't see why people of both sexes can't have access to these common backgrounds and myths without saying that some are for both sexes but some are women only and, perforce, less worthy. This is so much a preoccupation of critics in the popular magazines, but academics often echo—putting Virginia Woolf only in women's literature classes, for instance. In one case at [University of California at] Davis, one of my male colleagues taught a course called something like 'Sex in Literature' and it contained no books by women.

"I approve of all the legal and consciousness-raising and militant things about feminism, though I don't do much. I try to support them. I don't approve of some of the doctrinaire bickering that you hear goes on, or of the wish to make everyone toe the mark. I got a terrific scolding from a female colleague over something I had written about Charlotte Brontë. She said, 'That's not what feminist criticism says.' Actually I am rather poorly read in feminist criticism."

I asked her whether her attitudes about women had changed over the past few years. She felt they had not. "I was raised without too much consciousness of female disadvantage. My brother had to do the dishes too, etc. When I did suddenly realize it, when I was about twenty, married, babies on the way, and the clear expectation that it would be me that stayed home and minded them and the house, I was shocked. Though I hadn't anything else in mind either. Through shock, my ideas about my personal arrangement developed quickly, and I still stick by most of the conclusions I came to then—this would be the late fifties, or early sixties—and I think they would hold true for other women: ideas about rights and duties, self-realization, doing one's work, taking one's work seriously.

"I suppose I feel uneasy at my own good fortune, when so many others don't have good fortunes, or seem to me to have sad lives. The precariousness of things is rather harrowing, the idea that things can take a turn for the worse. Up to now, though, I have found things less awful than I imagined they would be, in fact not awful at all.

"Politically my views do keep changing. I think, to paraphrase a character in one of my books, that I've given up on people and am become a rabid environmentalist instead."

Germaine Greer

Interviewed by
Joseph Kestner

Germaine Greer was born in January 1939, in Australia. She began her academic study in Gardenvale, Victoria, early achieving success: in 1956 alone she held a Diocesan Scholarship, a Senior Government Scholarship, and a Teacher's College Studentship. She graduated in 1959 from the University of Melbourne with B.A. honors in English and French language and literature. In 1962, she finished her master's degree with first-class honors at the University of Sydney. As a senior tutor in English, she taught at Sydney from 1963 to 1964.

In 1964, Germaine Greer became a Commonwealth Scholar at Newnham College, Cambridge University, from which she received her Doctor of Philosophy, concentrating on Renaissance studies, with a thesis on Shakespeare's early comedies. Following her graduation, she became assistant lecturer and then lecturer in English at the University of Warwick, Coventry, from 1967 to 1972. During this time she was briefly married to Paul du Feu.

With the publication of The Female Eunuch *by McGibbon and Kee in 1969, Germaine Greer became one of the most erudite of the leaders of the international women's movement. In 1972 she became a columnist for the* Sunday Times, *London, and began reviewing for such journals as the* Spectator *and the* New Statesman. *This career included broadcasting as well: in 1972, she covered the Democratic Convention for* Harper's. *Meanwhile, in 1971 she participated in a landmark, much-celebrated debate with Norman Mailer at Town Hall, New York, about the women's movement.*

The year 1979 saw Germaine Greer take another academic direction. In autumn, 1979, she was appointed visiting professor in the Graduate Faculty of

Modern Letters at The University of Tulsa. Several months later she was appointed
a permanent member of the Graduate Faculty as professor. She became director of
the Tulsa Center for the Study of Women's Literature. In October 1979, her second
book, The Obstacle Race: The Fortunes of Women Painters and Their
Works, *was co-published by Secker and Warburg and Farrar, Straus and*
Giroux.

Presently, Germaine Greer spends most of her energies at the Tulsa Center,
often sixty or more hours per week. "One of the greatest problems confronting the
student of literature by women is the scarcity and undeveloped state of the texts,
even those by the best-known writers. Moreover, a larger proportion of women's
work was extensively edited and even bowdlerised," she has written. To correct this
situation, the Center "is looking at the works of seventy-four women poets," with
some emphasis currently on the eighteenth century. She has said, "We are not a
women's studies center. It's a common misconception. We specialize in women's
literature." Germaine Greer will, in connection with the Center, be editor of Tulsa
Studies in Women's Literature. *In 1980 she delivered the keynote address at*
the Nineteenth-Century Women Writers Conference at Hofstra University.

Germaine Greer is a demanding professor. She remarks, "Once students
are in my class for a half hour, they realize it's going to be hard work. Those who
think they will kibitz through will be dismissed. Some say I expect too much of
students, that my standards are too high. I agree, but tell them, 'You can come up
to mine because I won't come down to yours.'"

Germaine Greer's current interests, both discussed in the subsequent
interview, are fertility and Shakespeare. Her next book is titled The Politics of
Fertility. *In that study she will discuss "reproductive rights," focusing on the*
relationship of government to fertility. "This is probably the most important book
I've ever written," she has noted. Her subsequent work, to be published by Oxford
University Press, will involve Shakespeare.

The following interview was conducted during the autumn term, 1980,
at The University of Tulsa, Graduate Faculty of Modern Letters.

Germaine Greer: I think to speak of a "community" of women authors is
to overstate the case. We are all in the same position. The language is
principally spoken by others. We come to it as borrowers or as servants
who have stolen their master's clothing, in a way. We teach everybody to
speak — women teach children to speak, but when it comes to
establishing the language of a tribe, purifying it, defining it, women
haven't traditionally done that. There are still certain realms, I think, that

are closed to women, which women struggle to open, only to find they are a sort of Pandora's box, because the language is even repulsive.

Take George Eliot as a case in point. George Eliot imagined when she was writing *Middlemarch* that she was writing an archetypal novel. She wrote a frontpiece and an endpiece of the novel in which she described what she thought she was doing about Dorothea's having to find another way out because it wasn't the time of heroism and it wasn't the time of St. Theresa of Avila, but like St. Theresa of Avila she went off looking for martyrdom and probably was condemned to survival. That's not really what the novel is about. The novel is about ever so much more than that. However, its true profundity occurs on a different scale. It couldn't be described in that way. Its true profundity occurs in the way Eliot describes the mating of Lydgate and Rosamond, the dishonesties at its base, the way dishonesties become institutionalized in the relationship, the effect that the relationship has on both people. It's a great tragic depiction, and yet it doesn't have any immediate bearing on that theme. That theme is the theme in capital letters which will do to justify the book to the aliens — it says it was the excuse for the book, but the actual achievement of the book is something quite different. The Dorothea theme doesn't mean what Eliot thought it meant. In knowing that the two stories of Lydgate and Dorothea have to be wedded, she was responding to artistic truth. She was absolutely right; they did have to be wedded. The book has more in common with something like James's *Portrait of a Lady* than it does with *War and Peace*, one of the novels of grand sweep and small penetration. When you look at it, when you actually confront what is staggering about the relationship between Dorothea and Will, it is that Dorothea makes a decision that disappoints the reader because the reader has this silly expectation that she is going to marry a great man. Eliot knows that her only salvation is to marry a man who needs her, which is a completely different thing. In the examination of how those attitudes are shaped by day-to-day contacts and progress in knowing each other, familiarity and so on, Eliot really has the same genius as Jane Austen. It's dressed in different trappings, dressed in the Victorian multivolume novel trappings. But the skill exists, and it's absurd to call it miniaturist. It infuriates me that people call Jane Austen a miniaturist. A miniaturist is not one who persuades you of the greatness of the small things of everyday life; a miniaturist is one who takes huge subjects and makes idiotic references to them in a tiny scale. You can make an icon on ivory which encapsulates eternal truth. And to suddenly have said, oh yes, ivory, that means that she's a miniaturist — wrong — mistake. It's just that you draw a different line. It's like the difference between an etching where you are allowed no pentimenti, where you are drawing straight onto the plate, and something that you can puddle around with and rework and paint over and so on. All the thinking has to be done before you make the next stroke, and everything is in the tension in a single line.

In reference to Charlotte Brontë's hostility to Jane Austen, you find examples of that all the way through. You see, that's the problem. The problem is that every woman faced with this unpleasant reality that she is trying to creep up the back stairs into the drawing room has to think that the women who have already made it and have suffered in the drawing room, have done it in some way that is illegitimate. You have this phenomenon which you find everywhere, the phenomenon of horizontal hostility. There is so much hostility that you reach out and grab the person you can actually get hold of. You are hostile to the person who is close to you, but different. Charlotte Brontë was a desperately passionate and a desperately frustrated woman, and she would have loathed Jane Austen's achievements of artistic balance and stasis, and she may well not have been aware of the heroic struggle to achieve that. She may have thought it came easy because it is very easy to misunderstand the culture that immediately precedes yours because so much of your growing-up was a rejection of that. I am troubled by the hostility that women writers express to each other. All women artists for that matter. They do it all the time and it is unworthy of them. It is completely self-defeating. But it is inevitable. Remember that women don't want to be put in that hamper that says "women writers." They want to be the one woman writer who doesn't have to go in the hamper.

Fanny Burney is an absolute bitch. She is the harshest judge that any woman had. You just can't believe the gratuitous sniping by Fanny Burney. Fanny Burney is the sort of person that the more history you do, the more you hate her because she crops up all the time; she is always unreliable, she is always destructive, and she is always self-seeking and self-aggrandizing. She drove people crazy. For example, take one case. Dear old Mrs. Delany, the most civilized woman who ever lived, who never said an ungraceful thing, never did an ungenerous one. A life spent in avoiding doing evil is really spent quite well, and Fanny Burney just insisted on cultivating Mrs. Delany, who really couldn't bear her. She was a little vulgarian, and Mrs. Delany could see quite well what was going on, that she was being used to improve the reputation of one Fanny Burney. Of course Jane Austen was right to admire her because in a way, because of her complete thick skin, Fanny Burney wrote things that nobody else could write.

There has been far too much stress upon the lack of sympathy to women writers, because they really didn't have all that much difficulty getting published. Nobody did, and in fact you've got the giveaway, because you actually do have poems published as if by young ladies which were actually by young gentlemen because there was more interest in young ladies. It was easy to be published, as a freak. It was also quite easy to raise a subscription. Now, for example, if you take Mary Barber. Mary Barber was a friend of Swift's. She smuggled some of his more dangerous manuscripts to England for him, and she wrote, like hundreds of people who wrote Augustan verse and hundreds of people [who] got published. Grub Street was a reality, publishers would publish anything — once. Mrs. Barber's poems, if I'm not mistaken, were published by subscription, and lots of women poets were published by subscription. Now that meant that all the people in her immediate circle agreed to buy copies of the book, and when you got five hundred people or five hundred copies, somebody might take twenty and give them to friends; then you could afford to publish and went ahead and published. That's an extraordinary situation.

I think the chance to publish is really fairly good most of the time. If you take Mrs. Barber, I have just chosen her at random. Mrs. Barber's poems were really rather illiterate, but they showed some sort of promise. So Swift and Delany and Mrs. Grierson — Constantia Grierson, a classic scholar who was married to a bookseller — worked on the poems and prepared them for publication. Now you can look at that in another way. You can say, Oh well, they damn well rewrote them. But if they did, Mrs. Barber was only too happy to stand forth publicly as the author of this elegant volume that finally came out of Dublin. This happens hundreds of times. Eighteen-year-old milkmaids write tolerably well in verse and somebody shows up and pays for it, and then Byron comes along and says, "Oh God, with all these carpenters and milkmaids babbling on all sides," and he is perfectly right, and there's not much value to it. There were literally hundreds of women writers in the eighteenth century who got a chance, and the same is true in the nineteenth century. It's what happens next after the chance. You can't necessarily make a living, but it was tough even for Pope to make a living. Living is difficult, publication is easy. So of course the palm goes to the amateurs of the upper middle class who get themselves published on very slight credentials.

As far as a distinctly women's language or style is concerned, one day we will have machines that will do that. We will just feed books into them and ask them to give us a scatograph of the kind of language that they used, and I think that we would probably find that Ambrose Phillips is indistinguishable from Miss Namby Pamby Nimmininy Tit or whatever she is called. But if you take the case of Virginia Woolf, it is rather interesting because I really find great difficulty with the style of Virginia Woolf's novels. I find it slippery and self-feminizing. She is projecting an image of femininity: this liquidity of the images that slosh together, the glancing attention to everything in a room, the sort of coyness occasionally, the effectiveness of the touch. I find *Orlando*, for example, impossible to read. I just want to beat my head against the wall. I don't know what she is playing at. Then I come to something like *The Common Reader* and I think, "My God, why don't you do this in the novels—why can't I have this marvelously original, nonpompous, razor-sharp perception, beautifully expressed, this learning lightly worn, going straight to the heart of the thing—encapsulating the character you are talking about in six or seven words that could never be better?" The shock of recognition sounds in every line in the essays, and when you read the novels, there is no shock of recognition at all. You are actually being beaten with silk scarves. It is just infuriating. If you have got a situation where women are seeking for a female style, what you are going to have is a parody of a female style in the same way as women in the past have written a parody of a male style.

It's a lie, and it's something interposed between the writer and truth. It's another obstacle to climb over, and I just don't know what the solution could be. The thing that interests me is the way Virginia Woolf wrote the essays in *The Common Reader*. There was no Leonard Woolf standing over her shoulder; she was writing for deadlines. She was writing for a public that had to be told something, and occasionally she cared more about the subject, even if it was Letitia Pilkington, another eighteenth-century writer. She just wanted to get the subject before you quickly, and give you her perception of it, and she was all intelligence and no creativity, except that she is much more creative when she is all intelligence. It's when she is being creative that we would say, "Stop it, Virginia, just stop mannerizing the subject." It is the false standards of

Bloomsbury. A lot of it is Leonard Woolf. I do not have the usual view of Leonard Woolf. Leonard Woolf was Virginia's problem, not her salvation. I wish she had had a room of her own or a fellowship at Girton or something, anything. She is absolutely right about that. Space is important, and most women don't have any. Everybody, everyone was on Virginia's case. Everybody, not just Leonard. Jane Austen knew exactly what she was doing with the creaking stair. But it is much more important than that because what you have got to stop is men's surveillance. I can't believe that men still do this, even men who ought to know better, even if I write something and I'm living with a man who has something to do with letters. (I hardly ever am.) My way of having a creaking stair is that I generally make love to men who haven't read a word I have ever written and never will.

When men hear the typewriter going, they just wait for the typing to stop so they can have dinner, and they say, "Have you finished typing, dear?" Then they will say, "What did you write today?" Because it doesn't matter if the man is a sort of tenth-rate academic who has never been published; he will still look at the sheet in the typewriter and say, "Oh, did you mean that?" or "I think there are too many adjectives," and the thing about it is, you haven't finished with it — you are still drafting it and here you are getting an unsolicited opinion about it. When you say, "Mind your own business," or "Go away," or "Go publish your own novel," it's an amazing thing. Men with very little achievement still consider that they should advise women.

Jean Rhys maddens me because she's got this wonderful art-deco prose style, and all it does is paint the same picture of the thwarted woman who's got out of an unbearable relationship but who sees nothing before her except the possibility of another unbearable relationship which she'll be in just as long as she can bear it, and then she'll be back sitting in the corner of this café with some single glass of absinthe that she has to make last for four hours because she can only afford one glass. This is after leaving Mr. Mackenzie and before meeting Mr. Somebody Else. I think, "Oh, Jean, for God's sake" — this is so empty and so self-regarding, an exquisite piece of nothing. Just paper cutouts.

Authors creating male and female characters is an interesting situation. Defoe's women are a special case in more than one way because lower-class women just don't have any voice in literature at all at this time, so you might consider that he is writing about *Born Free*, what was the lioness's name? It is that sort of thing, Elsa, the lioness in *Born Free*.

Defoe is writing about an interesting species and he is fascinated by it, as well he should be; it is wonderful, but it has no voice of its own. It can only be hymned by people like him and it can't be hymned by other women because they have never encountered such a thing as a bawd or a self-seeker or a survivor. However, and it certainly puzzles me, men can create women characters in a way that women cannot create men characters, like Flaubert in *Madame Bovary*. You see, we don't really understand how much of men "c'est nous" because we are hypnotized by the alien quality of men at the moment. So it is in history traditionally: we have always written about men as lay figures; it is really strange. Think of Eliot as a case in point. The women are so much better than the men in Eliot always, more fully developed, more paradoxical, more interesting, more alive. Daniel Deronda is a complete yawn. Now, what can you do with that character, how could she do that? (I would take the one exception of Lydgate.) But I can think of other cases. I can think of Henry Handel Richardson's Morris Guest. Morris Guest just doesn't work at all, I think. He's just not there.

Well, why does anybody not succeed? I am trying to think of a single example. You see, even someone like Gissing writes well about women. I *know* the women he is talking about. He writes about them with tremendous compassion and insight and lets them be active in a way in which he wouldn't even have found particularly attractive or comprehensible. I love *The Odd Women*. It is a wonderful book, and I had never read any Gissing before until Virago did that book. The achievement of *The Odd Women* is the creation of those independent women and the following through of the decision to reject heterosexual love. I mean, the two things are very difficult to do. He must make you feel all the intensity. You know how much of the working of the novel is making the reader desire what you are going to get the characters to do; that's what *Pride and Prejudice* is all about. So Gissing gets you to really desire that these two characters will mate, and then he does the toughest thing of all. He has the woman reject it for reasons which are perfectly valid, but not easy for a man to sympathize with because generally the view is, you know, she teased me, she led me on, she wasted my time, she's frigid, she's a lesbian, she's something or other. Gissing does it so well because you realize it is also the only possible decision. I hadn't realized he was a novelist of that stature. I didn't think he had that in him. I can't bear to think about *The Mill on the Floss*. It is just so ungraspable, that novel. It's a great novel. Maggie is set for destruction from the very beginning.

The eighteenth century would have thought of the suffering heroine as a tasteless and sentimental indulgence in unhealthy thoughts, but the amusing thing about that is, it seems to me, that the Augustan insistence upon social life, social values, grace, moderation, derives from a very close and vivid apprehension of the alternative. You have a population which for various reasons is beset by all kinds of neurasthenia so that the spleen is a disease which has possibly fatal results. I don't even know yet what the spleen is — I'm not happy with any of the modern definitions of what the eighteenth century meant by it. But it seems to me that the eighteenth century saw the people lose their bearings and go mad. Possibly because of white lead poisoning, stupid reasons, I don't know why. Poor old Swift had an infection in his middle ear which meant he lost his sense of balance and his sense of orientation, and so he thought he was mad. His great fear of being mad drove him mad, and that was the sort of Augustan reality. Johnson was a chronic depressive who had tremendous difficulty moving from one day to the other, so when he wrote in defense of sanity and independence and the stoic virtues of self-sufficiency and so on, he wrote with all the passion and the yearning of somebody who knew that those virtues were beyond him. Somehow or other, by the time we get to the nineteenth century, life is eased for many people. There is a whole new stolid robust middle class that is making a lot of money and wants to see its own values perpetuated, and suddenly, the first thing that happens is the romantics began to court madness and to value melancholy. They are actually trying to diversify their experience by playing with things of which the eighteenth century was mortally afraid and so these things lose their terror. You start having an aesthetic approach to people at the end of the tether, people that are falling to pieces, and you start to exploit them as a rarity. There is no point in exploiting when your sister is upstairs and has been prey to hysteria for months and months and is dying because she won't hold any food down and so on and so forth. You wouldn't dream of going to an opera about a woman who was dying of love. It just would be gross. But women stopped dying of love or whatever it was that they were dying of; they were probably dying of completely different things, but it all got parceled up in a psychosomatic package of madness and decline and so on. Remember that even Charlotte Brontë vomited herself to death in a pregnancy. She died of dehydration.

It is quite clear in reading poets like Anne Finch that the spleen was a disease caused in many ways by inactivity, by enforced inactivity, by frustration and the turning of the vital powers inward. The alternative was to be married and to risk your life in childbirth and to run a house and then you were actually being put to work so the usual thesis was, oh well, frustrated motherhood is killing these women. But it was more than that. It was being deprived of any function in the world, and Finch makes more claims for melancholy or spleen or atrobilious fit than other people do. When you get to the nineteenth century, Dickens has various cases of men going to pieces. It is called hysteria because it is supposed to arise from the womb, but Freud made it very clear that he had male hysteric patients. We don't really define any situation as hysteria. They are given other names instead. Nothing is so protean as mental disease. Amazing. It very much changes according to the way people sense them. What the hell was a brain fever?

You see, right now what I am trying to do is, I am trying to get pictures of these little groups of women. Because they worked very hard to hold the groups there, the group is part of their achievement. We've been told to respect Anne Finch Countess of Winchilsea for the fact that she is a preromantic. Even the woman who is editing a new edition of her [work] actually called her unique in an essay because she was both an Augustan and a woman. I felt shocked and upset, and so would Anne Finch have been shocked and upset because she wrote always to other people, to Arminda, to Ophelia, to Clarissa, to Clarinda, to Saranissa; but she was not unique in that she was a woman and an Augustan, and not even unique in that she was a woman, an Augustan, and a poet, because they were all writing poetry to each other. It was just in her case she was more gifted than other people, and the poetry actually survived and the other women's poetry didn't survive. Maybe it wasn't poetry they wrote, maybe they sent flowers or seeds for the garden or patterns for embroidery or something, but it's all part of this wonderful lightly drawn society which has got these terribly delicate sinews and lines of connection like Pope's simile of the spider. It's the lines between these women that vibrate with all these tender and complex feelings which are also ceremonious as the occasion demands it, and extremely sympathetic and sometimes slightly malicious, and sometimes difficult, and so on. If you imprison her in uniqueness, then you have already imposed a really false value which is a sort of masculine value, where writers are respected the more they separate themselves from their background and the more they stand out as original or strange or consciously exploit themselves, even to the point of driving themselves clean around the bend.

It's become more and more like that. In the twentieth century I suspect you have to reach into their bowels and pin them onto the page. The big peaks for me—I don't know—I have spent more time studying Byron and Shakespeare than anything else in my life. Both of them are men who understood a great deal about women and were enraged and disgusted with women a lot of the time, but also had no doubt at all that women were capable of anything once certain massive drags upon their lives were eased. Look at Rosalind. It's a way—you actually take off the social role when you take off the clothing. Suddenly your character is able to take a longer stride and argue with people and be pert because she is desexed of all that feminine trivia. That includes, by the way, the whole program of fecundity, childbirth and so on. It is very hard for us to grasp; just like going over Niagara Falls in a barrel, you can make all the plans you like for living with somebody. Millamant and Mirabell in *The Way of the World* were getting on very well until she has her first miscarriage and is sick for two years because nobody can stop her bleeding, and so she just bled. "Well, terrific, I had three fucks, look at me." What do you do about that? Shakespeare is far too intelligent and far too sensuous a man to ignore it. There are certain devastating physiological imperatives which have got to be shaken off too if men and women are able to look each other in the eye. That's why the obvious love is between men and boys or between boys because there is all kind of sexual fulfillment possible without this abominable aftermath. That's really traumatic, that.

The Professor is the wishful woman's story of how it should have been. I find it so moving, that *Professor*. The whole thing about *Jane Eyre*, and for that matter about *Wuthering Heights*, is the way they've lighted on a really rich vein of female fantasy. Nobody can fail to be overwhelmed by it. I hesitate to use the word archetypal because it has been misused so much, I don't know anymore what it means but there is a kind of centrality in that theme, whereas *Villette* is much more oblique, much more personal except that there is a whole genre of the female "school" novel, and school is a very good paradigm for the way in which society alienates women from themselves. *The Getting of Wisdom* is one. There are no men in it, and it is almost a perfect novel about the destruction of a woman's innocence. The turning of the woman who would have been straightforward and witty and energetic into somebody conniving, and I don't think even Henry Handel Richardson knew what she did with that book. It's a wonderful book, I think.

In the Brontë family, we will never know if the geniuses were only the sisters. We'll never know what it was about Branwell. I think the girls—and I've seen this in other English families—were all more aware of Branwell than they would ever be of any other man. But because of their shared puberty and all those intense experiences, they were susceptible to him—physically, mentally, and emotionally. (You see, that's what is so wonderful about the Brontës, it's as if they had one artistic ego to share between them all.) The same is true of Rossetti and Dante Gabriel. I think the Brontë sisters did destroy Branwell because of the intensity of their expectations and their enormous faith in him. So if he'd had any ability it just would have shattered under this kind of strain, the drug-taking and so on. Also, if you remember, the girls were —well, it's hard to grasp how badly shocked they were by his sexual liaison with the wife of one of his employers. Anne was employed by the same people. The real thing there was jealousy and outrage [that] he could have done such a thing. I see his doing such a thing as a desperate way to get out of the terrific force field of all those women. They were the most passionate women in history. Charlotte Brontë was an absolute geyser of passion. She's amazing. It's amazing to me she was able to have that much sexual energy in the circumstances. It was only because of their father being too busy and their mother being dead.

It is a necessity to exorcise the mother in order to reclaim the mother. I always say to feminists who want to know what they can do, I usually say, "Well, you can start talking to your mother." They go, "Oh, my God!" Well, that's the problem, your mother is the problem. You must find a way to love her and to purge the fear and resentment. Everyone has this resentment. Your mother socialized you. If your feeling is that your socialization has castrated you, which in most women it has, then you feel anger. What else could you feel? Why is it that I cannot wear trousers without wearing a girdle? Because my mother said I mustn't, and I feel uncomfortable because I can hear my mother saying, "You look ridiculous." It really goes right back to toilet training and everything, and girls are expected to be much neater than boys at a much earlier age, and so on. Freud said toilet training is inexcusable, and it is inexcusable. The mother is identified with all that. Everybody hates the mother, and the crimes against the mother proliferate all the time. The only thing is we have never been aware of how many crimes against the mother were perpetrated by daughters. I am now at the age where most of my girlfriends are mothers, and I had no insight into that situation until I saw it. I didn't realize how adolescent girls wound their mothers and what vicious satisfaction they take in it. They know exactly where to hurt them.

I've never seen such pain so clearly given as in that relationship, and I hadn't really understood it at all. The terrible thing is that the mothers have this blind love for these girls and can't even touch them because the last thing the girls want is physical closeness.

I don't understand why so many women are in conventional analysis. It's really because there's no one to talk to and you pay a bunch of money to somebody, and he has to listen to you whether he likes it or not. An awful lot of psychoanalysis is being allowed to talk about yourself, and that's probably why so many women are in it, because there really isn't a chance to talk so seriously about themselves any other way. Most women having anything to do with children know that Freud didn't understand the female side at all. If you've ever spent any time with a little three-year-old girl, you'd realize that she's extremely genital, she's extremely vagina-conscious, she knows exactly who she is and what she wants, to the point where she's very disruptive. She can be a real danger. She's quite capable of making sexual advances to a man, or to anybody. She's likely to hide beads and little things inside her vagina, so you have to check it before you put her in bed. She's supposed to have a hymen; it's all nonsense. I don't know when they had hymens, they certainly don't seem to have them now. So I say, "Come on, sweetheart, what have you put up there today." They have this feral female smell. You realize that Freud reflected his male paradigm onto females by accusing them of penis envy, and an adolescent girl lacking a penis, and blah, blah, blah, and seeking a penis and women wanting children, women wanting a penis, and so on. You think, this just will not do. If that's the truth, then *penis* means something we don't understand. Let's start again and work out what is in this little sausage. I hope that somebody — I wonder if anyone has — dealt with the sexuality of very small girls.

I don't think anyone has ever realized how many problems are going to stem from the simple fact that most children are wanted. I think it's terrifying. There was a time when children just came along. They were there, and you had to accept them. It gave the children a measure of autonomy in a perverse sort of way — "well, I'm here and you'll just have to buckle under." So people adjusted maybe begrudgingly, building extra rooms onto their houses — bought baby stuff, and worried about how they'd be able to get out, go to the movies. Now you have a different situation where you get people saying, "Now I'm ready to have a child, I don't ever want to go to the movies again, and I've got enough money that I can afford a nurse, and so on and so on. And I want a child that I can really spend time on." That child would become an extension of the personality of the people who want it. I'm really worried for that child, that poor child. You know, "We're going to do this, study music," or whatever. There's going to be a tremendous concealed hostility in that situation, and it's going to be like Branwell Brontë. "I was president of Exxon Corporation, and I came home and stayed in bed for nine months because I was too old to have a baby, and I had seven doctors in attendance and out you came. And look at you, you won't study!" "Of course I won't fucking study." I can see it being just diabolical. I find that people have tremendous guilt about leaving children on their own. If mothers only knew how children yearn to be left on their own when they interpret as neglect the fact that they occasionally take telephone calls during nursery hour. It's all crazy, this sort of blackmail.

Women are still in the position of being eunuchs. But they're not the only eunuchs, you see. They will always be until something extraordinary happens to the world. They will always be as long as sex is a commodity and as long as consumerism is organized the way it is, as long as the house is the principal unit of consumption and the woman presides over the house, until people start living out, as long as couples is the accepted mode. In fact, there's all the evidence that resentment against women is getting stronger and stronger rather than less and less. Crimes against women are more violent and they are more frequent now.

It's not so much that things have declined. It's that at the beginning, feminism had this enormous media success. There was a tremendous change, a real change, in the attitudes of women working in the media and in the attitudes of the media towards their readers. That's a very important change, it's a real cultural change. It'll have long-reaching effects, but we didn't win the right to abortion, we didn't actually win anything. Certain of our demands coincided with the spirit of the time and with other people's priorities. The right to abortion was granted to women around the same time as the thesis of "Lifeboat" earth became an enormously widespread fear. In fact, I don't think we'll lose that access to abortion, either. The government's under pressure from various powerful pressure groups who have always been able to pressurize this government, and in fact they can pressurize governments anywhere, and so they're going to have to backtrack and try to conceal their sponsorship of abortion in various ways. But I don't think there's any possibility that we will see a major rollback. I just don't see that happening. The only thing that really concerns me is that legislators and public alike don't know what abortion is any more. It's changed so much in ten years, [but] people are still talking about babies in plastic bags thrown into rubbish bins. It's not really like that at all. So we now know much more about contraception and we're not nearly so gung-ho about it as we used to be. It's very worrying to me that so many liberal people become illiberal on the question of pregnancy and childbirth. We are in the middle of a regression now. I heard a man who has forged his reputation in liberterian circles say that he thought that some women should be compulsorily sterilized, women of weak intellect who are on welfare and who already have three children. He also said that some people should be forced to undergo abortion, it should be open to them as the only option. The even more seductive idea, even for liberals, is that the state should not support children just because they're born, that people who have children, when they already have two or three, should not get any state support, should not get any welfare or whatever. I can't believe that I'm hearing these people say these things because it seems to me to be an absolute liberal principle that any child who is born must be assured of the basic requirements to grow to reasonable intelligence and self-sufficiency and have a bearable life. We can't say to children born of poor and ignorant people that they are condemned to a life of poverty and no medical care. It'll have results, they'll die; they often do.

One of the things that anthropologists have found hard to explain is how few primitive societies have any degree of illegitimate births. They rack their brains to find out how that is, because they see in Polynesian societies and African societies that pubescent children are allowed to engage in all kinds of genital encounters, boys sucking each other's penises and girls rubbing each other and children having intercourse. Generally what that seems to represent is that all kinds of sexual activity are all right between children who cannot conceive. But there also seem to be some supporting rules for that. In the case of Africa, generally speaking, some form of stereotyped intercourse is allowed for teenagers. It's usually what's called intercourse *inter crura*, between the thighs, and the boy knows he mustn't insert the penis into the vagina. He can have intercourse *inter crura*. Now the thing about that of course is that it can be very satisfying to the woman because all the pressure is on her external genitalia. It's been spelt out to us a thousand times and it's true, that the female orgasm originates in the clitoris anyway. So who's idea is it that penetration is the be-all and end-all of sexual pleasure? It clearly isn't. One of the most extraordinary things about the West is, on the one hand, most of us who call ourselves liberals have hit the street to demand the right of homosexuals to make love anywhere they like, to use any orifice they please, and to use any degree of fantasy, or whatever. Every store has a dildo in the window and all that sort of thing. And then at the same time, heterosexual relationships rely entirely on intromission, that's considered to be normal sex. A woman who says she doesn't want intromission and that she's sick and tired of taking pills and diaphragms and IUDs and so on, can there please be some other way, can we make love some other way, would be considered to be extremely unreasonable, mad in fact. I find this really interesting that we now believe stereotyped intercourse is as bad as we once believed masturbation to be. Now we accept masturbation, and we find doctors telling women *ad nauseam* to masturbate, it's good for the tone of your uterus — all of which is nonsense — there's no proof of any of that. It's become a kind of therapy. Doctors tell women who are suffering preabortion anxiety to go ahead and masturbate, which is almost impossible to do because she's so anxious. But on the one hand, masturbation is good for you and do it often; and on the other hand, stereotyped intercourse makes people tense, uptight, miserable, and affects their orgastic impulses. None of it's been proved. The irony is that Masters and Johnson used stereotyped intercourse as their physical treatment for impotence.

Americans are beginning to realize that no matter how much Masters and Johnson do for you or no matter how much your new sex therapy class improves your capacity for orgasm, you really cannot go on fucking the same person day in, day out, at the level of frequency you've been told is normal without some loss of tension, loss of excitement, and what have you. So they say, "Oh, perhaps celibacy has a part to play." I very much doubt whether celibacy has any part to play at all unless there are very strong compensations for complete celibacy, which there are of course in terms of career and whatnot. People react like this instead of understanding the pacing of sexuality, its indulgence, its control, the amount of access you give yourself to sexual opportunity, instead of understanding that it's all a very subtle and sophisticated thing. A husband and wife can't leap at each other like wild animals and fuck away like mad for the first six months and fall back exhausted and full of rage and disappointment, and then take each other to the divorce court; that's obviously absurd. In fact safeguards were built into all those systems of betrothal, which generally allowed stereotyped intercourse until the Victorian period anyway, and limited access of husbands and wives, husbands working in one place, wives staying in another, periodic visits to the parents, and so on and so forth. All of this is an attempt to control the sexual urge within marriage and keep it in a state of vitality. All kinds of formality between spouses and limitations on what spouses can do to each other and so on and so forth. Instead of understanding that, Americans are now talking about the new celibacy, which means you never make love at all. The abortion thing was the same, swinging between wildly extreme points of view, instead of seeing that the moderate way was the most suitable. For example, we were suddenly talking about abortion as though it was terrific — "Wow, isn't this great, we can have abortions." Everybody forgot there is another side to that, which is when will the day come when we can say, "Great, we can have babies." Most of us who have abortions are not really sure whether we absolutely and utterly do not want a child under any circumstances. We are usually much more aware of the fact that we can't afford a child; [that] we'd lose our place in the race for distinction, whatever it is we're involved in — be it university or work; that the penalties of having a child are so great that we know we would take them out on the child, and the child's life would be a misery. So we go ahead and go and do it. But it's equally important to say, "When will women have their children, when will they not have to make ignoble bargains in order to have children?" That angle was always ignored. Now comes this terrific backlash, and people are producing more and more evidence that abortion destroys them, makes them miserable — you have long-range psychological consequences. It's been studied a hundred times, and it's interesting because you have never seen a subject in which researcher bias was more obvious. They get completely conflicting results. They look at groups which are matched and balanced, and obviously if you question women about abortion in a certain context you will produce the psychological results.

It's interesting about the films, women's pictures. I didn't see *The Turning Point*, but I certainly saw *Julia* — in fact, I hardly go to the movies any more. But it seemed to me they were all very earnest, serious pictures, and they dealt with women's problems in a respectful, nay, reverent, sort of way, which is an odd thing when you think of it happening with someone like Lillian Hellman, who was brought up under the iron rule of style: if you couldn't do it with style, don't do it at all. Don't for Christ's sake moan, because it's not stylish to moan. By all means wisecrack and cut down to size, but don't complain. Complaining is a totally nonstylish activity. Now my favorite films for women are the films that were made in the Depression era like *Mr. Deeds Goes to Town*, or whatever. And one of my favorite films of all time, which was redone and I bet it wasn't anywhere near as good, is *My Girl Friday* with Rosalind Russell. Look at those women, and even the character played by Joan Crawford in *Grand Hotel*. In that she plays a girl who goes out as a casual typist. She gets sent to visiting dignitaries in hotel rooms, and it's pretty well understood that they're going to come on to her and she probably, if the odds are right and the price is right, she may even be more to them than a mere secretary for the time that they're in town. She's completely unapologetic about that, she's completely streetwise: when someone comes on to her in a bar she gets rid of him in two seconds flat because he's a wolf. He's not a gentleman and he isn't going to take her out to dinner and pay for a good dinner and maybe buy her a present, and all the other things. It's really a brilliant piece of characterization by Vicki Baum in the original, and it's even better when Joan Crawford does it in the film, before Joan Crawford became the heroine of the weepies. I love that period, and that too was short-lived, and it was all to do with the Depression and people coming from under to on top. I'll tell you what we're back to which is even more distressing. I haven't seen the film, but I noticed it in New York, the Godard film with Isabelle Huppert, which seems to star Isabelle Huppert's behind, judging from the still they've used here. The film is called *Every Man for Himself*; well, there you are.

The restriction on women by cultural factors never, never really went away. They've always had a degree of self-expression and a degree of freedom. They've always had a degree, but it's never been enough, it's barely been enough to start screaming. It's like saying, "Well, everyone in prison is free because he can scream." But no one can understand what he's saying, least of all himself. There won't be any freedom for anybody. I'm amazed how beaten down people are in American civilization, and I'm amazed that I can have a student come to me six weeks into term and say, "I have to pull out of class because my husband's been moved to Oklahoma City." I say, "But you've just come to Tulsa." She says, "Yes, I've been four and a half months in Tulsa, we have a new house, I've just finished furnishing it, and now I've got to put it up for sale and start again." I think, my God, does nobody give any thought to the role these people play in their community, the friends they will have made, the friends their children will have made — which is even more important in terms of their ultimate socialization. How can they do this, uproot these people and fling them around the country like this? And so you talk about degrees of freedom. That woman would say she has a degree of freedom because she's coming to do a university course. I would agree with you. I would then say her chances of making anything out of the course are seriously limited by her background. I can't strip away her pretenses. She's taking a tiny step forward and it's now being negated by the fact that she has to move. But still, she'll start again next year and keep on going. It's just like watching a dog trying to get out of a swimming pool, tearing its claws off, just making the same gesture over and over again. It seems to me it's infinitesimal: you realize, what we're watching is history. We're not watching news so you don't expect to see it day by day.

One of the problems with the American feminist movement is it's too upfront. The ERA is meaningless, really. It's only meaningful when it comes to training women for political struggles. It's training them the hard way, and learning the hard way, organizing and grouping, but they're not able to do anything else while they're doing this. And what will be the upshot? The upshot will be a clause in the Constitution which makes America the most feminist nation in the world. That's a ludicrous proposition. America is actually directly responsible for the most horrifying oppression of women outside its own borders, let alone what it does inside. USA ideas have been a scourge to women in the world. And there are too many people who know that. That it should have "feminist United States" written on it! You realize that people in the East think of American feminism as just an aspect of the perversion of this country, that women are so noisy. They also see that women have no real power and that women spend all their time in the men's pockets.

When I was a little girl I used to paint, and I should have gone on doing it but I gave it up in my final years at college because I couldn't get my folio ready in time and get As in all the other things as well. When I was at university I was singing as well as studying literature, and I was also working in the theatre, and I've done that in every university. I've been in three universities as a student, and that way I wound up being Actress of the Year in Cambridge. By then the singing had kind of faded out. I had to sing sometimes on stage, but the music was still there. If anything, the painting had taken a back seat. I think that what's happening to me as I grow older, and it's worried me a bit, is I'm becoming less and less interested in people and more and more interested in anything but people, less and less interested in social life and more and more interested in finding out the things I don't know. I read about people all the time, and I'm a bit like Alice in Wonderland—I don't like books without conversations or pictures. I do make things personal; I have that female habit of turning all abstract suggestions into something that I can relate to, human, personal.

Women do nothing but wait. It's a great theme in women's poetry, the waiting. That marvelous Rossetti poem about lying there and waiting for the knock on the door. It's meant to be Christ, but it's not of course. Well, I think there's a fundamental personality difference between men and women. This may very well be an aspect of oppression. But it may be an aspect of oppression which we ought to cherish. It's a bit like Pudd'nhead Wilson, that the slave turns out to be a nicer person than his master by virtue of being a slave. For example, women do not claim attention in the same measure as men do. It's especially obvious in their art because they don't go for the forms which draw a distinct barrier between the art form and the unsynthesized manifold around it. For example, women are very good essayists, they are among the best. They are very good letter writers. [Those] are art forms which are thoroughly imbued with real life, they are continuous with life. There is no frame separating the letter. Now they are also very good novelists. The novel is also the hybrid form which is up to its knees in history.

I've never studied it, the novel, precisely because of that. I've never spent much time on it because it's an ignominious hybrid, it just doesn't turn me on. Well, so you read *Middlemarch* and there you are wondering, well, it is partly about the spread of the railways in the United Kingdom, and you think, well, did she observe that correctly, and so on and so forth. They are legitimate questions to ask about novels, and you can use the novel with extreme limitations which must be observed every inch of the way. You can use it as some evidence about social attitudes and values. So you can say, "Yes, ladies taking gruel to the poor; behind the facade of the country house there were workers' cottages which were unsanitary." But the novel has this continuity with reality as well, that reality illumines the novel and the novel illumines reality in a journalistic way, a day-to-day way. Now, I'm much more interested in poetry, which is like painting rather than ceramics or weaving because poetry also draws a big frame in white paper around itself. It is also discontinuous with the unsynthesized manifold. It is a freestanding work of art, it makes its own rules, and it must satisfy them within eight lines if necessary. It's what I've always studied when I've given my attention to poetry, this higher form of truth which doesn't have to relate to any lower form. The novel sometimes achieves it, but it doesn't have to, it's not part of the deal. Now it seems to me that women are not good painters and they're not good poets either. Well, it doesn't *seem* to me, we know they're not. It's useless going on and on and on, saying, "Well, we'll find a painter some day." The chances are you never will.

It's this business about the personality structure, you see. I don't believe that women can be so utterly singleminded and pour all their energy into that constricted space, and also demand that the rest of the world regard that restricted space and defer to it. They just don't see the point. They may do it, they may appear to do it. But when you look further into it, you see they haven't really done that at all. For example, take again Rossetti. Rossetti spent more time making cutout picture books for the hospitals than she did writing poetry. She made thousands of these books of cutout transfer things, and they were all given away, and it's pretty obvious that she hardly ever revised a poem. She wrote them in white heat. She wrote them at a certain level of intensity and she didn't work to screw that level up further, sometimes it's really limp. Well, Emily Dickinson did draw a frame around herself. Emily Dickinson drew a frame around that whole little drawing room that she used to retreat to upstairs — her sense of separateness and self-distillation. Even there, there would have been another way of doing it. Even there, the poems are continuous with life in a strange way. They're full of personal allusions so that people go on elucidating them and remembering them — the name of her dog and the nextdoor neighbor. They are still important, I think. Obviously Emily Dickinson is another case, and I think Marianne Moore's a different sort of case, too. There'll be more and more poets who self-consciously draw the frame of white paper around what they're doing. But then you see the one who really does have a new voice is Sylvia Plath. That long scream of agony which is what we prize in her was directly related to real life. It finishes in its culmination in that masculine act of suicide, which is the ultimate drawing of a frame around your life, and saying, "It ends, here." It does turn your life into an art form.

If I read one more feminist criticism paper on literature being about the woman's search for herself — every time that's given to me as the theme of a novel I know it's bullshit. It's been the theme of every novel ever written. It can't all be about anything so deeply boring as the search for the self.

There is narcissism in women's writing today. The protagonist has just turned forty and her husband has left her. Coincidentally, the authoress has just turned forty and her husband has left her. She has had an affair with a man who borrows five hundred pounds and disappears. Coincidentally, the principal character in this book is having an affair with a man who blah, blah, blah. I'm *so* tired of it, the narcissism of the lady novelists; it's *so* tedious. A portraitist always paints his own face. But when someone like Raphael paints Castiglione, there's something about the immense warmth and tenderness and gentleness of representation, which is Raphael's own values. But I know that Castiglione did look like that, and indeed he felt like that too. It's the way the face is seen, the way he got the sitter to sit, the way he chose — so that it's up close, the way he put against that gentle, laughing face that huge velour sleeve, like a mossy hill that he could put his face on.

George Eliot is obviously all those people. She's Maggie Tulliver, and she's Gwendolyn, and she's less Dorothea than she thought. What goes wrong with Dorothea is that she falls in love with Dorothea, she abandons her ironic stance and starts fawning on her and calling her beautiful when she called her everything but in the first few chapters. George Eliot wasn't all that honest. She lived a lie, I'm afraid. For a long time, I think she did. That sort of hypocrisy, the concealing of the relationship with Lewes, and then calling herself Mrs. Lewes when she wasn't, and then Lewes' death, and then that extraordinary ignominious marriage with that other whoever-he-was — the sort of piety of it, the broad streak of vulgarity and hypocrisy that overlay that.

I don't get very worked up over Doris Lessing. I find that I have to go on reading Doris Lessing by act of will, I'm not being carried along. I was thinking of someone else before I picked Doris Lessing as well . . . who was I thinking of? I don't want people to think that's what I think about modern writers. I was thinking of one person in particular when I said that, and it would be the distinguished Margaret Drabble, who drives me crazy. I think she has tried to write a book that wasn't necessarily about her in the same way, and it didn't really work. Mary McCarthy writes beyond that and has written classic short stories as well, which is a genre I'm particularly interested in. And she's better than that. Simone de Beauvoir, of course, tried to write on a different scale . . . looked for a larger canvas. But whether the canvas got pulled in or not I don't know. Erica Jong is a narcissist again. It's not just that it's narcissistic, this way of writing, but it's about one's self. It might very well be about oneself, if it took an interesting attitude to one's self. But what makes me crazy is it doesn't. They're so subtly self-congratulatory. We're given little clues that the heroine is really a fascinating woman and that nobody can really ultimately resist her. She is hurt by people, but it's their inadequacy. The point is not whether it corresponds to the writer's diary but whether it corresponds to the writer's preferred self-image. I would like to see women writing ironic novels about themselves, making themselves look stupid for a change.

I didn't really indict Mailer. I tried to rescue Mailer from what I thought was a really ham-fisted job that Kate Millett did by taking him so literally. I've had this same conversation with Fellini. Fellini gets furious because, for example, women attacked his film *Casanova* in Italy. He says that all these objections are in *primo piano*, they take the literal content of the film as if it were the content of the film "They think because I make a film about Casanova, I approve of Casanova!" Whereas he approves of Casanova so little that in fact when I saw the film at a special screening before it was released, I just sat in this hall carved out of onyx and jasper and gold and cried with laughter, because I felt so sorry for the penis in its dreadful loneliness. We'd had a quarrel about the film early on when it was being put together, and then I was delighted with him when he put all Casanova's favorite fantasies at the end and they were all threadbare, and the threadbareness is so obvious, so he ends up dancing with the mechanical doll because that's all he can use, the mechanical doll. All those feminists screamed and shouted and yelled, that Fellini was antifeminist of the week, the month, the year, the decade, the galaxy, you name it. He kept saying, "Don't they see, don't they understand anything about ironic distance, don't they see why I did it this way and not that way?" It was no, no, no, you should never have shown women being used that way; that was what women used to say: "No, we won't have that, we can't have women as dolls." The point is that men are not able to cope with women unless they make dolls of them, can't you understand that's the point made on *your* side. "No, no, Fellini has no right to do it." If a woman had done it! I mean, they let Wertmuller do much more vicious things than that.

There seems to be a tremendous desire to punish male artists. And you know, punishment's a completely self-defeating activity. I keep saying, "Let's not punish anybody, let's do it ourselves in a different way." When they say, "We want to get into these bars where men drink." Oh, fuck it, I don't want to get into bars where men drink. Let us buy a bar of our own and make it more exciting and more wonderful, so the men are turning themselves to our bar. Now, why should I scream and shout to be somewhere I'm not wanted? There's no law in the world that's going to make them want my company. I've never understood all that part of it. I can have a club to exclude people with red hair, if I want.

Mark Gerson

Margaret Drabble

Interviewed by
Gillian Parker and Janet Todd

Margaret Drabble was born in 1939 in Sheffield, Yorkshire, an industrial town in the north of England. She is the daughter of John Drabble, a circuit judge, and the former Kathleen Bloor; her father was also an author, and her mother had taught English; while her sister Antonia (A.S. Byatt) is a well-known novelist. Margaret Drabble was educated at the Mount School, a Quaker boarding school in York and at Newnham College, Cambridge. After a distinguished undergraduate career she graduated with honors in 1960, and married the actor Clive Swift in the same year. She had planned to go on the stage, and acted in Shakespeare, but marriage and children prevented her from pursuing her career.

Instead of acting Drabble took up writing, with immediate success. She completed her first novel backstage, while expecting her first child, and her next two novels during her subsequent pregnancies. The marriage continued, through difficulties, until 1975, during which time the author lived a "domestic" life, in her own words, mostly in her house in London, writing prolifically (novels, plays, short stories, criticism), and looking after her three children, two sons and a daughter. She continues to live in North London, taking on, as her children have grown, a more public role: she appears on television in discussion programs, sits on committees for progressive causes, teaches at a London college, and has undertaken the daunting task of editing the new Oxford Companion to English Literature. *Her most recent appearance (June 1981) was with the World Disarmament Campaign protest outside the House of Commons.*

Although Margaret Drabble began writing her novels before the feminist resurgence, many of them deal with what were later to become key issues. For example, in 1965 the heroine of The Millstone *(entitled* Thank You All Very Much *in the United States), Rosamund, finds in the midst of writing her dissertation that she is pregnant; she decides to have the child on her own, finishes her doctorate simultaneously with the pregnancy, and sets off with the baby on a teaching career. Instead of a man and marriage, the resolution is a child and a career. Because of their central concern with the contradictions facing women in recent years, the novels have attracted a feminist interest, and controversy: her recognition of the importance of motherhood, for example, was an unwelcome position until fairly recently, when there has been a shift in opinion on the issue.*

Margaret Drabble's novels follow the trajectory of her own life. In the early works the focus is on the situations of women who are having to make their lives cohere around a jumble of partly lapsed, partly operating rules, as they struggle to maintain their own direction in life, often in the midst of marriage and childrearing. The later novels move out of the house into the larger community, where the social forces that were previously presented indirectly, as they affected the heroine's survival, become increasingly the direct object of focus.

While the novels assume a world in which the moral guidelines have suddenly been cut loose, they are nonetheless deliberately traditional in form, a sign of Drabble's refusal to accept chaos as the norm. In this she differs from the tenets of much current literary theory and practice. Her characters are still struggling to achieve some sort of order: they recognize, in most cases, the inadequacy of the solutions they reach, but also know and reject what the alternatives entail. Emma Evans, in The Garrick Year *(1964), disastrously married with two small children, has an affair with a glamorous acquaintance; while she is talking with him in the park one of the children falls in the dangerously flooded river, and she turns away from the man to the child, in an instantaneous leap. While Drabble has Emma remain in her marriage, the final scene acknowledges Emma's recognition of her situation. During a reconciliatory picnic, in an idyllic English pastoral setting, Emma is the only one to notice among the flock of sheep one that cannot move, paralyzed by a snake clutching its belly, and sees it as an emblem of her own present state.*

The imagery of Paradise in that scene—lost, spoiled, and longed for—introduces what is an important element in Drabble's work: the language and metaphors of the Bible, or of the old Dissenting interpretation of the Bible. Perhaps because she was raised in the North, the stronghold of Dissent, Drabble uses the language with natural ease, not like a literary device. In The Millstone

Rosamund initially rejects such an outlook, the outlook of her parents, "their blend of socialist principle and middle-class scruple, the way they had carried the more painful characteristics of their non-conformist inheritance into their own political and moral attitudes . . . ," but it is an outlook to which Rosamund will return. Like Rosamund, Drabble also returns to this inheritance, using it increasingly in her later works to provide their structural and moral basis. Although the form it takes is thoroughly secular, the protagonists of Jerusalem the Golden *(1967),* The Needle's Eye *(1972), and* The Ice Age *(1977), are, in very different ways, engaged in the quest for salvation, for a way of life redeemed from chaos, and made part of a coherent whole. Beneath the account of people's messy daily lives lies a pattern, the search for the right path through the wilderness to the promised land. In this Drabble taps, of course, a strong strain in English writing, going back to Milton and beyond. It is in keeping with this element that Drabble's novels have become increasingly concerned with community —particularly in* The Needle's Eye, *and in* The Ice Age—*with its present failure and fragmentation.*

Gillian Parker/Janet Todd: As a novelist, do you think that there is a female tradition or imagination in literature?

Margaret Drabble: Yes, I do. I think in the novel there is. Poetry is another matter. I think there is a female tradition. It is highly significant that Jane Austen and Fanny Burney were at the beginning of the non-picaresque novel —Burney I suppose is picaresque too—that they were writing about social behavior and marriage and villages and domestic life in a way that had never been done before. A lot of men took this over, but it remains a dominant thread and I entirely agree with Virginia Woolf in *A Room of One's Own* when she says that there are links and we owe debts. I do feel that very strongly.

Gillian Parker/Janet Todd: You find then that there is a female content?

Margaret Drabble: There is a female content. I'd even say there is a female style. Jane Austen's sentences are so deceptively normal: that is a female style rather than a male style, I would have thought. One could make a fairly good case for Dorothy Richardson and Virginia Woolf being conscious of the female sentence. I think there is such a thing. Not all female writers write in it and not all male writers don't write in it but I think there is a discernible tradition. . . .

G.P./J.T.: And continuity from Jane Austen through Richardson and Woolf?

M.D.: I think there is—with gaps. There is a continuity and I think that women writers are very often conscious of their heritage, not only in subject matter but also in prose and treatment.

G.P./J.T.: If you had to give one or two women writers who had influenced you most, who would they be?

M.C.: I suppose I would say Jane Austen and George Eliot. They influenced me when I started writing. Of course I've read a lot more since then. I didn't read Virginia Woolf until I'd written two or three books of my own, so she didn't influence my formative years. She's certainly influenced me since, and so has Doris Lessing, for example. So has Mary McCarthy—a completely different kind of writer but in whose work I find a lot of kinship. So there are a lot of women writers I feel close to.

G.P./J.T.: You put Mary McCarthy in a slightly different group there.

M.D.: She has a desire to research and bring in fact, which is slightly alien to the female tradition. Of course she's always put herself in a position where she can do harder research than a lot of domestic, housebound female writers have been able to do. So she does introduce a new element. Also she's satiric—Jane Austen is too—but she's satiric in a way that George Eliot and Virginia Woolf never aspire to be.

G.P./J.T.: McCarthy of course is American while the others are English. Do you feel that if there is a female tradition or style, it's not peculiar to a specific country?

M.D.: I don't think it is specific. But I don't think it exists in French, and it doesn't exist at all in German. So it probably is an English-language tradition and it is only recently that I've started rereading early female authors from the States like Kate Chopin or Willa Cather—I've only read those in the last three years. I now see kinship but obviously wasn't influenced by them. I do have a sense it was a less conscious tradition and less upheld as a model than it is here, that women writers in the States have had a tougher time. Perhaps in Mary McCarthy's case she had to be more masculine in her presentation because the others hadn't really made such an impact. The tradition was stronger here, so it was more easy to write in it.

G.P./J.T.: Since graduating from Cambridge in 1960 you've raised three children, pursued an academic career, written eight novels, two literary studies, and a history text. How have you been able to do all this, to break out of the "silences" that Tillie Olsen has described as the typical lot of women writers?

M.D.: I never thought it was a problem. It never crossed my mind I should shut up because I had children. In fact in a way the writing sprang very much out of having children because I started to write when the children were very small — indeed when I was expecting the first one. It was my way of refusing to be sentenced because I was prevented from doing a lot of other things through being pregnant and having small children. It was the only thing left to me to do, which is very much what the single writers of the nineteenth century felt. It was the only job they could do, so they did it. I don't think there's any need to be silenced. I've never really understood that point myself — I can see if you've got ten small children but if you want to write you don't have ten children. You make a choice not to. I think it's perfectly possible to bring up small children and work. Perhaps it's easier now than it used to be — certainly it is. I like working hard. I've always felt I ought to be working somewhere or other.

G.P./J.T.: Your first novel, *A Summer Bird-cage* [1962], ends with a discussion between the two sisters over whether or not to have children. Recently this has become very much the issue — perhaps because a lot of the original supporters of the women's movement who remained childless are now reaching their late thirties. Childraising, rather than say sexual freedom or economic parity, is now being increasingly recognized as the central contradiction for women, a recognition you came to early in your work. Would you agree that this has been a fundamental theme in your novels?

M.D.: Yes, I mean I noticed this at twenty-one because I had my first baby at twenty-one, and it was immediately apparent that this was an extremely important issue and one not written about very much. It was my life. I was facing the problem every day and it was an entirely natural thing to write about. And I'm very much in favor of having children, which is obvious from my work, but it does create problems.

G.P./J.T.: I was a bit disturbed by the introduction of the *au pair* in *The Waterfall* [1969] as a method of coping. How do you feel about the use of other women for domestic chores — a necessity for the working mother or a social anachronism?

M.D.: It's a terribly difficult point this — something that has plagued me all my life. At the moment to my great joy I don't need anybody. There have been points in my life — as in any working life — where you do need somebody: your children are off school etc. When the children were very little I used to have three afternoons a week when a girl in the village used to walk them round, but once you try to do anything more organized you do get into awful feelings of guilt, of using other people. I don't know whether this is proper because I like to do my own dirty work but in a way I'm creating a lot of trouble for myself and annoying the children by involving them in my principles. I think it's a very interesting question, this, but I don't think it's resolvable. I'm delighted that now I don't have to get people to look after my children. It's a great relief.

G.P./J.T.:   I think that it is significant that we are talking here about how you managed your life. How other women cope is an abiding interest, in life and in books. Perhaps it's one of the reasons why women read novels. This raises a tricky question of course — the writer's responsibility to provide role models. Since your heroines are dealing with the same problems of self-definition as your readers are struggling with, the characters tend to be judged as models. *The Waterfall*, again, has been criticized because its heroine, Jane Grey, is essentially passive, a noncoper, and finds her solution in romantic love. How do you feel about this sort of criticism?

M.D.:   It's a very peculiar book. I can see why it could be found disquieting. I can see why feminists don't like it — because it's about a passionate heterosexual love affair which disturbs everything. It disturbs all one's preconceptions about what's important in life. I think passionate heterosexual love affairs are extremely important and that whole book is devoted to one. People who don't like that kind of stuff aren't going to like the book. They're going to disbelieve the premise that this emotion is real. So they find the heroine unattractive and her submission to her fate lamentable and the texture of the book unpleasant. I don't care about that. I wasn't writing it for them. When I wrote that book there was no feminist criticism around. It was written in 1967 or so, before the first of the feminist critical books, and so I was not in a way conscious of any feminist reaction. I don't suppose I would have cared if I had been. I think that Mary Ellmann's book came out in 1968; that really began the whole conscious movement. Obviously people had been thinking in these terms before — as indeed I had myself — but it wasn't organized in the way it is now, so in writing *The Waterfall* I just wrote what seemed to me to be the book.

G.P./J.T.:   Out of all your novels *The Realms of Gold* [1975] has received the most attention in America, and its heroine, Frances Wingate, the most approval. Did you intend her to be simply exemplary? At one point, after a few drinks, her thoughts become subversive of her high-powered professional life: "All one has to do, she told herself, with a part of herself, is to keep moving, keep talking, and don't spend too much time alone. And you'll survive. What for? Don't ask, don't be naive." Then there is your own rather dry comment to your readers, suggesting why they find Frances, rather than her ordinary-housewife cousin Janet, a more welcome character: "Because Frances Wingate's life moves faster, it is therefore more entertaining . . . It is depressing to read about depression. Frances Wingate, as you will have noticed, rarely feels depressed for long, and her opportunities for distraction are varied. Whereas Janet Bird's best hope of distraction is an evening class." What do you expect your reader's attitude to be towards Frances Wingate?

M.D.: Well my attitude is ambivalent, which is why I put in these asides. I thoroughly approve of the energy with which she leads her life. I also can see that she's been very lucky. Janet Bird hasn't been lucky. There's a lot of luck in life—something I'm keen to emphasize—and consequently in Frances Wingate's success and certain side disasters. We don't see much of Karel's wife who disappears quietly to a lesbian commune conveniently. If I'd been writing the book as a tragedy rather than a comedy that would have to have been given rather more space. In a comedy you can brush people away in a comic plot ending—that's all right for them. But it's never wholly satisfactory—even in Shakespearean comedy when characters are forced to marry people they didn't want for the sake of the plot or go to a lesbian commune for the sake of the plot. A sort of uneasiness creeps in that the winners have won and everyone else has lost and it would seem to me unfair to create a character whose actions had no ill side effects—of course they do. But I approve of Frances. I approve of people who keep busy and keep moving. I don't approve of inertia. But on the other hand it's no use telling someone like Janet Bird to pull herself together—how can she? So I do approve of Frances—she's in many ways admirable, but rather selfish, but you have to be selfish. . . .

G.P./J.T.: To be admirable?

M.D.: Yes, that's the paradox that's worth writing about.

G.P./J.T.: If Frances is generally admired as a winner, another of your heroines, Rose in *The Needle's Eye*, has come under attack as a loser. She chooses a modest, "harmless" as you say, way of life, deliberately at odds with the competitive imperatives of society. She has been criticized as an antifeminist heroine. What do you make of such criticism?

M.D.: Well, I think it would be very nice if everyone could be winners: but they can't be—that wouldn't leave many people to write about, would it? I admire Rose immensely. I don't see any reason why everyone should go out for material success and career success. I think Rose's decisions are perfectly valid and I admire her way of life. She's not a loser at all — she's extremely resilient and psychologically success for her is avoiding what her history had destined her to be, which was to be a rich woman. She's avoided that extremely successfully. She's a success in terms of what she meant to do and she remains one. . . .

It's a prescriptive way of looking at books — telling you what your heroine ought to have done. And it's very easy to look around the street and say well, she should never have married him — but she did. And what's interesting is that she did and how she copes with it when she's done it. We all do wrong things — Rose does wrong things — she makes mistakes. But it's how you cope with the mistakes you've made that makes a person interesting.

G.P./J.T.:   I'd like to ask you some questions about how you write, about your method as a novelist. How do your novels come into being and grow? Do you start with a character, a conflict, or a plot? Did you, for instance, with *The Millstone*, begin with the character of Rosamund, or with thoughts about the conflict between old and new moralities, or with an idea for a story about a single mother?

M.D.:   That book came almost entirely out of the idea of having a baby. I wrote it while I was having my third baby and I was very interested in what made people different, between people who had babies and people who didn't, and whether it changed you or not. So that was the plot really — whether having a baby changed you. I made her a single mother because that is the most acute transformation, because there's nothing else to blame, simply the isolated fact of having a baby. But the novels vary. They seem to grow out of a lot of related ideas. If they relate themselves enough, they turn into a novel. I very rarely begin with a character, a predicament more.

G.P./J.T.:   You spent some time as an actress. Did this background help when it came to writing novels? Dickens apparently acted out parts as he wrote them — do you?

M.D.:   Not at all. I'm a lousy mimic. As an actress I was no good at impersonation. The only link, I would think, between acting and writing is that I quite often do readings from my own work and I think that they all read in a spoken voice. Some prose doesn't read in a spoken voice, but I think mine does. It has a speech rhythm to it. I always hear it spoken. That applies not only to the dialogue, but also to thoughts, description, and everything. I hear them in terms of, I suppose, my own voice, I myself saying it and that's a kind of mimicry I suppose. In terms of characters—I was the kind of actress who, when I played a part, never read the rest of the play. I didn't know what the play was about. So it is a very different activity—acting a part. In a book you've got to do all the parts. It's a different kind of identification altogether.

G.P./J.T.:   At one point in *The Realms of Gold* you tell the reader that you have intended one of the characters (David Ollerenshaw) to play a larger part in the narrative, "but the more I looked at him the more incomprehensible he became." This suggests that your characters take form as you write about them, that the novel develops its own inner necessity as you proceed. Is this usually the case, or are you more likely to have the analysis of the characters and what will happen to them worked out in advance?

M.D.:   Well, it's not really true that they develop as I write. The fact is that they preexist and by contemplating them I cease to understand them. I don't get any nearer to them. It's like people in real life. You actually think about them a great deal and in the end you give up and say, I don't actually understand why William is as he is, but you can still use him in a book because he exists, there he is, and he does what he does. But you can't actually understand enough of why he's doing it to use him that little more in the action. It's not as though I have control over them. I know they're there but I can't actually control their movements in the way I had hoped to be able to do.

G.P./J.T.:   So it's not a matter of coming to the end of them by contemplating them more; they keep that mystery of ordinary people.

M.D.:   Yes, they remain aloof.

G.P./J.T.:   Your point-of-view seems to mesh with that of your heroines who provide the reader with analyses of themselves and others as they cope with their moral predicaments in an admirably clear-sighted way. Yet there usually comes a point in the plot when this gives way and dreadful things happen, come suddenly lurching up to disrupt the narrative: I'm thinking of Emma Evans when the baby nearly drowns [*The Garrick Year*] and she dives into the river, or Rosamund [*The Millstone*] who screams until the hospital staff do what she wants, and even Frances Wingate [*The Realms of Gold*] with her attacks of silent despair. At these points are you, as the author, separating yourself from the characters' perspectives to reveal the chaos that finally lurks beyond the reach of their competence, and of their way of narrating their tales?

M.D.:   I think we delude ourselves if we think we can control events by understanding them. These moments are bound to happen and I suppose as a writer I'm showing that you can't control things. But then you can control them; they all go fighting back and restore order as soon as chaos has broken out. If chaos never broke out, there'd never be any action, would there? No one would ever do anything. They'd just think about it. Events have to dominate characters from time to time. I don't like events to dominate them too much. I like a degree of self-control and self-propulsion, but that may be a deep psychological flaw in me.

G.P./J.T.:   Of course you're the author and you control the whole show anyway . . .

M.D.:   Well, not really. You can't control what's represented. You have to represent the reality that your character would inhabit. You're at the mercy of that. It would be an absolute travesty to portray a life in which everything went according to plan, in which the consciousness dominated everything. If you did, you'd have to do it ironically and show that the character was losing out on a lot. In that case I wouldn't be able to like them very much, because I'd be criticizing their control. I suppose I like to show that my characters fail but I like to feel sympathetic to them in their failures.

G.P./J.T.:   One of my favorite metaphors is the tatty plaster lion outside the Alexandra Palace which Rose regards affectionately at the end of *The Needle's Eye* as a symbol of the sort of society England has become. How do you arrive at your symbols? Can you recall any particular one that exactly summed up the meaning you were pursuing at the time?

M.D.:   Yes, I was very pleased with the lion. It does in fact exist. I got it very late in the book because I went to the Alexandra Palace, not having been there for quite a long time. I'd nearly finished the book — I thought, I bet if I go there I shall find something. And there it was. So, there really is a lot of crossover between the outside world and the inside world. I find often when I'm writing a book, I go to the place towards the end and see something there that does offer an image for what I'm writing about. The octopus at the beginning of *The Realms of Gold* was a similar thing. I actually saw such an octopus — I think it was in Naples — and it just seemed a very interesting image combined with a television program about octopuses I'd seen. It seemed a very interesting image of imprisonment and maternity and so on. You store them up. You do both — store them up and actively seek them.

G.P./J.T.:   So it is fortuitous and sought?

M.D.:   Yes. The amazing thing is — and I think most writers would agree — that when you're in the middle of writing, everywhere you look is packed with relevant symbols. The whole world seems to be full of useful materials and you see it all in terms of what you're writing about.

G.P./J.T.:   Your study of Arnold Bennett [1974] places him firmly in his time and culture. When you teach, do you deal with the writer's period or only with the work itself? Do you see literature as text and context, or as text alone?

M.D.:   No. I see it as social context. Also I see it a lot in terms of a writer's personal biography. I was taught not to pay any attention to it, but I find it increasingly interesting. It's so obvious that writers are influenced by the way their parents behaved. It seems to me ridiculous to isolate a text, in fact almost meaningless.

G.P./J.T.:   Do you teach your own novels? If so, how? Do you place them in a social context?

M.D.:   No, I don't teach them. I think I had one free-for-all discussion once. My students said let's do one and I said OK. But they just asked me a lot of questions about where I'd seen something — which seemed perfectly legitimate curiosity.

G.P./J.T.:   Let me push it. If you were going to teach them, to what historical context would you link them?

M.D.:   I don't think I'd be able to — it would be far too complicated because I know too much. I wouldn't know where to begin.

G.P./J.T.:   I had in mind the way in which your later novels have been increasingly concerned with the larger historical context. The question of justice in society seems to have become increasingly central to your work. Rose's story in *The Needle's Eye* is a series of legal battles and she feels pursued by judgment; *The Ice Age* has two main characters in prison, and another awaiting trial. Are these legal matters metaphors, ways of talking about the larger issue of social justice?

M.D.:   Yes, they must be. I don't know whether prison is a very good metaphor for justice. I think in using prisons so much in *The Ice Age* I was trying to use it more as an image of being frozen and stuck and unable to move, which a lot of people felt at that time — and to some extent now. Yes, I think *The Needle's Eye* is certainly about the relationship of justice and the law, but I don't think I think in quite such grand terms when I'm writing. You know, you can look back later and ask, why have I used this — but it doesn't occur quite in those terms when I'm writing. I'm more interested in equality than justice, which is very hard to write about — fairness. There's a difference between social justice, legal justice, and fairness. I suppose it's the relationship between these things that preoccupy me.

G.P./J.T.:   The most sympathetic characters in your novels are often working class: Maureen in *The Ice Age*, Rose who has chosen to live a working-class way of life in *The Needle's Eye*, and various passing characters on the periphery of your main characters' consciousness — the old lady in the off-license in the opening scene of *The Needle's Eye*, or Ned in the pub in *The Ice Age*, for example. There seems to be something fundamental to your moral outlook here, would you agree?

M.D.:   It probably is a moral statement. I would feel extremely edgy if I introduced a working-class villain or a Jewish villain; I had great difficulties in *The Ice Age* avoiding Jewish villains in the property market — it's not something I wished to write about because you then drag in such a backwash or other issues that drown what you're saying. Of course these things are moral judgments. About the working-class characters — I have a great respect for ordinary carrying-on kind of people who just carry on being kind to one another and being neighborly and doing what they should. I do have a great respect for that. I don't think all the working class are uniformly benevolent and noble, but I suppose it is a moral point that the ones I introduce are.

G.P./J.T.:   Your main characters are representatives of the bright educated middle-class men and women who found unexpected affluence in the England of the sixties and seventies. Was it, on the whole, an altogether happy discovery, do you think?

M.D.:   Well, they've slightly lost it in the seventies; the middle class are complaining like anything these days — from '73 onwards. People got frightened round about '73 or '74 with the oil crisis and one heard nothing but the moanings of the middle class about their frozen incomes and inflation and so on. But even so they have frankly a much higher standard of living than when I was a girl. So they are more affluent, but perpetually discontented. Affluence makes people discontented in some curious way. It doesn't make me discontented — I think it's absolutely wonderful to be able to buy a pound of bananas — but this is the war-baby thing — that one's grateful for small mercies. A lot of people aren't. This is partly what *The Ice Age* is about, affluence making people discontented rather than contented. We all expect a standard of living which is untenable and we're going to have to reconcile ourselves to either a freeze or a positive drop in living standards and consumption. So the answer comes in terms of the characters in the novels. It makes the ones who can adapt happy and those who worry about it unhappy, and those who always expect more than they've got unhappy as well.

G.P./J.T.:   So you think that in the decline into which we have certainly entered — whenever one sets its beginning — you wouldn't expect the proportion of happy vs. unhappy to change?

M.D.:   No, I don't think so. Some people welcome the decline as a leveler. People who enjoy affluence tend to be people like Frances Wingate who are doing very well . . .

G.P./J.T.:   Simon Camish in *The Needle's Eye* married his wife out of a sense of obligation; but, since he was poor while she was new-rich, in fact he acted out the old role of marrying for money. From this follows, without regard for his motives, the traditional misery associated with such an act. On a separate issue you observe how "with a faint and recurring shock of astonishment" Simon recognizes "in his own behavior an eternal pattern of corruption." Your characters often start off with new motives and intentions but nonetheless end up in traditional forms of social dilemma or corruption. Do you see this as a central experience of a generation?

M.D.:   I think it a central experience of history — to think you're doing something new and to find out you're doing something old. It's very difficult to do something new. You think you've made a revolutionary or subversive decision and you find you're doing exactly what your parents did before you, only in a new form.

G.P./J.T.:   You often, indeed, find yourself doing the same things — but it's more surprising to find yourself in the same kind of moral dilemmas.

M.D.:   I suppose it is. That's how I see it. You can't free yourself from them: they pursue you and in order not to be pursued by moral dilemma and doubt, you have to, as Frances Wingate says, forget about that, forget about the doubt and get on with it. And if Simon had said that about his marriage, he'd have been all right. He's not doing anything very awful — his motives were mixed in marrying. I mean like a Henry James situation, you're not quite sure what dominated. I'm not at all sure and he's not at all sure either.

G.P./J.T.:   In creating your protagonists you are good at giving form to certain characteristically new types of consciousness that have emerged under the pressure of headlong social change: to take the men, for example, there is Simon Camish, the scholarship boy who makes it out of the working class to become a Hampstead lawyer, and who is now in a state of despair; or Anthony Keating, who goes from being the arts graduate with the usual English distaste for business and making money to becoming a millionaire property developer. Does the responsibility of taking a new and undefined state and placing it morally trouble you when you write?

M.D.:   That's a terribly difficult question but it's absolutely fascinating. I don't think of it in those terms when I'm writing but obviously the interesting areas to describe are the areas of change. A different economic climate lays a different moral stress on making money or being in the television world or the arts. And in fact my attitude to Anthony Keating is extremely mixed. He was a brave man to risk going out into a new world. And I think he would have been an absolute coward if he'd stayed in the BBC, turning out investigative programs and earning a high income, and living very comfortably. I think that's compromising morally. He may be misguided but he's taken a leap. That's why I wrote the book. I don't think I understand what I feel about it. I don't understand what I feel about industry, about capitalism, etc., and trying to define the new moral areas. What I would like to do — something that Angus Wilson does so marvelously — is to describe the successful businessman who thought it was legitimate and fruitful for the community to make money in industry and so on. I would like to do that — I can't do it for the moment.

G.P./J.T.:   Certainly businessmen are a little-represented group in literature.

M.D.:   Indeed. There are hardly any. They did it in the nineteenth century — people like Balzac and Zola wrote about this — the overreaching financier. They wrote about this world with great energy and vigor. . . .

G.P./J.T.:   Your last novel, *The Ice Age*, gave a rather grim depiction of the state of the nation and the national mind. Do you feel that all has been lost in England, or does some saving grace, or remnant, exist?

M.D.:   Britain will recover. I deeply believe that. I think this is a wonderful country in many ways and when it's got over its empire crisis, its middle-age crisis, it will be perfectly all right. It is still a very good country to live in and this is something that tends to be misunderstood between the States and England. When the English complain about England they love complaining and they don't actually mean it's the end of the world, I mean they don't see the end within five years. It's not as simple as that. I have great faith in a lot of things in this country. It's a place where you can lead a private and eccentric life better than anywhere else in the world, I'd imagine, and without a craving for material success. It would be quite easy in fact to interpret a lot of the economic problems of the moment in terms of the fact that people tend to put other things above material success: fairness and class solidarity. It's not simply material gain that people are fighting about. They're fighting about relationships, which is honorable. . . . In England we've been through so many slumps, crises, disasters, wars, that in a way it's part of the national habit, looking at these things. There is, as I say somewhere in *The Ice Age*, a national affection for queuing for bread. And when the lights go out and you have to have your supper by candlelight you don't think the end of the world has come. You think, Oh yes, here we are again, and this is quite fun really and you'll cope. That's very powerful — it sounds sentimental — but it is in fact a very powerful force in the British character and it's a great surviving force — that people don't expect life to be easy — it hasn't been and they don't expect it to be.

G.P./J.T.:   The last part of *The Ice Age* has Anthony Keating going off on a rather unexpected jaunt as a spy, getting caught in crossfire in an East European airport while clutching a John le Carré paperback. Since the novel as a whole is dealing with the decline of England and looking for and unable to find solutions, was this a way of rejecting the sort of solution a le Carré novel presents — a latter-day, almost self-parodying return to patriotism as the way out of paralysis?

M.D.:   Well, I've never managed to read a le Carré novel, so I'm not really clear what they're about. It was partly a joke and I think it is quite easy these days to step into a joke nightmare when abroad. A lot of people do it. They find themselves in prison very unexpectedly. And I suppose it has something to do with patriotism and the decline of Britain, but I'm not quite sure what.

G.P./J.T.:   Am I imposing pretentiousness on you?

M.D.:   Yes, I think slightly. I was haunted by a vision of the end which was violent but with characteristic compromise I've left Anthony not shot to pieces but simply frozen like everybody else in the book has been. And somebody actually thought I meant the Red Peril was on the way from the East — I don't think this is what I meant at all. That episode was based partly on some awful British catastrophe in Albania where I think we sent in a lot of men who got killed in a latter-day misconception of our role after the Second World War. I suppose I was seeing Anthony as standing up for old-world British chivalric imperialism. He's gone out on a meaningless mission to rescue a meaningless girl, but he nevertheless thinks it's better to do that than to refuse to do it — which I suppose is an image of a declining empire, a declining faith — you do what you should do even though you no longer believe in the meaning of it.

G.P./J.T.: You keep your interest in the outside world — you don't find yourself becoming more subjective?

M.D.: No. I find the outside world absolutely fascinating and constantly changing: you're always running to keep up. I can see there could be a problem since the material changes so quickly. I've heard older novelists say that the world changes so rapidly now that they simply can't be bothered with it any more; they reach an Olympian state where every little tide of opinion is predictable and they can't deal with it. Perhaps that comes when you're round about sixty. I think that the novelists who are still confronting a reality sometimes turn away from contemporary reality towards a working out of the relations between art and reality, a sort of Thomas Mann kind of preoccupation with what art is at all and whether we need it. And I can see if you really can't face standing at the bus stop in the pouring rain and pondering the punk situation, you might find yourself doing that, but one's deserved it by that age. There are some things you haven't the energy or adaptability to cope with.

G.P./J.T.: In your future novels do you think you will continue your concern for the moral state not only of individual lives, but of society as a whole?

M.D.: Morality is so relative and writing novels is a constant process of relating shifting morality to shifting society and working out where it's going to. I can't imagine myself ever going into a Lawrentian condemnatory blast about the evils of society. I don't see it like that at all. I mean I'm not a moralist in the denunciatory sense.

G.P./J.T.: Can you say something about *The Middle Ground* [1980], your newest novel?

M.D.: It's about a woman journalist and a group of her middle-aged friends, and it's about the state of London rather than the state of Britain. It's very much a London novel. It's also about feminism slightly. It's called *The Middle Ground* and it's about maintaining the middle ground — which is just what I said Britain was quite good at doing — not being pushed into political or sexist extremism, yet not rejecting new light. I think feminism is a new light, and my character is struggling with her feeling both that it is a new light and that it is being betrayed in some fashion. It's more about being female than *The Ice Age* was. It's got no plot; it's very much a texture novel. Because London life is so immediate and rapidly changing I wanted to write about the texture of it.

G.P./J.T.: Have you started your next novel or do you have a breathing space?

M.D.: Well, I have started one or two, but I keep throwing them away. I'm working at the moment on an intimidating project, which is reediting *The Oxford Companion to English Literature* —a five-year plan. I've been working on it so hard and I have so many irons in the fire I haven't been able to sit down with a novel. But I will do, I suppose, in a year or so.

G.P./J.T.: How do you feel about being officially honored —you were recently made a Companion of the British Empire.

M.D.: I was both amused and delighted. I'd worked jolly hard on many committees and going to lecture in various places, but I love doing it all and I feel slightly guilty about the fact that the things I love doing should be rewarded. But on the other hand, people say it is very good for literature and women to be honored and it is also useful in various professional ways to have these letters after one's name, so, yes, I'm delighted. I'm also absolutely enraptured by royalty in a very curious way. I find royalty absolutely fascinating —the whole thing is so interesting. I can't work out why I'm so interested but I can't deny that I am.

G.P./J.T.: You share it with the whole country. It's an extraordinary phenomenon.

M.D.: It's so deeply rooted. One can laugh at it, one can be republican and vote for the Socialist party, which I always have done, but nevertheless there is something there. And when you read Shakespeare or books on the Commonwealth, you see that you can't forget all that. There is something peculiarly interesting about them.

G.P./J.T.: Would you say success has changed your relationship with your family —parents and children?

M.D.: No, it would have to have changed one an awful lot to change relationships with one's children. My parents have been very pleased for me and that's nice, but no, it doesn't change your relationship with people you're very close to at all. It *does* change your relationship with certain peripheral people.

G.P./J.T.: What about your sister, who's also a writer —A. S. Byatt —do you have sibling rivalry or is it more a fear of influence?

M.D.: I don't really consider it. I don't think we actually read each other very much, but that may be because we'd be afraid of influence if we did.

G.P./J.T.:   You received acclaim very young. Do you feel guilt for being so feted, for not being the unfeted artist in the attic?

M.D.:   Of course I do. I feel a lot of guilt about it. I can also tell you it unleashes a lot of malice. You pay for your success in many ways — in other writers and other people. So it's not as though it's all joy — and therefore one feels guilt because one is made very much aware by people who let you know that it's not fair and they're much better than you are. And in some cases they are very good. The people who make me feel deeply uneasy are the people whose work I profoundly respect and who haven't had the acclaim they should have done. You go on telling them you admire their work and doing what you can to force others to like it, but it doesn't always work. I also think I've been extraordinarily lucky in writing at the moment in history when I did. But there in a sense we created the moment in history — a whole group of us who have a lot in common — who I suppose did start writing about these things when they had to be written about; so I suppose it is not wholly luck. But I do feel guilt and then there are days when I feel absolutely wonderful and cheerful. The nicest thing about success is that old friends know where to find you and they write to you after twenty years and say, I've been thinking about you, I saw your name, let's meet. Also you make new friends whom you otherwise wouldn't have been in a position to meet. To meet colleagues whose work I like very much and whom I enjoy talking to is wonderful.

A. S. Byatt

Interviewed by
Juliet A. Dusinberre

A. S. Byatt published two novels in the 1960s, Shadow of a Sun
(1964) and The Game *(1967).* The Virgin in the Garden, *which first
appeared in 1978 and was reissued by Penguin in 1981, is the first volume in a
projected quartet of novels: the author is at present writing the second. She is a
well-known critic who has written on Iris Murdoch and Wordsworth and
Coleridge, and edited* The Mill on the Floss *as well as the Virago editions of
Willa Cather's novels. She reviews, broadcasts, and has published articles on the
contemporary novel, and has a particular interest in American writing. She is
senior lecturer in English and American literature at University College, London.*

Although The Virgin in the Garden *is far from being an
autobiographical novel, it reflects crucial elements in A. S. Byatt's own life. Born
in 1936, she was three when war was declared and her father, who was called up
to the air force, was only a visitor at home for the next six years. She grew up, as
do Stephanie and Frederica, the two sisters in the novel, in a world colored by
adult fears and the scarcity of material things. Like Frederica, she was seventeen
in 1953, Coronation year, the time of the novel's main action. The family, who
lived in Yorkshire where the novel is set, invites comparison with the Brontës: three
clever and literary sisters, the youngest now an art historian, and a brother
fourteen years younger than A. S. Byatt, the first-born. The author's mother
taught before marriage at The Mount, an old-established Quaker boarding school
in York which the sisters attended. A. S. Byatt took an Open Scholarship to
Newnham College, Cambridge, to read English. After graduating with first-class
honors, she spent a year in Bryn Mawr on an English-Speaking Union Fellowship*

where she developed the interest in American literature that is significant in her teaching and writing now. She returned to Oxford for postgraduate research on allegory in Renaissance literature between The Faerie Queene *and* Paradise Lost, *and her fascination with Renaissance iconography surfaces in* The Virgin in the Garden *in Alexander's play about Elizabeth I, a drama that links the lavishness and idealism of the past Elizabethans with the renewed energy and excitement that heralded the accession of the second Elizabeth. The suggestive double time scheme of the novel is made more complex and resonant by a prologue set in 1968, where the characters who had been in the heyday of youth in 1953 can look back on that seeming golden age from a world which has moved on, much as Alexander, in the play* Astraea, *looks back to the special glamour of Renaissance England.*

A. S. Byatt, who was married in 1959 and had a daughter and a son in the early 1960s, dedicated the novel to her son, who died while she was writing it, and the book owes some of its richness of texture to her power to accommodate both comedy and tragedy within its broad compass. She has since remarried and has two school-age daughters. She belongs to that postwar generation which was urged back into domestic life, and, like many professional women in the 1960s, struggled with part-time work while bringing up her children. She first went to work full-time at the age of thirty-six, shortly after her son's death.

A. S. Byatt remains deeply interested in Iris Murdoch, another writer of academic standing who had to establish herself before the contemporary women's movement had gathered any momentum, certainly in Britain. Byatt's first critical work, Degrees of Freedom *(1965), identifies Murdoch's concern to create both "real people and images" (a phrase Murdoch had used in an essay on modern fiction called "Against Dryness").* The Virgin in the Garden *is in a tradition of realist fiction which goes back to George Eliot, but draws on modernist images and on contemporary interest in the novel as a mirror of itself.*

Juliet A. Dusinberre: Were you conscious of a battle between real people and images while you were writing *The Virgin in the Garden?*
A. S. Byatt: Yes, but there is a third element, which is the rest of creation, neither people nor images, just what is there. Painters know naturally that the artist is concerned with that third element, but writers don't always. I think it is very important to see what is there before any of it becomes related.
Juliet A. Dusinberre: When you use language to describe experience, do you feel that you have controlled that experience and that that is what writing is about?

A. S. Byatt: I think there is an order underlying language which one searches for endlessly, partly through metaphor. In all three novels I found that the material came together when the metaphors cohered. But language relates things as well as controlling them. When I wrote in *The Virgin* about Elizabeth and the red and white rose quartered in her face, which is a heraldic image from a poem about her, it made me think of hanging, drawing, and quartering. That was linked with the image of meat in the butcher's shop, one of the original germs of the novel, which led on to "All flesh is as grass," a primary theme in the book. One also finds language breaking away from one's control, as in the description of sexual excitement. That happened in the scenes with Lucas Simmonds [a master at the school who studies cosmogony] and Marcus [younger brother of Stephanie and Frederica]; I found the language was full of blossoming sexual images. In fact I found that aspect of it alarming and became frightened of the involuntary way language took over.

J.A.D.:   You have written on both Iris Murdoch and George Eliot, and in *The Virgin in the Garden* Edmund Wilkie teases the younger sister, Frederica, for planning to write a novel "by Proust out of George Eliot," and the two characters seem to refer back to George Eliot's scathing attack on "Silly Lady Novelists." Amidst the brilliant invective in that piece George Eliot declared that novels written by women have at their finest "a precious speciality, lying quite apart from masculine aptitudes and experience." Would you agree?

A.S.B.:   I probably would, and fifteen years ago I would have expatiated on it at great length. But now that everybody else is doing so I don't want to talk about it. It's no longer something I can say in my own voice, and the artist must always speak with her own voice or she ceases to be an artist.

I derive my sense of an order behind things from T. S. Eliot and Pound. I write the way I do from James *via* T. S. Eliot rather than from a line of women writers. There is another tradition of writing which is less of a symbolist aesthetic, from Ford Madox Ford and Pound and Willa Cather. This is plainer, starker, and more descriptive: a word for each object. My second novel in the quartet is going to have this plainer style. It's called *Still Life*. The third one moves on again to some kind of linguistic crack-up, to the gap between private and public language, the saying of the same things in different ways. Its title is *Evidence*.

J.A.D.:   Virginia Woolf said that the novel needed a new form which was adapted to what women wanted to say, and that there might even be a different kind of sentence structure which would be more amenable to expressing a woman's vision. She herself praised Dorothy Richardson, and *Pilgrimage* offers new models of how to write and of what to write about. Are you conscious of trying to forge your own special sentence structure?

A.S.B.:   I like writing very long sentences, but I think that comes from Henry James and Proust and Eliot rather than from a tradition of women's writing.

J.A.D.:   I can think of one very long sentence in *The Virgin* which reminds me of Proust. It describes Frederica looking back in middle age at the 1953 celebrations and at the production of Alexander's play, in which she was the young Elizabeth:

> Disembarrassed, in the sixties, of the awkwardness of being seventeen, a virgin, and snubbed, she was able to fill her memory theatre with a brightly solid scene which she polished and gilded as it receded, burnishing the image of Marina Yeo's genius, after Marina Yeo's slow and painful death from throat cancer, seeing the Bevy, as they developed into housewives, gym mistresses, social workers, boutique assistants, an alcoholic and another dead actress, as having been indeed golden girls, with a golden bloom still on them, seeing the lawns, the avenues, the lanterns in the branches and the light winking on half-obscured singing bottles, in the still eternal light through which we see the infinite unchanging vistas we make, from the height of one year old, out of suburban gardens or municipal parks in summer, endless grassy horizons and alleys which we always hope to revisit, rediscover, inhabit in real life, whatever that is.
>
> [p. 317]

A.S.B.:   That sentence echoes Proust's at the end of Part II of *Du côté de chez Swann,* in *À la recherche du temps perdu*, both in the vistas and in its way of going back to an experience through literature and through childhood. Everything is seen from the height of a child. The Bevy is in *The Faerie Queene.* "Golden girls" is *Cymbeline*: "Golden lads and girls all must, /As chimney-sweepers, come to dust." The "memory theatre" is the title of Frances Yates's book on the Elizabethan theatre.

J.A.D.:   Yet despite all these inherited associations I feel that the search for "real life, whatever that is" is at the heart of your book, in which you seem to suggest that things become real by moving into the past, and also that literature creates a reality more durable than lived experience.

A.S.B.:   When I read I inhabit a world which is more real than the world in which I live, or perhaps I should say that I am more alive in it. It is a language world. Language tries to capture and make permanent a moment in time which won't be captured. This was what I was trying to say when I described my characters watching the Coronation on television. I draw on T. S. Eliot's "now and England." Then. The present only becomes a real point in time when time has moved on and made it past.

J.A.D.:   When I heard you lecture on George Eliot you said how voraciously she read while she was writing and that this seemed to feed her creativity, but that sometimes the reading, as in the preparation for *Romola*, got in the way and she got stuck. You are a person who obviously has the passion for reading which you give to Stephanie in the novel; and Alexander, the playwright in the novel, worries about finding a voice of his own because his language, like yours, is a tissue of literary echoes and inherited images. Have you ever worried about having a voice of your own?

A.S.B.:   Yes, I have, but I feel that it's possible to recognize literary models, as I would recognize Coleridge, T. S. Eliot, Pound, even Wallace Stevens, and still make the language which you've inherited from them express your own voice. All the great writers have drawn on literary models and this has made the language as rich and expressive a medium as it is.

J.A.D.:   That's certainly true of Shakespeare who constantly drew on literary sources, and yet one feels his language to be totally his own. When you were pointing out all the echoes in that one sentence I was thinking how much I felt it to be your sentence, with your tone of voice and particular way of looking at things. But I wonder if you could say anything about Stephanie's dream before her marriage, which seemed to me to embody the artist's fear that she will cease to be able to create. It's all about drowning and the submerging of identity, and comes at a point in the book when the novel itself might lose direction and color and come to a standstill.

A.S.B.:   Stephanie's dream is about her fear that marriage will preclude creativity, which is a fear I used to have, a terror that you can't do both, though I don't have that fear now. When I wrote that chapter it seemed like a dream, I didn't labor over it at all. It draws on the fifth book of Wordsworth's *Prelude*, which is about books.

J.A.D.:   Yes, and the two forms that the poet sees are language and geometry, which are the forms of art in your novel: language is the medium for thought and feeling for Stephanie and Frederica and their father Bill, and for Alexander, and for Lucas Simmonds who goes mad because of failing to keep images separate from each other. But Marcus, the brother, sees in geometrical shapes and visual forms. I felt that your image of Marcus's mind being the "true survey" of another landscape was a graphic one for the writer's own created world which is not the actual world itself, but another plane of experience where his mind wanders and discovers new forms. Do you feel that feminist critics such as Ellen Moers and Elaine Showalter have contributed to an understanding of the artist's landscape?

A.S.B.:   I liked both critics and I thought Moers was very good on the female sexual landscape, though I'm sure I've encountered it as much in male writers as in female. What frightens me about a critic like Moers is that I'm going to have my interest in literature taken away by women who see literature as a source of interest in women. I don't need that. I'm interested in women anyway. Literature has always been my way out, my escape from the limits of being female. I don't want to have to get back in. That is one of the reasons for my dislike of the women's fiction which Julia Corbett writes in *The Game*: it's self-indulgent creation, the "waste fertility" with which Comus tempts the Lady in Milton's *Comus*, a denial of real fertility and real freedom. I don't want to be part of a school or movement. I have to hang on to my individuality, my lone voice, because that is the source of my identity as an artist. For me being part of a group would be the death of creativity, because I need to be separate from other people. I still believe in the liberal concept of the individual.

J.A.D.:   Do you prefer not to be considered as a woman writer?

A.S.B.:   A journalist interviewed me once who had just interviewed Iris Murdoch and Doris Lessing, and he said that all the women writers he had seen had one thing in common, their terror of the feminist critic, because they felt that they were being pushed into being spokeswomen when they didn't want that kind of mission. The novel is an agnostic form and a comic form; we don't want to have to be believers and to have to make other people believe.

J.A.D.:   Do you think that the women's movement has influenced the way you write about women?

A.S.B.:   Feminist criticism can get in the way of what one really wants to write about by forcing one to consider self-consciously things that one would otherwise do naturally, like creating women characters. The writer's profession is one of the few where immense sexual-political battles don't have to be fought. There have not been deep prejudices against women writers, except that a woman writer may be set aside and praised like a dog for walking on its hind legs, what Johnson said about being gratified not that it is done well but that it is done at all. It does women a disservice to elevate them as women rather than as writers because it prevents their being judged on merit. George Eliot is amazingly good on women but amazingly good on other things as well. I started thinking about *The Virgin in the Garden* because someone in an adult class asked me why no one could write a novel like *Middlemarch* now, and I tried to list the different elements in *Middlemarch* which we've lost in contemporary novels: the large numbers of characters, wide cultural relevance, complex language. I'd rather talk about George Eliot's views on German philosophy than her views on women. Politicians and media people have to talk about women because they have to reflect other people's attitudes. But writers don't. It's important for a writer to have a capacity for seeing what is going on in the world around her, to see facts as well as fictions.

J.A.D.: Do you admire the women's studies programs which have been established in some universities?

A.S.B.: I feel unhappy about the separation of women's studies courses from literature courses. I think writers like George Eliot and the Brontës and Virginia Woolf ought to be taught in mainstream literature courses. I don't write specially for women and I would be distressed if men didn't read my books. If women writers are studied exclusively in women's studies I think this seems like choosing a new kind of second-class citizenship. Iris Murdoch gets into a blazing rage about it, saying that women are more than 50 percent of the population and that they ought to stay right there in the middle of it rather than occupying some place which it is going to be easy to call the sidelines. I have, however, nothing but admiration for a woman like Carmen Callil whose Virago Press is a necessary and very successful publishing venture as well as a women's organization.

J.A.D.: Do you perhaps feel cautious about the ideal of sisterhood?

A.S.B.: I am, apart from anything else, unashamedly heterosexual. I like working with men and I like teaching men. I think there is a danger that sisterhood could be the enemy of objective truth, in that one is so busy supporting and being supported by other women that one becomes cocooned against unpalatable realities and criticisms which might create growth.

J.A.D.: Both you and your own sisters have achieved a great deal. Were you brought up to be achievers?

A.S.B.:   Yes, we were. A lot of pressure was put on us as children, although not overtly. It was always assumed that we were clever and had an obligation to make our mark. Because of my father being away at the war we were a household of women: my brother is much younger, and I think this meant that I never felt myself to be part of the second sex in the way that women do who are brought up with brothers close to them. My mother came from a working-class family in the Potteries in Staffordshire, Arnold Bennett country, and had read English at Newnham, Cambridge, which she was justly proud of, and she wanted me to follow in her footsteps. She met my father when they were both at grammar school [academic secondary school]. His father owned a small sweet factory, and my father went into the family business to save money to read law at Cambridge, and eventually he became a judge. I went to a Quaker school because my family were sympathetic to the Quakers, but unlike the Corbett family in *The Game*, which was taken from the family of a friend of mine, we were not ourselves Quakers.

J.A.D.:   Did you find the Quaker environment conducive to being a writer?

A.S.B.:   No. At the Mount there was a strong sense of the virtue of dedication and contemplation but the school's ethic was against individual achievement. Iris Murdoch is right about the opposition between the artist and the saint. The saint queries the artist's values, and I think the artist queries the saint's. But the artist can't discard the saint; in a way she's got to be both. That's why it's important for a writer to have a large canvas and plenty of characters, so that she can enter into other people's beings instead of just mirroring her own. That's one of the things I don't like about women's fiction, that it tends to concentrate on one or two main figures. Murdoch points out that the encounter with Shakespeare is an encounter with disparate worlds fully realized, solid and independent, and that this openness is at the heart of moral life as well as of artistic life. But the Quakers, because they have so few rules, put enormous moral pressure on you and this becomes a kind of imprisoning, one of the things I was trying to say in *The Game*. On the other hand, a religion without Bible or priests does recognize the significance of words, and Quaker emphasis on silence creates an awareness of the value of words, of what they can do, and it also reminds one of what words can't do, of where their limits are, which a novelist needs to know.

J.A.D.:   The Quakers have a very good record on women. Was that an influence on you when you were growing up?

A.S.B.:   My mother had taught at The Mount after she left university. When she got married she automatically lost her job. Modern feminism has ensured that that couldn't happen now. Even today with the recession married women are not going to be the first to go, except unfortunately in part-time work. Although as an artist I don't want to be part of the women's movement, I am a back-to-the-wall feminist on things like tax, divorce laws, equal pay, married women's property, even abortion, though I am more equivocal about that. I think the choice ought to be there, but I wouldn't go out and march for it.

The feminist I admire the most is Betty Friedan, because *The Feminine Mystique* was written for my generation, who had been brainwashed into thinking that a woman's place, whatever her training and talents, was back in the home bringing up children. Child psychologists like Bowlby made you feel that you ought to be with your children all the time, whereas Betty Friedan did try to get women back to work, and I believe in the right to work. I value my job as a form of independence, because I am a woman. It means a lot to me to have a salary and an office and a desk and adult company during the day. I'm against feminist demands for very long maternity leaves. I think there should be maternity leave, but if you ask for a year or more of leave you create impossible conditions for employers and then they won't employ women, so it works against women's rights in the long run. If you train someone for a job, particularly in the sciences, and then she is out for a year or more, she gets out of touch with the subject. I want my daughters to work, but I also want them to marry and have children. I have no ambition to be a grandmother; I want a breathing space first. I've been tagging along with children for twenty years. I just want to walk faster now.

J.A.D.:   You went to a women's college at Cambridge when there were no mixed colleges. Would you rather have gone to a coeducational one?

A.S.B.:   If I'd had the choice when I was eighteen I probably would have gone to a mixed college, but I think I would like now to go to Newnham [which has remained single sex]. One of the things the women's movement has done is to make it easier for women to talk to other women. When Virginia Woolf says in *A Room of One's Own* that two women were friends, she is right that that is an important step forward. When I was at college I didn't have many women friends; one went out of college for one's social life. When my children were little I did find it hard talking to women at the school gate. They envy you your double life and hope you won't be able to manage: you are a threat to them. It was difficult not to become rather schizoid. I went through a very irascible stage when my children were young. My daughters go to a single-sex school because I wanted them to go to an academic school, and there isn't an academic mixed school in London. But I do now have close women friends, mostly people I've met through working. The women's movement has taken away the idea that women can't enjoy themselves together.

J.A.D.:   Your sister, Margaret Drabble, is a novelist, and there are pairs of sisters in both *The Game* and *The Virgin in the Garden*. Do you think Stephanie and Frederica are portraits of you and your sister?

A.S.B.:   Although one is interested in sisters because of having them, Stephanie and Frederica are both in many ways different sides of me, as also are Marcus, and Daniel, who didn't have a true-life model. [Daniel is the curate whom Stephanie marries.] Frederica is like me in her intellectual equipment, her obsession with words and patterns, and also in her sexual greed and curiosity. There is perhaps more sympathy towards both sisters in that novel because I put more of myself into each of them. I had a lot of trouble with both Julia and Cassandra, the novelist and the don in *The Game*, and felt very alienated from each of them in turn.

J.A.D.:   It's obviously tempting to compare your family with the Brontës', and indeed the Brontës are a presence in both those novels. Do you think there are disadvantages, as well as stimulus, attached to growing up in a literary family?

A.S.B.:   It was difficult for me to find enough space to be myself. Sometimes one felt like not beginning to write for lack of mental and emotional space. It is also hard to have shared memories with another writer. So much of art is a transmutation of memory, and this needs to be private, not communal, or it is in danger of being destroyed. The northern landscape matters to me a great deal: I'm always looking for hills. There is a very strong Puritan element in the North. Perhaps it's significant that the novel develops out of the Puritan seventeenth century which also marks the beginning of individualism: the artist and the saint again. The Puritan instinct forces one to map out the consequences of one's own actions which is partly what I meant when I was drawing Anna's adolescence in *Shadow of a Sun*. I wrote it when I was adolescent myself, and it was much easier to describe Frederica in *The Virgin* from a stance of looking back on that age. Cambridge was my southern Garden of Eden. I played the Lady in *Comus* in a production in Trinity Hall, and that image of the Garden as both fertility and growth and temptation is there in *The Virgin in the Garden*. I should have stayed at Cambridge to do research but I went to America instead. That was because of needing space to be myself.

J.A.D.:   You said that Marcus was to some extent you. I wondered how much of your own life goes into your novels?

A.S.B.:   One always does put things in from one's own life, but I place and time them differently so that they become something new. Every writer has to tackle the problem of how much to use her own experience. George Eliot had great difficulties with *The Mill on the Floss* because of describing her own childhood and her relations, and she did not avoid offending people. Lucas Simmonds's mad cosmogony is real.

J.A.D.:   When Frederica makes up an address for the traveler in dolls it is half invention and half truth and she feels that this gives it more plausibility than total invention. Is that how you feel about making a fiction?

A.S.B.:   Yes, it is. I am a very private person and I think the artist has to be private even though her work becomes public. That is perhaps why Alexander remains a slightly shadowy figure in *The Virgin*: it is his play which is real. Art can only exist if the artist is private and I think some feminist critics don't realize this. They never seem satisfied with the artifact but want to go behind it and that can become an invasion which destroys the conditions which create art.

J.A.D.:   Alexander's play in some ways seems to be a mirror image of the novel itself. What is said about his style, that it is highly wrought, glittery, and adjectival, might also be said about yours, and of course of the subject matter as well, in that he deals with an Elizabethan age and so do you.

A.S.B.:   The images in Alexander's play, blood and stone, flesh and grass, music and silence, the heard and the unheard melody, the red and the white rose, are the images of my novel. I had some trouble with Alexander's play and kept asking myself, what is Alexander writing? This question continues to obtrude in the next novel, where he is writing about Van Gogh and Impressionism, and I feel afraid that he is going to write a rather good play, which I hadn't intended.

J.A.D.:   You said in "People in Paper Houses" in *The Contemporary Novel* that one way in which writers can comment on the fictiveness of fiction is by writing parody or pastiche. When Alexander reflects on his play he says that in the early stages he felt some natural tendency in the warp of the word towards parody and pastiche, and I wondered if you felt that pull in your own novel, in that you recognize George Eliot and Proust as models?

A.S.B.:   If one writes about writers there is a possibility that the novel will become in-turned and self-engrossed. That's why I value Daniel and Marcus: they are both nonliterary. Daniel lives rather than reads, and he doesn't relate what happens to him to what happens to people in books. When I made Frederica and Wilkie discuss the kind of novel she might write, by Proust out of George Eliot, it was meant to be the other way round and to be an androgynous joke, but it got straightened out in the printing.

J.A.B.:   How important is androgyny as a theme in the book?

A.S.B.:   Both Coleridge and Virginia Woolf said that all artists were androgynous. Alexander has in his room the purest picture of the androgynous being in Picasso's *Boy with a Pipe*, who might be man or woman.

J.A.D.:   Alexander strikes me as an androgynous being, and I wondered whether you felt that you had represented in him yourself as artist, with a different sexual identity? His interest in Elizabeth I is also related to this theme because he is fascinated by the man-woman counterpointing in Elizabeth's character, just as she herself was deeply aware of it and exploited it in every possible way, with strong masculine references to her weak womanhood.

A.S.B.:   Jung points out in *Psychology and Alchemy* that the philosopher's stone sought to reconcile the masculine and the feminine principle, as Shakespeare does with the union of the twins at the end of *Twelfth Night*. Alexander, like Elizabeth I, is fascinated with clothes, which are an important part of being human, and of sexual identity. That goes back to *Lear* and unaccommodated man. But of course clothes also confuse sexual identity: Daniel as a cleric wears a skirt. Alexander remains afraid of real women. He never becomes sexually involved with Frederica in any real way.

J.A.D.:   No, in fact I felt that he fell in love with her because she played the part of his imagined Virgin Queen, archetypally untouchable, and he lost interest when she returned to her role of ordinary real woman.

A.S.B.:   Yes, and Frederica lost interest too. They were both in love with words and wanted to prove that you could love with words. But of course there are passions which are too powerful to be expressed with words.

J.A.D.:   In your preface to Willa Cather's *The Lost Lady* you said that Cather saw her characters as portraits and forms of energy, particularly of sexual energy. Is this how you see yours?

A.S.B.:   Sexual identity can be a form of energy, but also the refusal to be bound by sexual identity releases creative energy which is perhaps why androgyny is such a compelling symbol for the artist.

J.A.D.:   In *The Game* the serpent is both the literal reptile tamed by Simon for television viewers, and Coleridge's symbol of the imagination forever uncoiling. I wonder whether the serpent doesn't have for you the multiple mythology of being on the one hand the tempter, the discordant element in the Garden, and on the other, the source of wisdom and art, the image for creativity?

A.S.B.:   The serpent is both sex and destruction, and imagination and preservation, and these two are curiously and intimately combined. Coleridge certainly knew that his serpent of the imagination was also derived from Milton's depiction of Satan.

In *The Virgin in the Garden* I wanted to substitute a female mythology for a male one. The male mythology is the Dying God and Resurrection. The female one is birth and Renaissance, and that is what the Elizabethans recognized, and what Alexander wanted to show in his play. I'm interested in Renaissance because things go on being born. In Shakespeare's last plays the daughter is the restoration of something. T. S. Eliot talks of a dissociation of sensibility after the Elizabethan age, when feeling and thought become separated, whereas for Donne's contemporaries thought had the odor of the rose. Alexander's play celebrates the wholeness of which Elizabeth is a symbol.

J.A.D.:   You seem to find stimulus for writing novels in intellectual work. Is this so?

A.S.B.:   I need to write a theoretical book at the same time as I write a novel. The gap between creative writers and critics has closed markedly in the last ten or twenty years, partly through the influence of structuralism. There are now academic theorists, novelists who are academics, and critics like Harold Bloom who think criticism is a form of creative writing. I don't. I think critical writing is a way of finding out how to write well. I had to throw off the burden of Leavis who thought that to write any book of criticism, however second-rate, was better than to write a second-rate novel. I always put novel writing higher. But I'm different from novelists like David Lodge and Malcolm Bradbury, because I don't try to keep abreast of critical theory.

J.A.D.:   What is the intellectual background of the next novel in the sequence going to be?

A.S.B.:   It focuses on Van Gogh and Impressionist art. The book centers on the public and the private. I have been haunted by the figure of Betty Maguire whose children were killed in an IRA attack, and eventually she killed herself, but not till she had tried to get over it in a very macabre way, by having another child and calling it by the same name as the dead one. Van Gogh's mother did the same with him. He was born on the same day as a brother who had died a year earlier and whom she called Vincent Van Gogh, and she used to take him to look at the grave.

J.A.D.:   There's a good deal in *The Virgin in the Garden* about how Alexander's way of writing, though relished by a fifties' consciousness, went out of fashion later and was dismissed in the seventies as overblown pastiche. Willa Cather said that all great art was simplification, and Benjamin Lodge in the novel keeps trying to pare away the literary references in Alexander's text, accusing him of vulgar ostentation where Alexander protests that the literary associations come naturally. When you move on from the period of Alexander's play, the fifties, will you also discard that highly literate and decorated mode of writing?

A.S.B.:   I don't agree with Cather, because I think you have to learn how to write a complicated language before you can discard it for a plain one, and that is what she herself did. Her mode of writing becomes more and more simple. I had planned to write the second novel in a very spare language without any metaphor at all. But I have been reading some books on metaphor which have started to persuade me that metaphorical writing is not necessarily the antithesis of literal writing, but that metaphor itself can be literal. The theoretical book behind this novel is going to be on theory of prose from Flaubert to Pound and William Carlos Williams.

J.A.D.:   When you said that the female mythology of *The Virgin* is birth and Renaissance rather than the Dying God and Resurrection one remembers the argument between Bill and Winifred, just before Marcus is conceived, about *The Winter's Tale*, and Bill's rage with his class who had tried to tell him that the play saw the pains of life reconciled in art.

A.S.B.:   I agree with Bill about that: I think *Lear* is a much truer image of suffering ordered into the forms of art. Lear's madness is real in a way that Lucas Simmonds's is not. Winifred's feelings at Marcus's birth, the rage that he was just like his father, and her love for him, were mine when I had my son.

J.A.D.:   Is Marcus like your son?

A.S.B.:   No, my son was very easy and outgoing. Marcus is more like me in his "spread" consciousness, which I afterwards discovered was exactly the word used by Wordsworth in *The Prelude* for that experience of feeling the spirit outside the body; and also in his asthma. My son died while I was writing the novel and I did put some things into it, about Daniel's father dying in a crash and about Mrs. Thone's son being killed, because of that. I had to in order to keep on writing. But I think that was the one time when I was really grateful for the novel as a form which transcends the personal, which is not just a medium for the writer to express her conflicts, but which exists in its own right. Because the form was there I had to keep on writing in it and that kept me going in spite of all the things which were happening in my life.

J.A.D.: And yet I think the end of the book is despairing. Willa Cather wrote that the novelist cannot describe elemental passions, she can only describe a passion in detailed form in its partial human manifestation. Would you agree with her?

A.S.B.: Yes, and that is how I tried to show the despair in the book. The ending is rushed. Endings are very difficult, you just have to stop at a certain point.

J.A.D.: But happily, in the ending is the beginning of the next novel, and perhaps the female mythology of birth and Renaissance may provide an image for the renewal of the real people to whom you have given life and identity.

Antony Miles Ltd.

Joan Barton

Interviewed by
Janet Todd

Joan Barton: I was born in Bristol in 1908. My parents never had a bean, but people were so stupid then — they tried to keep up a face. I was the eldest of three children and was terribly jealous of my brother who was only about fourteen months younger and important because he was a boy. I've been very influenced by this jealousy. My sister was nearly five years younger than I was and very pretty; I was always the plain, difficult one. I don't think Joan will ever get married, was my mother's attitude. I was fairly, though not extremely, close to my sister — she died when she was fifty-one. There's no one left.

My parents were much more important to each other than the children were to them. I lived with them a long time — until I was thirty or so — but never told them anything about myself. I was staggered when my sister said after my mother's death that she'd kept all my letters from abroad, sure I was going to be famous, poor mum!

I went to a little dame school and then a council school which was terrifying. At eleven I got a scholarship to Coleston's where I became head girl and had a marvelous English teacher. I wanted to go to Oxford and I got in but had no scholarship, so I went to Bristol University, which I absolutely loathed. At nineteen I became ill with a sort of hyperthyroidism and I was in bed for months and months — just when I was growing up. I wrote a lot during this time. I had been writing since I was six or seven and had things in the school magazine but I couldn't write for a living — I hadn't got any money.

It was very hard in those days. I had had a grant for books because I was going to teach, but when I went back for a term and said I wasn't going to finish or teach—I knew school life wasn't my sort of thing—I had to pay back the grant—only £12, but it was murder raising it. I needed a job, so I took one in Bristol in George's, a big bookshop, but there was absolutely no money. The man who'd been there fifty years earned £5 a week and an accountant of thirty-five years standing earned £4.10d. When he died, I asked for his job and got it for £2.5d, exactly what I was getting already. But the rest was perfect. The books were there and, when the seniors were having their long one-and-one-half hour lunch times and there were no customers, I never did a thing but wander round the shelves looking.

Because of the low money I had to get another job and I went to the BBC in Bristol as a registry clerk. But an office was awfully dull after a shop, where there's always people. Anyway I stayed there nearly five years and then at the beginning of the war people came from London and it wasn't a local office any longer. So I got fed up and left.

I wrote up to 1940. When I was at George's, I had a friend I went to stay with; she was rather good at drawing and we decided to make "rhyme sheets" and send them to Walter de la Mare—her mother thought it was terrible of us. He didn't think anything particular of the rhyme sheets but he rather liked my poems.

Walter de la Mare was the kindest man. He read many of my poems and he sent them places for me. He even sent me stamps so I could submit them. I've got about 100 letters from him criticizing, but so kindly and gently. I met him too—I was frightfully provincial and he had a butler and all the rest of it. When I wrote a novel, I sent him the beginning and he sent it to Faber for me, which was the greatest mistake because they criticized it rather harshly and I never wrote another word of it. I went on with poetry though and in about 1935 when Auden and Spender were all boiling up, I thought, I'm awfully old-fashioned and I began then to write unrhymed poems, although Walter de la Mare had said he thought the digging for rhymes produced gold. I wrote on till 1940 and then stopped. I don't think it was the war.

I moved to the Somerset County Council to the Treasurer's Department where I turned out to be quite good at finance. I went out to do audits. One was at a workhouse. I found out the first thing people had to do when taken into this workhouse—men and women separately of course—was to knit their own grave stockings and make their own shrouds. This was 1940! The stockings and shrouds were all put away on shelves and we had to take stock of the things.

After eighteen months I got a job as county secretary to the Women's Land Army in Hampshire — 1,000 land girls and 250 voluntary workers. I had a big staff and princely salary of £350 a year but I knew I would have to work for a living after the war and I needed something more permanent. So I went to the British Council and in less than a year headed a department of forty people evacuated to Oxfordshire. We moved to Blenheim Palace where John Betjeman had the overall care. He was very kind to me and a great inspiration to have around. He thought a lot of my poems and wanted to send them for publication, but I considered this wrong as I was sure then I was never going to write any more. So that was that.

I stayed at the Council until 1947 when Barbara Watson (my deputy there) and I decided to start a bookshop. I've been living with her for thirty-five years as companions (there's no emotional thing but we get on awfully well). I left the Council because it was quite obvious that when the men came home from the war I shouldn't keep a department — no woman was going to — and already I was doing a lot of interviewing of men who had left as office boys and were coming back as full colonels. Obviously they were not going to be office boys any more, although they had no experience of the work. So Barbara and I decided to risk it on our own and after a lot of hunting around we found a house in Marlborough and we started the White Horse Bookshop. We didn't make any money but it was a great success and we had lots of fun.

But still I didn't write — not until about 1956, when I started again. My religion had meant a great deal to me as an adolescent — I was brought up in high church with music and ceremony. I never rejected it but it suddenly just ceased to mean anything. Yet I had this awful nostalgia for it. I can't talk about it but about 1956 both Barbara and I went back to the church and now my religion means everything to me.

I wrote quite a lot after that — much as I had before — though perhaps I was more self-critical. I wrote most of the poems in *The Mistress* at this time. (Philip Larkin chose the title poem for the *Oxford Book of Twentieth Century Verse*.)

I've always been isolated in my work except for Walter de la Mare and John Betjeman, and my living was other things. Lots of people say they write but it can mean absolutely nothing. I've been influenced mostly by older poets whose books we sell. Tennyson, Browning, and the seventeenth-century poets mean far more to me than the moderns though I like Joy Scovell, some of Anne Stevenson. I've dipped into Americans too — I enjoy Eliot very much and Robert Frost, some of William Carlos Williams. But I can't read Robert Lowell — he means absolutely nothing to me, nor does John Berryman, partly because their minds are so utterly different from mine and their whole attitude to life so alien. Masculine thinking can be so different from women's and I can't cope with it. Men are so much harder in their outlook, more selfish, not in a nasty way, I mean. So I don't care much for modern poets — an occasional poem, that's all. I like old-fashioned people best, like Alice Meynell. I think she's very good though nobody cares about her now. Reading her poems I feel, yes, we are together.

In Marlborough we were very much in the book trade, going to sales and so on. I adore sales and bidding at them, meeting other booksellers. Some of my poetry has grown out of bookselling — I'm not inventive. In 1961 I started editing the parish magazine — it was a sixteen-page printed thing and really hard work. It was all I could to to keep this up and my full-time work. So I wrote no poetry till we left Marlborough and came here to Salisbury in 1966, continuing bookselling but without the shop. At this time I had a letter from Edwin (Ted) Tarling praising my poems and asking for some. So I got them out — I'd had a few published in between at the suggestion of John Betjeman. Tarling did eight numbers of *Wave*. Then Philip Larkin asked for something. Whenever anyone asked I produced.

I haven't written much really — about 100 poems in an extensive life. I make few false starts. But until now I never really had much time — the books had come first — this is the trouble with having to earn money. Nowadays people don't mind — they go on social security — but you couldn't in my day. And if you were self-employed as we were, it's very difficult even to get sick pay.

Then in 1978 I saw this advertisement saying literary bursaries were being offered by the Southern Arts Association and I thought, I'd never had a thing out of the state, why shouldn't I get something for a change. So I tried and was shortlisted. I went for an interview but was so disgusted — they were abominably rude. I came back wondering why I'd let myself in for this and feeling diminished; I planned to write a fierce letter saying that as a person who provides the money for these bursaries I strongly objected to the way I'd been treated. But while I was composing all this, I had a letter offering me one!

So then I thought I must do something. I couldn't just accept money. I made a study in a spare bedroom, sat down, and suddenly found I'd written three poems in no time. I was staggered because I'd been used to writing about four or five a year. Well, I wrote something like thirteen or fourteen in the next twelve months. Then I got frightened because I wrote two that I could tell were no good. Now I haven't written anything for a while but I expect I shall start again.

These last poems started like the others — in bookselling and so on. Then after a while they became personal. It was a great surprise to me. Until this last year I steered away from writing anything that could divulge me to anyone else — no one must know me, I thought — I wrote through a male person or I made a mask. Then in the last eighteen months the mask dropped and I've written personally.

I have no strong family feeling. My father hadn't got it either. I've got a thousand nephews and nieces but my brother and sister are dead. I've loved people but I can't bring myself to talk about it. I have sometimes thought I was a bit like the Miller of Dee.

The Mistress

The short cut home lay through the cemetery —
A suburban shrubbery swallowing up old graves
Iron palings tipped with rusted fleur-de-lys
A sort of cottage orne at the gates,
Ridiculous and sad;

And lost in their laurel groves,
Eaten up by moss,
Stained marble, flaking stone like hatches down,
The unloved unvisited dead:

In the no-man's-land of dusk a short cut home —
The exultant sense of life a trail of fire
Drawn into that tunnel roofed with the cypress smell
And walled with silence adding year to year:

Too far, too far: always
Under the smothering boughs in airless dark
The spirit dwindled, and the fire
Flickered then failed:

Gently implacably from the shade
The indecipherable dedications spoke
"Dear wife" . . . "devoted mother" . . .
"Beloved child" . . .

[*1959*]

From *The Mistress and Other Poems*, Sonus Press, 1972; reprinted in *A House Under Old Sarum*, Harry Chambers/Peterloo Poets, 1981.

Lot 304: Various Books

There are always lives
Left between the leaves
Scattering as I dust
The honeymoon edelweiss
Pressed ferns from prayer-books
Seed lists and hints on puddings
Deprecatory letters from old cousins
Proposing to come for Easter
And always clouded negatives
The ghost dogs in the vanishing gardens:

Fading ephemera of non-events,
Whoever owned it
(Dead or cut adrift or homeless in a home)
Nothing to me, a number, or if a name
Then meaningless,
Yet always as I touch a current flows,
The poles connect, the wards latch into place,
A life extends me—
Love-hate; grief; faith; wonder;
Tenderness.

[*1970*]

From *The Mistress and Other Poems*; reprinted in *A House Under Old Sarum*.

Gay News

". . . What a disaster year!
I advertised in *The Times* last summer
for a holiday friend
to motor south —
those endless thousand miles.
I had to ditch him there.

"*I* have been ditched since then —
'fussing and fretting' he raged
'like an old hen!'
Such cheek! After all
he was only a ship's steward;
but he was young. And now it's lonely.

"Desperate, I remembered Christopher
—so idiotic yet so beautiful
in his Anglican fig,
(ashamed of his people but he married well).
I telephoned:
'A Voice from the Past!'
Silence. 'Kit, are you there!'
He spoke at last:
'I thought you were some old woman!'
And that was all he said,
yes, that was all. . . ."

[*1978*]

The Major — An Epitaph

No I never knew him — at least until
he died. His books were up for sale
and sitting at his desk I knew him then.
French windows opening on a squared-off lawn,
brown as an Indian compound,
a flagstaff with the halyards hanging loose,
a hedge of pampas grass
bordering the green canal,
the stagnant evening sticky with thunder flies:

The neat deaf housekeeper brought sherry on a tray
"To help you sort things out:
the Major would have wished it.
Quiet but firm and always 'on parade'.
The flag was raised and lowered every day,
the Major set great store by that."
And had he lived here long? "Just since the war.
Not old, but maybe sixty-odd.
He never married and his friends were dead."

Predictable books: Ian Hay; *The Hill*;
Buchan; *Tell England*; Kipling; Forester;
old Army Lists; Teach Yourself this and that;
no secret sex, all clean and decent stuff.
Good with his hands, but nothing definite,
fixed up some tricky switches for the light,
built his own graceless desk and shelves of deal.
On the Parish Council; sidesman at the church. . . .
He should have been all right.

I found the diaries then. Useful for scrap.
And flipped them through to see
what should be burned.
Blank after blank; but here and there a date —
a Service Dinner, Legion Poppy Day,
Conservative Rally, village fayre or fete —
dry scattered bones to chart the way across
deserts of non-involvement. . . .
Why foolscap size? That seemed to make it worse.

Back a few years and catching at the eye
a longer entry, numbered: *Points in Common*.
Our faith in God. Devotion to the Queen.
War service overseas. Then, *Sentiment,*
L for each other, also A and T. And last
Dislike of "scum" government.
I should have burned them first.
And faced with his
My own life — nothing special — suddenly blazed.

When did it all start going wrong? Why should I care?
What use was pity now? Or love?

The time for that had finished long before.
He never married and his friends had died.
Why after twenty years should I still care?
Not out of pity, now, nor out of love;
guilt is the motive power—and fear:
how loneliness comes sifting silting down
and men are buried in it still alive.

[*1973*]

From *Ten Poems*, privately printed by The Perdix Press, Sutton Mandeville,
Wiltshire, 1979. Reprinted in *A House Under Old Sarum*.

Last Days

Come to the chattering ward
at Visiting Hours
and you will always find her
high on the pillows
flanked by cards and flowers,
and pretty still
lips and cheeks made up
eyelids carefully blue
on brilliant eyes;
and all her talk is plans
plans for afterwards
after the patient
waiting to get well.

But these are flags
bravely at sunset flying
in an approaching dusk
to be brought down.
For come too early,
quietly and alone,
and find her sleeping,
leaden shadows lying
on eyelids paper-thin,
on cheek and brow,
the straightened sheet
plain as a linen shroud
beneath the chin,
then you will know

for sure what hour it is:
how soon must come
the stripped and empty bed,
her folded clothes
put ready to take home.

[1979]

From *A House Under Old Sarum.*

Lord Let Me Know My End

Daily I read that notice in *The Times*
Miss Smith, aged ninety, dead
on such and such a date,
no given name, no kith and kin, no home,
too old for anyone to know
how or whence she came.
And I can hear her cry
"But once I had a name
they knew me by,
those fading generations whom I taught."

Daily I read how some Miss Brown has died,
of two forgotten people long since gone
the last surviving child —
all else unknown.
And then I hear her cry
"But I was never theirs,
I was myself, my own,
did I deserve this
I who was faithful
through those lost dead years?"

So do these ghosts each day cry out to me,
the spinster nurses, teachers,
servants of the state,
the last surviving daughters:
and I who never knew them promise them
"I will remember
keep a year's mind for you, say prayers,
not for your death

but for those last years, columns long, alone."
Or is it myself I promise
buying off my fears
lest I even I should be
that nameless, homeless, unremembered one?

[*1979*]

From *A House Under Old Sarum.*

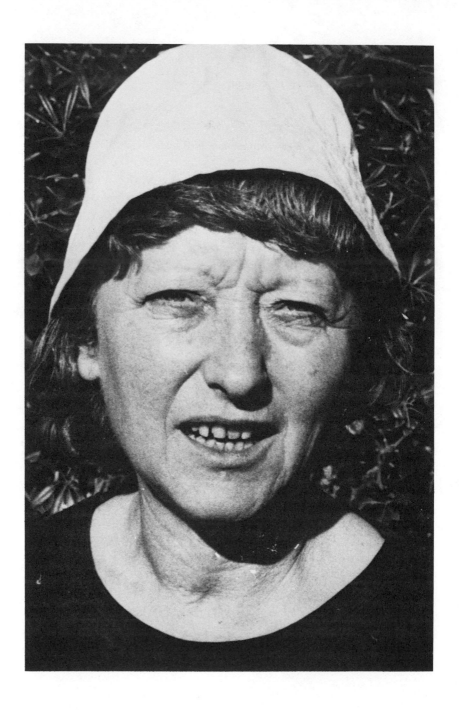

Christiane Rochefort

Interviewed by
Georgiana Colvile

The extremely limited biographical information given at the beginning of each of her books is an accurate indication of Christiane Rochefort's keen sense of privacy. All that is known is that she was born in Paris, in the Fourteenth District, and is consequently a true Parisian (quite a rare species!). Her broad and varied interests were already apparent in the wide range of subjects she chose to study at university: medicine, psychiatry, psychology, and ethnology among others. She generally found institutionalized learning to be restrictive and unsatisfactory and often preferred self-teaching to completing courses and taking exams. Her feelings towards the different jobs she has held were similar. She tried her hand at office work, journalism, and working with film people at the Cannes Festival, but the only position she truly enjoyed was working with Henri Langlois at the Paris Cinémathèque.

For many years, Christiane's creative energy was so great that she refused to limit herself to one genre: she was all at once a painter, a sculptor, a musician, and a writer. Over the years, writing has eclipsed the other arts but her keen interest in them has never waned.

Ideologically, Christiane is very clear as to her position, which she once defined as follows: "I would be an anarchist if that were not already a label!" Her sympathies with the women's movement form part of her more general outcry in defense of all oppressed minorities and individuals. In all her novels a need to escape from the bondage of social restraints predominates.

Christiane is basically a loner as a person and as a writer "I have become like a wild boar," she told me. She was once married and sums up that situation from a woman's point of view as a somewhat grotesque golden cage in her third and only autobiographical novel *Cats Don't Care for Money* (New York: Doubleday, 1965). Now she merely smiles and says: "That gentleman couldn't understand that I wanted to write at night, he kept asking me to come to bed, so I had to choose: obviously, I wasn't going to give up my writing. I have never regretted it."

Christiane Rochefort is widely read in France where all her novels (except *A Rose for Morrison*, Paris: Grasset, 1966) are available in paperback.[1] She published ten books between 1958 and 1978, seven of which are novels, one an essay on how she wrote her fifth novel *Spring in the Parking Lot* (Paris: Grasset, 1969), one sociological essay on the oppression of children, and finally that delightful collage which I can only call a mock-autobiography. She is at present finishing an eighth novel and has so far never let more than three years elapse between publications. She has also translated John Lennon's *In His Own Write* into French (1965) with Rachel Mizrahi and two books by her friend Amos Kenan from Hebrew into French: *The Finished Horse* and *Holocaust II* (my translation of the titles). These last translations, and her partiality to various Jewish writers such as Rachel Mizrahi and Amos Kenan, prompted me to ask her what her affiliations were with various branches of Jewish culture. Her answer was that, in spite of her hated fair hair and blue eyes, she felt part of an underdeveloped minority and ("thank heaven!", she said) excluded from the white adult male community. She has always felt a strong attraction for oppressed groups and there was a time when she was often the "Saturday-night goy" in an all-Jewish gathering. She even learned Hebrew—"I am a natural-born bastard," she declared, "and luckily I have Celtic blood"—but her main objective is to remain outside of any specific race or culture, as a free individual. This has not been easy.

Christiane Rochefort can certainly be considered one of the pioneers of the women's movement in France. She was an active participant, in the early years, in the women's encounter groups that grew out of May '68 and in the various demonstrations of the early 1970s for free legal abortion and against the traditional domestic role assigned to women by society. In France, as in America and indeed on an international level, a small group had quietly set out, no more no less, to change the world. A whole mentality was being shaken, history was on the move, great possibilities for radical change were opening up, thanks to a few courageous women. At that time, MLF—*Mouvement de libération de la femme*—was just a general term, a banner under which all resisting women could unite.

Then the inevitable happened: various destructive forces soon began to weaken, divide, and destroy that initial surge of positive energy and the solidarity which had prevailed at first among most women. Christiane sensed the danger early. First of all, various left-wing political groups, such as Trotskyites, Maoists, socialists, et alia, tried to annex the women's movement to their own ends, while remaining quite oblivious to the women's objectives. Many women, unused to operating under political pressure, allowed themselves to be manipulated, while others continued to struggle for their autonomy. Secondly, the mass media soon began to exploit the movement, using the MLF acronym in order to promote their productions and performances, as indeed did commercial advertising. Finally, various ambitious women soon proved that their sole concern with the movement was to take advantage of it as a means of getting as much power as possible for themselves.

At the beginning of the movement, Christiane wrote three strong articles that were warnings against the dangers besetting it. One was against centralism, the second against the MLF acronym, and the third against the establishment of a bureaucracy and a centralized treasury within the movement. These articles are out of print now; they appeared in the early feminist paper *Le Torchon brûle* [Dishcloths are being burned] and in *Les Temps modernes* in the early 1970s. Alas, no one paid any attention to the articles, except the few who were already aware of the dangers. Some, such as the novelist Monique Wittig, joined Christiane in her outcry, but they all felt they were preaching in the desert.

To her mind, women can only fight for freedom in a kind of anonymity—that is, not clandestinely, but in total avoidance of power patterns, which fatally engender a mechanism of degradation. Amongst the people who have struggled for women's rights, Simone de Beauvoir is one of those Christiane respects the most: "For women's problems we would turn to Simone and for class and racial issues to Sartre," she said.

Christiane still looks back upon the beginning of the movement as a time of true searching, of the flowering of a new and free ideology, of creativity and beauty. Her favorite novel, the utopian *Archaos* (Paris: Grasset, 1975), which she considers to be her only positive work, grew out of that time. She feels that the women's movement followed a pattern of development similar to that of the black civil rights movement and probably also to that of the 1917 proletarian revolution, both of which started out well and then degenerated. If we are to read Christiane's novels as prophecies (*A Rose for Morrison* certainly predicted May '68), the next group to rebel against social pressures will be preteenage children.

Natalie Sarraute once said that being a woman had never made any difference to her as a writer. Christiane Rochefort agrees with Sarraute on the whole, but feels that this issue cannot be considered as a whole, but on three separate levels: "form, content, and feedback from readers!"

As far as her own personal experience goes, when she was a child and scribbling her first attempts at writing, she had no idea of the social implications of being a woman. When she was little she wrote little pieces that bore no specific mark of her sex or gender. She was just somebody and as an adolescent she wrote poems and analytic essays and like most adolescents she combined insecurity with a narcissistic vanity. She identified with Rimbaud and his line of thought and it never occurred to her that Rimbaud's status was male (and indeed is it?). In short, she saw no difference and still sees none, on the level of style and form, between men and women writers.

However when it comes to the level of content, one enters into social considerations. The differences between the messages conveyed by a man and a woman could be compared to that between what a black African from the jungle and a Parisian executive might write. The difference stems from the individual and his particular experience of life. A black man and a white man from the same city may or may not write in a similar fashion. Different people have met with different obstacles and received different caresses from their mothers in infancy. For example at times there may be a considerable affinity between what a militant black man and a feminist woman write. Here Christiane suggested that a writer like Maya Angelou offers a kind of synthesis between women and blacks.

She insisted that there is no such thing as race, but only culture(s) and that the whole issue is not biological but cultural. Before the biological differences can be so much as considered the cultural ones will have to be thoroughly analyzed and determined. This would require years of research by a professional team of scientists, perhaps in an institution such as MIT, with the help of a computer. A mass of information would result from such a project and the classification and in-depth study of these data might finally reveal the correct facts concerning the effects of cultural conditioning upon human beings of both sexes. Christiane is personally convinced that as far as artistic expression is concerned, there are greater discrepancies to be found between individuals than between whole groups.

There is a third level, besides form and content, which also constitutes part of the social aspect of writing, this time on the receiving end; that is, the way readers see and hear the text. Here the attitudes of both professionals (critics, journalists, etc.) and amateurs can be so different towards men and women, that early in her career Christiane seriously considered writing under an assumed name. She would have chosen a neutral first name such as Claude, Camille or Dominique, like George Sand. Realizing that this would mean leading a complicated existence of hiding and dodging the public eye, she decided against it: "Shit!" she said — and insisted that I include that in the interview — "I am the way I am and need no masks!"

Christiane is very skeptical concerning Judy Chicago's research on the difference between men and women as expressed through their style of drawing. Although she considers her intentions to be quite sincere, she feels that the American artist is falling into the trap of biology without considering the impact of culture. To Rochefort the kind of conclusion reached by Judy, for example that women tend to draw in curves and men in jagged lines,[2] is not only gratuitous and grossly psychoanalytic but furthermore creates a kind of stereotyped mentality and encourages discrimination. Neither does she believe in Hélène Cixous' theory of "feminine writing" which claims that women write according to a natural biological flow and stream of consciousness, whereas men's works remain cramped within binary structures and a bureaucraticlike organization.[3] Christiane sees no real contradiction here between structured and free-flowing writing.

This led Christiane Rochefort to examine a specific influence of culture over biology. She maintains that the cultural phenomena resulting in the general confining of women to a passive domestic role have led to a further development in women of the right-hand brain, which transmits intuitive information and visual perception (for left-handed people the sides of the brain are reversed), as opposed to the left-hand brain, which codes information into language and tends to be less evolved in females. Men, on the other hand, have had their left-hand brain overexpanded by society and the work role it has assigned them; they consequently want to formulate everything by means of linguistic codes such as technical jargons, whereas their right-hand brain is likely to be almost atrophied. This does not make male intelligence any more logical; one only has to look at any male-dominated bureaucracy, administration, government, or the world at large to be confronted with one vast absurd chaos. On the other hand, the right-hand brain produces structures and a logic of its own, closer to the subconscious. Here, in an aside, Christiane recommended the dissident Russian writer Zinoviev as one of the best logicians in the world and his book *The Yawning Heights*[4] as the first real treatise in logic she has ever read. In this monumental work (Christiane Rochefort admits in *My Life, Revised and Corrected by the Author* [Paris: Stock, 1978] that she took two months to read it!) he analyzes the illogical aspects of language, including scientific jargon and the power syndromes involved.

Christiane feels that her true initiation to creative writing (incidentally, this is about the only university discipline she approves of) was achieved through studying the works of William Faulkner. She was hardly influenced by the French literary tradition but feels that the writers of what she calls the Golden Age of American literature: Faulkner, Steinbeck, Caldwell, Lowry, as well as Joyce and Kafka, were her literary fathers. Her passionate interest in their books resided not in the content but in the structures. Those great Americans, she told me, were structural masters, long before anyone had heard of the French structuralists. She dismisses the latter as petty little critics, who have contributed nothing new and have not even grasped what is obvious and essential about literary structures. As a budding writer, Christiane Rochefort would spend hours making charts and diagrams of *Light in August* and *The Sound and the Fury*. She went through a phase of imitation but not in any of her published works. Now she says: "Thank God, I don't write like Faulkner!" Faulkner was her passage into her own writing, as were to a lesser degree Joyce and Kafka.

Among French writers, Christiane Rochefort much appreciates Queneau, whose linguistic games influenced some of her writing, and has a special love for Boris Vian. She relates in *Writing Is a Strange Experience,* (Paris: Grasset, 1970; Canadian Version: *Journal de printemps — Spring Diary*, Montreal: L'Entincelle, 1977) how she could feel his presence while writing *A Rose for Morrison*, in fact he seemed to be dictating the first third of the book to her, as though she were a medium, and then left her to continue on her own! She does not look upon Vian as an influence, but more as a kind of literary lover.

For many years Christiane was certainly ahead of her time, or born too late to participate in the 1913 Avant Garde or Dada/Surrealism.

During the 1950s in France she felt quite alienated in her way of writing but later she began to feel part of a new tradition, as more recent writers like Ajar, Agnès Pavy, Raymond Lévy and Rachel Mizrahi[5] began to emerge in France. The bond between them is an attempt at transmitting spoken language or coming as close as possible to it in writing. This led me to mention Céline who had done this, also alone, much earlier; she replied that much as she dislikes him as a person, she has to admit to his stylistic breakthrough and feels closer to him than to more traditional novelists like François Mauriac.

Christiane was sorry to be able to include only very few women among her favorite writers. She feels that the reason for this is that they have been handicapped by social pressures in their creative attempts and consequently, until recently, have had no real literary tradition of their own. She then interestingly referred to a meeting of women poets, the group Hidden History, who had organized a reading of their works, which she attended in New York a few years ago and which was a revelation to her. It was the first time that she had felt roots among her sister writers, and the first time that they were numerous and varied enough to be able to present her with a real choice. She experienced the reading as a glimpse into a still far too hidden world. Her reaction to Marguerite Duras is complex. She especially admires her early works and, although she finds her present evolution through film interesting and is able to understand it, Christiane Rochefort feels unable to share it or be influenced by it. As for Marguerite Yourcenar, Rochefort's only comment was that it is shameful and grotesque that any woman (even more so than a man) should agree to become a member of such a reactionary institution as the Académie Française.

On the subject of critics, Christiane was adamant, as I already knew from earlier conversations with her in California. As a creator she has little or no patience with them. She calls criticism "commentary" and feels that this parasitic genre has invaded literature at the expense of creative writing. The present day profusion of critical texts appears to her as a sign of decadence. She considers it to be a "power trip." (She used this familiar American expression here.) To her mind criticism crushes its object and makes it more obscure instead of clearer. Furthermore a critic tends to strip the text from the reader by appropriating it to his own glory. She sees criticism as a malignant tumor that is poisoning French culture and compared it to advertising, which appropriates a product before making it available to consumers.

Christiane Rochefort does however approve of the idea of a sociology of literature, which she finds to be almost totally lacking except in the works of certain American feminists such as Kate Millett, and to a degree in those of Michel Foucault. This led to the question of feminist criticism: "Is there such a thing?" she asked.

Something struck me as soon as I entered Christiane's apartment, a cosy little nest just big enough for her and her two cats, neither tidy nor messy, just lived in; both functional and attractive in a simple way, it was first and foremost a writer's cell. Books lined all the walls and covered most of the furniture. There were also stacks of cassettes, a corner kitchen, a corner bathroom, two small bedrooms, a tiny backyard for greenery in a somewhat wild state, but above all a large table to write at and an easy chair for listening to music. To Christiane Rochefort writing comes first.

As she talked she led me further into a magic world, much like that of the Surrealists, into that fleeting space where the creative process unfolds. Although she doesn't talk much about her private life, she is quite willing to talk about her writing. Christiane Rochefort is a disciplined writer. She sits at her table and writes every day for several hours, even if she is not working on any specific opus. When she starts on a book, she plunges in and then works slowly; sometimes she has to stop and set it aside for a while. If, on the other hand, she is able to continue she becomes totally absorbed and leads a nunlike existence until it is finished. She then barricades herself in her apartment with adequate supplies of pens, paper, and food for a siege!

To Christiane Rochefort different states can be achieved in the process of writing. When she is able totally to lose herself in it, to let go and become immersed in a positively psychedelic trance, she is able to produce the work she is the most satisfied with. She rarely reaches such a state of grace or "high," which engenders the kind of automatic writing advocated by Breton (1886–1966), the founder of the Surrealist movement in France.

Warrior's Rest (Paris: Grasset, 1958; New York: Doubleday, 1962) is an impressive first novel. (Plot: Geneviève Le Theil becomes physically mesmerized and drawn out of her stuffy middle-class existence into marginality by the former writer, now down-and-out bum and alcoholic, Renaud Sarti, whom she has accidentally saved from suicide. He humiliates and mistreats her, but she is the one who survives the adventure, tubercular and pregnant, but a stronger person.) This book can perhaps be better understood now than in 1958, when it was conveniently dismissed as pornographic. After going through it with a fine-tooth comb and finding no single pornographic passage, Christiane concluded that the sexism of most readers had labeled her rather brutal style of writing pornographic — which could simply be translated as "unfeminine." The book was even compared to *Story of O*, which can truly be classified as obscene, especially on an ideological level, since it condones the sexual abuse of women. The real porno peddlers complained that *Warrior's Rest* was not "dirty" enough.

Later readings proved to be more interesting. After taking the book at surface value (Geneviève's point of view), people began to perceive the book's second layer (Renaud's muffled voice). Christiane has never much cared for autobiography and generally stays out of her novels, except for *Cats Don't Care for Money* and a brief appearance in this first book. "I, is another" wrote Rimbaud. In *Warrior's Rest* Christiane deliberately chose a character she could not identify with (Geneviève) as the first-person narrator. She sees this distance as a stylistic necessity. She feels close to Renaud, whom she considers to be trapped by the times: in the 1950s there was no way out, no hippie movement, no May '68 — only sex, drink, cigarettes, and sometimes drugs. His affair with Geneviève is just a way of killing time, himself, and her. His is the second voice; he talks little but his attitude cries out against the vacuum of his period. He cannot say "I," he is an object. A third voice makes a brief appearance, that of Rafaële, an androgynous girl, a kind of female reflection of Renaud, even more lost in the world than he is. Christiane finds Rafaële too sketchy and consequently a failure. She is even less satisfied with the other minor characters. She has now learned to work on even the most unimportant figures of a novel, but then only the main protagonists came to life.

Christiane Rochefort considers her second novel, *Children of Heaven* (New York: McKay, 1962) as completely successful, but she is not especially fond of it, probably on account of its utterly realistic, nightmarish content. (Plot: Josyane is the eldest of a working-class family, living in a HLM [*habitation à loyer modéré;* that is, a low-budget thin-walled concrete apartment building of the type built all over France in the early 1960s.] The Government Family Allowance prompts her parents to reproduce like rabbits. Josyane has to look after the brood. Her bright spirit is gradually dimmed, she has to leave school, and after a fling with a motorcycle gang, goes off "happily" married and pregnant, to live much like her mother, in a slightly higher-standard building.) In her essay *Writing Is a Strange Experience*, Christiane relates how she had a studio in one of these buildings for her sculpture. The grimness of the concrete surroundings prompted her to sow some grass under her window. When it grew, somebody deliberately uprooted it; she planted it again, they uprooted it again, and so it went on. The persistence of this destructive urge aroused her curiosity concerning the mentality which HLM living produces. *Children of Heaven* grew out of that tuft of grass, which she incidentally was never able to include in the book. *Children of Heaven* has a perfectly linear structure, but time is handled deceptively: years can pass by in one sentence, whereas whole chapters may cover only a few hours. The love scenes at the end contain a section of puppetlike dialogue taken piecemeal from a trashy magazine, which renders a perfect cliché.

Christiane Rochefort's second book is certainly one of the most powerful attacks on modern urban living. Little hope emerges except in the fact that Nicolas, Josyane's youngest brother, behaves like an unconventional rebel and is left alone because of his physical strength. When I asked Christiane whether Josyane's pregnancy at the end of *Children of Heaven*, and even Geneviève's in *Warrior's Rest*, was meant to place some hope on the future generation (May '68), she was hesitant. She sees both women as further alienated by pregnancy, especially Geneviève, whose child will have a tubercular mother and an alcoholic father. But Josyane may find her way into the women's movement later on, and her child could well be Christophe, the boy who runs away from his HLM home in *Spring in the Parking Lot* (Paris: Grasset, 1969); Christiane agrees that the latter in a way constitutes a more positive sequel to *Children of Heaven*.

However, Christiane's intentions in writing this novel were made clearer than ever seventeen years later, in *My Life, Revised and Corrected by the Author* (p. 260): "I was reproached with having given it a happy ending. Ha ha ha! If you really want to know it's a horror book. I was yelling: YOU'LL SEE, THOSE BUILDINGS ARE KILLERS."

Christiane considers *Cats Don't Care for Money* as her worst work, mainly on account of its autobiographical content: she was unable to put enough distance between herself and the main characters. In fact she would have liked all the characters to behave like marionettes, in automatic fashion, in order to obtain the desired satirical effect. She only succeeded in making the secondary male figure, Jean-Pierre Bigeon, into a puppet. (Plot: Céline, a carefree bohemian girl, falls in love with and reluctantly marries a very conventional, upper-middle-class young man, Philippe Aignan, who then proceeds to reform her. Bored and unhappy as a perfect bourgeoise housewife, Céline turns to Julia Bigeon, the wife of Jean-Pierre Bigeon, a business pal of Philippe's. Julia becomes her friend and lover. Julia's death in an absurd car accident and Philippe's flashy success in right-wing politics bring Céline back to life. She escapes and returns to her marginal world with the support and friendship of Philippe's younger brother and sister Bruno and Stéphanie (once again the May '68 generation).

This novel is a virulent attack on the French middle class, stereotyped image of marriage and indeed perhaps one of the first militant feminist novels in France. The upper middle class is in fact where the women's movement started.

Christiane considers the intimacy that develops between Céline and Julia as a natural alliance between two oppressed people, which logically turns into love. She actually wrote a "lesbian" love scene between the two but deliberately cut it out of the book so as to deprive her male readers of a certain voyeuristic pleasure. She subsequently discovered that this omission brought about a genuine stylistic improvement and helped the structure of the novel, which she is more satisfied with from that point on (about the last third). Coincidentally, in the final part, she no longer identifies with Céline and focuses more on the younger generation.

Unlike Roger Vadim's commercial screen adaptation of *Warrior's Rest,* Moshe Mizrahi's film of *Cats Don't Care for Money* remains true to the book and met with Christiane's approval. She was struck however by the effect of the script on the actors: the one playing the part of the husband would constantly attempt to soften the character and make excuses for him. Even the women, who at first liked their roles, felt uncomfortable at being involved in such an open battle between the sexes. The film was carefully kept out of commercial circuits. It is almost impossible to see in France. The producers, censors, et alia, obviously felt very threatened by it!

The next book, *A Rose for Morrison*, is one of Christiane's favorites. She calls it "politics-fiction." (Plot: in a *Brave New World* type of society, governed by people with names like Ruins, Senility, and Debris, a few young people, students, children, and workers still want to live, love, and be free. The students demonstrate, the workers go on strike, and the children subvert their schools' brainwashing system. A revolution blossoms, complete with music: the book is an uncanny prediction of May 1968.)

This book is very surrealistic; anything can happen, whether it be on the level of form or content, as in the novels of Queneau and Vian. *A Rose for Morrison* was written in twenty-four days, in a total state of trance, to a vast extent in automatic writing, under the sign of Boris Vian, as already mentioned. She had once more buried herself in her apartment, she told me, and a cooperative friend took care of all the housework, cooking, and shopping. He would also turn on the radio and often the news of the Vietnam War, which was in full swing in 1966, went straight into the text along with the rest of Christiane's automatic flow. Bob Dylan's records provided an almost constant background and his psychedelic antiwar songs permeated the novel and inspired the character of the singer Amok.

Stylistically, in this book Christiane was as ludic as she pleased and the text is constellated with surrealistic word games, invented expressions, and wittily contrived proper names, often deforming real ones, such as the "Pantygone" for the Pentagon. Christiane calls them "carnivorous rhetorical flowers."[6]

Here, really small children begin to play an important part. They are regularly sent to a clinic for special "brain treatment" whenever they refuse to conform. One little girl discovers the mechanism used by the doctors, who finally are outsmarted by the children. Similarly, young girls are trained for marriage to be passive, obedient, and frigid in prenuptial schools, where men can come and try them out. If they dare to experience pleasure or even ask for it, they are cruelly desensitized by means of a grater passed through their vagina. This idea sprang directly from Christiane Rochefort's automatic writing. Triton, a young girl thus ruined, becomes a singer (much like a castrato!) and assumes the name Amockingbird. Her most popular song, "The Last Days of May," inspires the final revolution which leads all oppressed groups to rebel. The general rebellion of workers, students, children is a kind of celebration of love, youth, and spring. All public registers are burned, no one officially exists anymore, and the beautiful young woman professor Sereine, who is at once a brilliant intellectual and a positive sex symbol, announces a fresh start; she deals in words in her classes and language too has been set free.

The title is a tribute to Norman Morrison, who had burned himself alive in front of the Pentagon in protest against the Vietnam War. Christiane especially loves this book and relates in *Writing Is a Strange*

Experience how her own optimism took her by surprise, precisely a quarter of the way through, after Vian had let her go: "My adolescents began to smash the whole works, just as I thought that I was writing a desperate book, and as I read it, I realized that I was more of an optimist than I thought. One certainly takes oneself by surprise at times."[7] The seeds of May '68 were already in the air. She told me an amusing anecdote. During the students' revolution in May 1968, she saw a drawing amidst the graffiti which covered most university walls, representing a policeman who had gone back to school and become genuinely absorbed in his studies, exactly like Cleoporte (Cloporte, in French, means a kind of bug or louse)—one of the characters in *A Rose for Morrison*. "It was really him," she said. Somehow she had jumped ahead in history. Unfortunately the book met with very little success.

Stylistically, her fifth novel, *Spring in the Parking Lot*, is more like the first three, with a clear linear structure, although its explosive content is reminiscent of *A Rose for Morrison*. (Plot: An adolescent boy, Christophe, leaves his HLM home on impulse and wanders into the Paris Latin Quarter where the students hang out. His free spirit makes him instantly popular with a group of students who help and adopt him. After spending a night with a girl and then turning down the courtship of Fabrice, a stereotyped homosexual, Chris is shocked into facing the mad passion which has mutually hit him and Thomas, a heterosexual male student. They break the social barriers, refuse any established labels for their new relationship, and their youthful ecstasy, which coincides with the coming of spring, wins over all their friends, who rejoice and celebrate with them.)

Christiane started this book in 1964, before *A Rose for Morrison*. *Spring in the Parking Lot* was a troublesome child and had to be rewritten three times. At first, Christiane Rochefort refused to accept what was happening to her characters, especially the nature of the relationship developing between Chris and Thomas. She had never really fully dealt with love in her previous books and this time it had to remain different and free from any of the stereotyped social patterns: the fact that both lovers happen to be male does not necessarily make them homosexuals. Christophe's spontaneous flight and the way he socially assumes it, turns him into an unusual and socially threatening creature: he radiates true freedom. "Why two men and not two women?" Christiane was asked over and over again. "Why not a green salad?" she replied. Part of the reason is that she wanted to create the necessary distance between herself and the characters, as with Renaud in *Warrior's Rest*. She is still not entirely happy with Chris's discourse.

The utopian vision which started with *A Rose* and lasted until *At Least Summer's Coming Soon* (Paris: Grasset, 1975) is definitely present here, and is as usual based on the idea of an escape from reality into a different world.

Since Christiane experienced such difficulties and complications with *Spring in the Parking Lot* and was still not satisfied with its ending, she could not quite let it go and decided to commit to paper the various adventures and obstacles that beset the writing of that book. Her notes during and after the composition of the novel grew into an essay: *Writing Is a Strange Experience*. At the beginning she mentions how she wrote some of her other books and what writing means to her in general. Christiane considers this book to be unique in its genre; if it is criticism it is only meant to criticize the present flow of "commentary" that has invaded modern literature. She does not "comment" on her book, but tells its story. She emphasizes the "happening" aspect of writing. For example, she describes an interest in adolescent boys that suddenly overcame her as she walked the streets. She realized later that this was merely a sign that she had temporarily become Thomas and needed to see the world through his eyes: when the book was finished, she no longer noticed adolescents any more than usual. This book needs very little "commentary"; it merely offers the reader the possibility of seeing a writer's world from the inside.

The next novel, *Archaos*, Christiane's longest novel, is also her favorite book. She has a real weakness for it and considers it to be the only entirely positive text she has ever produced: it does not merely contain utopian elements like several of her previous books but it actually is a utopia from beginning to end. Like *A Rose* it is a "politics-fiction" novel and, like *Spring*, it had to be written three times. (Plot: King Avatar and Queen Avanie are trying to produce an heir to the Throne of Archaos. Twins are born—first a girl, Onagre, whom the king sends away, and then a boy, Govan, who screams until his sister is restored to him in secret. Later the king is killed, and with the help of the unusual ecclesiast Erostase, Govan turns the country into a state of blissful freedom, from which all taboos, especially the sexual ones, have been lifted. If that country no longer exists, it is on account of its neighbors' jealousy.)

The book begins as a medieval epic and rapidly expands into a wild surrealistic fresco, far removed from any existing time or space. As in *A Rose*, the joys of spring play havoc with language as well as with social mores. Here Christiane wrote more consciously, creating a deliberate confusion. Her reversal of grammatical structures and conventional symbols, even the most elementary sexual "differences," is part of her literary strategy. On the level of content, the conventional social hierarchy of the first chapters, complete with King, Queen, Ministers, etc., gives way to a kind of pansexual pagan garden of Eden. Christiane is still not satisfied with the beginning, which remains more rigidly ensconced in the medieval epic/romance, but especially loves the end, written in a total trance. Those last three pages, which constitute a deliciously sensual love song made all-encompassing by the continual shifting of pronouns, could stand alone, without the bulk of the book.

If this book sings of joy and is Christiane's beloved child, it is again for historical reasons. It was written in 1972, when the women's movement was at its beginning and May '68 still remained an inspiration; people believed in change and had hope for the future. "Now," says Christiane sadly, "there is nothing utopian left in the world and I shall write no more utopias."

The role of children has been becoming increasingly important in Christiane Rochefort's books. They really begin to hold their own and create a nucleus of resistance in *A Rose* and in *Archaos* they live and love as freely as the utopian adults. Next, Christiane began to focus her interests more specifically on the younger generation. The following questions kept coming up:

—Are they not the most oppressed group in our society?

—What rights do they have?

In *At Least Summer's Coming Soon*, Christiane imagines them taking their lives into their own hands. (Plot: A whole class of twelve-year-olds, having been told for the third time by their teacher that they are good for nothing, leave their desks and drift into the countryside. Three of them, Grace, Regina, and Jean-Marie, are never found. It rapidly becomes an epidemic; children are missing all over the country and the young proctor, Mann, abandons his job to search for his beloved Regina. Gradually a clandestine network of marginal people is formed to help the children find food and an occasional shelter, away from the public eye. These supposedly "dumb" children discover their intelligence once they have left school. Now, at last, they can live and be free! When a few of them reappear in "civilization" their beauty is staggering, they have lost their insecurity and the authorities are baffled.)

The book was based on a real fact: a schoolteacher's repeated putdown of her class. Among the children's marginal protectors, women are shown in an especially favorable light; their love for the children overcomes their fear of law and order. Once again Christiane uses wordplay and describes a certain number of ideal situations, but the enthusiasm of *Archaos* no longer prevails.

This book led me to ask Christiane Rochefort about her views on communal living. She replied that we are not yet ready for such a formula and added that she herself had tried once and experienced it as a failure. The idyllic description in *At Least Summer's Coming Soon* of a commune run by friends of Mann's, the highlight of which is a young woman blissfully breast-feeding her beautiful golden baby, was done tongue-in-cheek, she said, and filled with irony. On the other hand, the three women living together (who also help the children at one point) seem better suited for team life, which appears to be less complicated without men.

This book is not surrealistic, but the plot is loosely arranged into a kind of "alternate montage," shifting from one group of runaways to another. On the level of content, the children's situation remains precarious and the title reminds the reader of the ephemeral nature of their adventure.

Children First (Paris: Grasset, 1976) is Christiane's only theoretical text and it belongs to a discipline of which she approves: sociology. In the book, she gives various facts and figures to support the thesis that children constitute an oppressed minority with no rights of their own, almost all over the world. From birth, they are taken over, labeled, conditioned, and trained to conform to adult stereotypes. They are in a kind of concentration camp without the least recourse to legal help. The most alive of all, they are in turn made to join the ranks of the living dead: adults. This book is a passionate outcry and reveals some alarming facts about IQ tests, school psychiatrists, parents' rights, et alia. It was the result of her intensive research on children's rights in several parts of the world, including the United States. She was particularly impressed by Dr. Frederick Leboyer's new approach to childbirth at the time:[8] at last somebody was trying to soften the trauma of birth by dimming lights, allowing for a first contact with the mother's body instead of with metal instruments, for example.

Christiane's objective in this book was not to "correct" society but merely to state some universally ignored facts concerning children. When asked about this book in the United States, while she was still writing it, she said that *Children First* was about "children's oppression." She met with puzzled glances, for her French accent (or was that the real reason?) had caused people to understand "children's operation." Needless to say, she found the slip interesting, especially when the notion of "children's oppression," once made clear, turned out to be equally foreign to her American audience, and in France, people could see no meaning in it whatever.

Both *At Least Summer's Coming Soon* and *Children First* met with an incredible amount of hostility and Christiane was viciously attacked by all of the participants in a French television program which was supposed to be a balanced debate between pros and cons. To her disappointment, mothers were angrier than anybody else and nobody could tolerate her maligning the cliché bourgeois family image.

As far as acting upon the thesis of the book is concerned, Christiane was more negative. She feels that in order to be able to do anything about children's conditions, one would first have to be realistic (which she feels she definitely is not) and secondly overthrow the ruling class (which is not about to happen). She does however credit Ivan Illich with the only possible suggestions for a solution,[9] for example the idea of allowing children to choose their own curricula and organize their studies themselves (as at Summerhill) and thus play an active/creative role in their learning process.

At this point, I asked the inevitable personal question: had Christiane ever wanted children? Her answer was that the pressures involved in our society are such that she could never determine whether in other circumstances she might have wanted them. She hates the possessiveness of the family structure and thinks that in a place like Samoa or the Trobriand Islands, where people don't "own" their children, but let them wander freely among groups of people, she might have had some. Here, everything would have to be turned upside down, which is nothing new in Rochefort's philosophy. "When people ask me that question," she said finally, "I usually just answer that I've never had time and that shuts them up!"

Christiane's latest book, *My Life, Revised and Corrected by the Author*, was, unlike the others, a publisher's request, not her own idea: "I stupidly accepted the commitment," she said. The original idea was a kind of literary experiment and seemed appealing enough. Maurice Chavardès was to interview her about her life and work and put the interview on tapes, which would supposedly provide the raw materials for a spontaneous text in oral style with very few written corrections. Such an experiment had already been successfully conducted by Marguerite Duras and Xavière Gauthier in *Les Parleuses* ("Women Talking," Paris: Editions de Minuit, 1974), in the form of a spontaneous dialogue between the two writers. Christiane had also experienced a similar flow of communication during a long discussion with some women friends, which she feels should have been taped and committed to paper. However, when she listened to Maurice Chavardès's tapes they struck her as a "bunch of shit" (her expression). In the artificial situation of that interview there had been a complete lack of communication. Having signed a contract, she decided in extremis to do something else.

The title is deceptive, which is hardly surprising considering Christiane's old dislike for autobiographical writing — her own, that is. At the beginning of the book she explains humorously that it would require eighteen thousand 700-page volumes for her to tell the story of her life. Besides, she warns the reader, she would rather not spend her life telling him/her about it, or his/hers for that matter, which would be worse. So let it be literature — as long as it is literature it can be contained in thirty pages or thirty lines or whatever.

This accidental book turned out to be a marvelous work of free expression, akin only to certain Surrealist texts. Christiane includes tributes to her writer and painter friends, mainly by putting contributions by them into the book, which expresses their importance in her life. There are texts by Amos Kenan and Rachel Mizrahi, who also helped Christiane compose the book and put together a series of word games, puns, and nonsense rhymes. Quantities of drawings by Misha Garrigue and a few by Ned Burgess and Amos Kenan add an aesthetic dimension to the text, in proportion with Christiane's own involvement with the plastic arts. They are subtly in tune with the text and its humor, without being conventional illustrations.

Anyone who knows Christiane will agree that this apparently random potpourri of thoughts, poems, proverbs, word games, lists of memories, militant statements, newspaper clippings, favorite recipes, and many other items, all full of humor and rebellion, gives the reader a far more accurate portrait of her than any conventional (auto)biography ever could.

Much of what she told me in our interview was included in this incredibly rich book. She refers to the composition of several of her novels, to her favorite writers and painters, and attacks the Paris urban planners, who have destroyed many an old building and several of her former homes with bulldozers, replacing them with ugly skyscrapers, the HLM of *Children of Heaven*. She tells us how the tax collectors emptied her apartment when she refused to pay a certain (small) tax, ironically congratulates the French government for the acquiring of the neutron bomb and reproduces piecemeal the prudish 1958 critical articles on *Warrior's Rest*. She neither spares her enemies nor forgets her friends. A nice little feminist dig at society is made in the passage where she deplores having so much mail to answer and trivial things to cope with in general: if only she had a wife to do it all for her — but then she could never impose that on someone she cared for, and could never live with anyone she didn't care for; how do they do it? This passage follows a mock advertisement for her own works.

The book radiates a great love for life, including the enjoyment of such things as good food and cooking — her recipes, by the way, are excellent! She shows us her life in fits and starts as she skips in and out of the pages laughing, drawing, singing, and sometimes raging, but never lets us look at it for any length of time; the book is on the move, in a perpetual state of escapade, like most of Rochefort's favorite characters.

The best joke of all appears at the end of the book: she simply lists all of Maurice Chavardès's 250 odd questions, each followed by one or several page references, leading back into the labyrinth of her text, to a more or less relevant passage. She cannot be accused of not including the interview, but she has kept it well outside of her *life!* "Textual analysis is the death of all writing," she says (p. 278). Indeed, *My Life* was not meant to be analyzed, but to be read and enjoyed. Bon appétit! It's a gourmet's delight.

Before *My Life* was commissioned, Christiane was already at work on a new novel, which she is now busy finishing.[10] "It's a pornographic book," she said earnestly. "The beginning was surrealistic and then I came across this masochist, a real one. He is a product of automatic writing: he is a heterosexual male masochist, not a homo leather-freak — that sort might well have led me in another direction, towards a kind of Nazism. — It isn't easy and it's the kind of porno book which won't excite its readers in the least."

"A sadistic book then?," I asked.

She laughed and said yes, in a way it was.

Indeed, there seems to be a connection between the present tendency to revert to the stagnant conservatism of the 1950s and Christiane Rochefort's actually doing what she was accused of doing in

Warrior's Rest. Then she was merely showing that there was "something rotten in the state of . . ."; now she is describing the rot, she is letting people have their smut but not enjoy it!

As is evident in the utopian books, and more spontaneously in *My Life*, Christiane is basically an idealist and cannot help trying to change the world. Although time passes, the spark of youth and her zest for life and freedom have never left her. She continues to protest against the numerous injustices of society, the oppression of minorities, the dishonesty of politics and to fight for the rights of the individual, precisely because she continues to love many people, children, animals, music, art, and the joys life can afford! The woman who is now transposing the colorless decadence of the 1980s into a sadly obscene story, also uses her tape recorder to capture the song of nightingales.

Notes

1. Unfortunately only three of Christiane's books are available in English, not for lack of translators or of a market for translations, but for absurd copyright reasons typical of French bureaucracy.

2. She gave me no precise reference here.

3. See Hélène Cixous, "The Laugh of the Medusa," translated by Keith Cohen and Paula Cohen, *Signs*, I, 4, (1976).

4. Alexandre Zinoviev: *Les hauteurs béantes* (Paris: l'âge d'homme, 1977), translated from Russian by Wladimir Berelowitch.

5. She mentions others in *My Life* (p. 168): "Hanska, Dufour, Moshe Zalcman . . ." Apart from Ajar most of these are not very well-known, even in France.

6. In the summary on the dust jacket.

7. My translation.

8. See Frédérick Leboyer, *Pour une naissance sans violence* [Birth Without Violence] (Paris: Seuil, 1974).

9. Ivan Illich, *Deschooling Society* (New York: Harper & Row, 1971).

10. It has since been published as *Quand tu ras chez les femmes* (Paris: Grasset, 1982).

Editions de Minuit

Luce Irigaray

Interviewed by
Lucienne Serrano and Elaine Hoffman Baruch

For all the feminist desire to recapture the reality of women and to cut through fantasy, there are some women who still take on mythological significance —faraway goddesses who remain out of one's reach. Such to me is Luce Irigaray, the brilliant, provocative analyst and writer. I have yet to see her. When I called her up in Paris last summer and she graciously consented to an interview, I asked my friend and colleague Lucienne Serrano if she would like to do one jointly. "Of course," was the answer. We set out to the fifteenth arrondissement, not quite knowing our way but somehow with the help of the trusty Paris red book (a collection of street maps and corresponding metro and bus lines) finding it. Irigaray was not at home. We were crushed. "She had to go to Grenoble to defend prostitutes," her friendly housekeeper explained. "She left a note for you." As if to soften our disappointment, the housekeeper tried to make us feel at home in an apartment that was all light and air. Unlike so many Paris dwellings, it was modern rather than nostalgic —with huge picture windows, white cabinets, beige shag rugs, abstract paintings on white walls. Since I had to leave the next day in order not to forfeit my vacation fare, it was left to Lucienne to do the interview alone, using questions that we had prepared together. Obviously there was a sympathy between the two women. Recognizing Lucienne's practice of yoga, Irigaray attributed to it her feeling of strength and serenity when the interview was over. The meeting took place with the two sitting on the floor drinking coffee in Irigaray's "office," a room that Lucienne describes as turning into a beach, what with its white sofa, its white rug with rocks on it, its sense of freedom and space —where the sky outside the floor-to-ceiling window seemed to turn into the sea. It would seem that something of fantasy exists in Irigaray's reality also.

Irigaray is a dissident psychoanalyst and writer who has also been extremely active in the French women's movement (Mouvement de liberation des femmes). *Largely untranslated, her revolutionary quality lies not in a creation of new fictional characters and worlds, but rather in the exploration and deconstruction of existing mythological, philosophical, and psychoanalytic systems. Her book* Speculum de l'autre femme (The Mirror of the Other Woman), *1974, rereads figures from Plato to Freud (but in reverse order).* Ce Sexe qui n'en est pas un (The Sex Which Is Not One), *1977, takes issue with Marx, Lévi-Strauss, and Jacques Lacan, who founded the Freudian School of Paris, a group to which Irigaray once belonged, but which she now questions.* Et l'une ne bouge pas sans l'autre (And One Does Not Stir Without the Other), *1979, is a poetic evocation of the troubled mother/daughter relationship as it exists in patriarchal society. Neither prose essay nor fiction, but partaking of both genres,* Amante marine (The Sea Lover), *1980, is a free-flowing rereading of* Nietzsche. *Irigaray's style—in her search for a* parler femme *("woman's language")—is fluid and open, a linguistic parallel to her view of the multiplicity of woman's sexuality. As Carolyn Burke points out, "A language of flux, it refuses rigid definitions and avoids images or metaphors that stabilize meaning in too permanent a manner." (See* Signs, *Autumn 1980, for Burke's introduction to and translation of Irigaray's essay "When Our Lips Speak Together." Other translations appear in* New French Feminisms, *edited by Elaine Marks and Isabelle de Courtivron* [Amherst: University of Massachusetts Press, 1980] *and* Signs, *Autumn 1981). "Open your lips," writes Irigaray, "but do not open them simply. I do not open them simply. We—you/I—are never open nor closed."*

Irigaray is highly controversial. While many feminists are minimalists, denying sexual differences beyond the purely reproductive, Irigaray might be called a maximalist, affirming the reality and importance of sexual difference. This has led to attacks on her as a follower of the patriarchal order. But such attacks are simplistic and fail to grasp Irigaray's subtle and profound disagreements with the patriarchal reading of anatomy as destiny. Irigaray feels we have yet to discover what the basic feminine morphology is. That is the quest that she is engaged in. Her attempts to recover pre-Oedipal sources of unity, to remove the distinction between subject and object, to reject a phallogocentric view of the universe (one marked by the exaltation of logical discourse and the phallus) in favor of one more in touch with touch, continuity, and also flux mark her as departing from patriarchal modes, a female explorer thinking and feeling her way along new shores of thought and feeling.

E.H.B.

Lucienne Serrano/Elaine Hoffman Baruch: Feminism has been considered simply another *ism* in the phallocratic system. Considering feminism in France, do you share this opinion?

Luce Irigaray: I don't particularly care for the term *feminism*. It is the word by which the social system designates the struggle of women. I am completely willing to abandon this word, namely because it is formed on the same model as the other great words of the culture that oppress us. I prefer to say the struggles of women, which reveals a plural and polymorphous character. But I think that when certain groups of women criticize and fight against feminism, they don't take into account the gesture they are making with regard to the dominant culture. After all, it is necessary to consider the way they attack us, and it is most generally under the label of feminism. In this case, it is necessary to claim the term back and then to refine it and say something else.

Lucienne Serrano/Elaine Hoffman Baruch: At present, in France, do you discern several feminisms, several currents in the women's movement?

Luce Irigaray: Yes, and I may perhaps forget to mention some of them. But I want to say first that the ideas that were defended by the militants in 1970 have now reached many strata of the population. That which interests me the most — and it is very important — is that women's liberation has gotten away from its old fights. It makes me very happy to know that women today are able to strike, not for the purposes of salary but in order to say, "You can no longer treat me like that," that is to say, on the basis of a sexist ideology. Certain women will no longer tolerate being treated no matter how. I remember a TV show called "Women's Work" ("Le Travail au féminin"), which showed a bank clerk, a worker, a high school teacher, a bus driver, apprentices in a factory who used the discourse of women's liberation. Before then I was a little discouraged by the conflicts among the militants, but while hearing these women I said to myself, "In all ways, we are winning." There may be conflicts, but the important thing is that it is spreading all over and that it be irreversible.

How then can one categorize the French current? It is, in my opinion, very split, from which comes the necessity to regroup people according to practical objectives. For example, I worked a great deal for the October 6, 1979, demonstration for abortion because it brought together all the different strains. We were not from one special group. The demonstration tried to mobilize all the women who were interested in legalizing abortion, whatever their persuasion.

To describe how the French movement is structured isn't easy. I would say that there is one faction which holds that feminism (and here I *am* using the word *feminism*) is secondary, and can arrive only after Marxism. The women in this group say that the struggle of the sexes can only occur after the resolution of the class struggle. But there are other feminists who are antisexists before all, and who emphasize the phenomenon of sexist exploitation before all class phenomena. Personally, I think that if one takes into account what Marx says, that the exploitation of man by man starts with the exploitation of the woman by the man, then the realization of Marxism would be the liberation of women, that is to say, the abolition of private property, the family, the state. This may look utopian, but this doesn't bother me. The most resistant, and at the same time the most explosive point in capitalist society would in fact be the liberation of women because women reproduce and nurture the labor force. In my opinion, the only thing which would be capable of upsetting capitalist society would be a general strike of women, not only the women in the field of production but a general strike of women; we would no longer submit to the social function in which they enclose us, that is to say, we would no longer do the housework, we would no longer have children, we would no longer make love, nor would we go to the factory any more. But it's not in the factory that we are most trapped — it is in the reproductive function.

In the description of the French movement, I haven't spoken until now of *Psych et Po* [*Psychanalyse et Politique*, a movement against all *isms*, in charge of and, according to some, asserting a tyranny over the important publishing house Librairie des femmes]. To tell the truth, I don't see very well how it is connected today with the other two big alternatives. This group sometimes attacks the term *feminism* in what seems to be a nontactical way. I don't see in fact what the practical politics of this group is, what its aims are. I would prefer that they themselves speak of these.

L.S./E.H.B.:   What is *your* connection with the women's liberation movement?

L.I.:   I have already answered that in part. I am in the French movement and also in the international one because I work with the women of other countries besides France and that is very important to me. Since 1970, I have refused to belong to any one faction. If a group excludes me, it is the group that excludes me, it is not me who excludes it, because I think that women's liberation is spreading everywhere, and there are things to say and to do everywhere. Without doubt I will never belong to any party in the cause of the women's struggle because I believe that my objective world and my political practice is above that. I don't want my commitment to be subjected to a contest of parties, which ultimately takes over and encodes it for electoral purposes. If the parties, under the pressures of the women's struggle, take into consideration the exploitation of women and make things happen, I would be delighted. But I think that, for what concerns me, I have to retain my total freedom. I make myself available beyond my analytic practice (and I do not standardize anyone in analysis; I don't think that anyone could say that I have directed her/him in one way or another) because women come to speak to me when they are lost and need me to listen to them, to guide them. My marginal position and my position in the struggle of women make me the one that they choose to call on. There are also my books, my writing. And politically, there is the fact of aiming, let us say, at practical objectives. I spoke to you about the October 6, 1979, demonstration. I also just went to Montreal where I was invited to speak in a colloquium on women and madness. When I participate in such a conference, I think that I am putting on an act, given what I say about militant feminism. But things happen which make me very happy — at least in foreign countries. Often, given my nonbelonging to any group, women from different groups come to me to regroup. I like that very much and it is very important to me.

L.S./E.H.B.:   What should women do in order to liberate themselves without falling into the quest for power like men?

L.I.:   I have the impression that power is a substitution or a palliative for impotence or the anxiety of impotence. To put this another way, power is like death; it is the work of the death drive, and if one wants to protect the values of the body, if one cares about a certain impulse towards pleasure and sensuality, power has no great interest. What's painful for me is the impression that with what I say, or write, or am, people are able to project distortions on me and can enfold me in those rags with which I have nothing to do. However, there is a question of political strategy. Is it good that at certain moments certain women occupy certain positions? Surely, if they can use them in order to make things move. The problem is whether they can remain women and not become total men. I think that this is not easy. But I am totally ready if they so desire to discuss things with women who are in this kind of position, and not to exclude them systematically. It depends on the women. I won't reject the women of the left who have chosen to be in political contests, for it is important to speak with them because of the place where they are. They can express certain things, on the making of laws for example.

L.S./E.H.B.:   For many women, equality is the most important concept. Do you think it would be possible to have difference and equality at the same time? Wouldn't hierarchy impose itself automatically with difference?

L.I.:   In a way that continues the question asked previously. I would say that equality signifies becoming totally like men. Do you agree?

L.S./E.H.B.:   Would it be possible to see equality as a halfway road between man and woman, the result of concessions made by one side and the other to reach a state of being instead of a state of possession?

L.I.:   I agree, but do you see that happening anywhere? As far as I am concerned, the overturn of power, the return to a matriarchy doesn't interest me at all. That which interests me is precisely sexual difference without hierarchy. As you have said, two parts of the world coming together is my wish. I don't think that could happen today. It could perhaps happen tomorrow. Let us say that my condition is feminine and that I try to speak from where I am and of the exploitation that is imposed on me without the least wish that women take power. On the contrary, I wish that women could succeed in checking certain power, that they would arrive at deconstructing and reconstructing another mode of living in society.

As for difference, just because it has always functioned in a hierarchical fashion doesn't mean that we have to reject it. I believe that it is necessary to make a double gesture, that is to say, both to interpret and deny that sexual difference should return to exploitation, to subordination, but at the same time to affirm the positive character of difference. To give a very simple example: just because there are anti-Semites doesn't mean that one should have to renounce the fact that one is Jewish. I believe that by putting it this way, people understand very easily what I mean — because I have searched for a long time how to say this in a very simple formula. There are many women today who are trapped by their refusals of difference, because difference has always served to exploit and I think that that is equivalent to saying: "I don't want to be Jewish any more because I have been exploited as a Jew." That is in effect to submit and to sacrifice oneself to hierarchy. The question is to discover the positive values in difference and to affirm them.

L.S./E.H.B.:   For you, to be a woman is to be different, but isn't vindicating this difference, in a sense, going along with the social structure which has constructed difference on the basis of so-called biological fact? In what way is your insistence on difference different from that of society?

L.I.: The men and the women today who deny difference are, in my opinion, indulging themselves in a type of unbridled idealism, for difference exists and society has been constructed on it. It's fine that the so-called intellectual militant women say: "Let's develop our masculine side and let the men develop their feminine side, and abolish difference since it has always served to exploit us." I would like that but it is to forget that women are enclosed as and in private property; that women are the underpaid workers, the foreigners subjected to all kinds of sexual mutilations. It is to deny the material, materialistic, social and cultural reality of difference. That reality exists. In fact it returns us to the question of how to distribute this difference. Women cannot be liberated from a reality other than a sexual one because this is the starting point from which they are exploited. Therefore one isn't able to renounce difference. That would be a false utopia.

How can we discover the positive characteristics of this difference? What I am trying to do is not to return to no matter what biology or anatomy, but rather to discover the specific morphological characteristics of the feminine. When others confront us with the concept of a feminine nature, we shouldn't let ourselves be taken in; it's important to answer that all of our culture in which we live depends on a masculine nature and a masculine morphology. All that which is valorized is connected to a masculine sexual morphology. So then, let us discover our own morphology and realize that our own vision of the world and our own fashion of creating, of building, is not, and is not able to be the same as that of men. Biology, anatomy have always made us the reproducers. The question to ask oneself is: "What can women in their difference produce? —Produce not in the sense of capitalist production?" There is something else on the imaginary level, on the symbolic, and beyond all consideration of reproduction.

L.S./E.H.B.: With regard to the symbolic, how do you define the term "eternal feminine"? Is there a connection between the eternal feminine and woman as merchandise, as object of exchange?

L.I.: The "eternal feminine" is not ours. It is a concept of patriarchal culture which, I think, idealizes us in a deathlike fashion. Within Christian culture, the eternal feminine refers to certain conceptions of the Virgin Mary. It is how men order their own ambivalence towards their mother and their wife to dissociate virgin and whore. I think that woman as merchandise belongs on the side of woman as whore, that is to say, that one exchanges her among men for use. It is complicated because merchandise is on the side of the fetish which measures itself according to a certain standard. There, I would say, there would be something of the phallus. And without doubt there is something of the phallic mother in the Virgin Mary. But is is not exactly a feminine phallic; it is a phallicism which is imputed to us. Therefore the eternal feminine is merchandise insofar as it is fetish, but there is also its value as use and usury, and there, it is on the side of the whore.

L.S./E.H.B.:   What do you think of the position taken by certain analysts that the major source of oppression stems from the mother?

L.I.:   That is true at a certain descriptive level. But it is to forget that even if this mother exerts a certain phantasmagoric power, in fact she has no social, economic, or cultural power. Given the exploitation that she submits to on the part of her father/husband, given her exclusion from social and creative activity, she reproduces the oppression to which she is subject. I understand what one wishes to say in denouncing the mother, and it's true at a certain level of the family. But the important thing is not to still and always crush the mother. The important thing is to try to understand why and how the mother could change in the actual system. But is is impossible; she cannot change. One might as well believe in Santa Claus. What can we do? Condemn her a little more? Freud says that our culture is built on a parricide. More fundamentally, our culture is built on a matricide: the matricide of the mother/lover — not of the woman as reproducer but of the woman as a lover, as a creator who has a specific desire and who fights for her desire. One sees this matricide at the beginning of our culture; our culture has been founded on it. When the fathers took power, they had already annihilated the mother. This can be seen in mythology, in Greek tragedy.

L.S./E.H.B.:   Therefore, according to you, the mother/daughter struggle is inscribed in the alienation to which a little girl is condemned from her birth by a mother who confirms this alienation and who is her sole respondent?

L.I.:   I have in a way answered that. If the mother is the alienator, it is because she has no identity as a woman. And this effectively plunges the mother and the little girl in the same nothingness. But the problem is neither to accuse the mother nor to say that it is the father who comes to liberate the little girl. The mother has to find her identity as a woman and from that point, she would be able to give an identity to her daughter. But this is the key point to which our system is most blind.

There is a theme that I take up again in *Amante marine*, which can be found in mythology and which seems to be at the foundation of patriarchal culture—in the great mythological figures one sees the structuring of the imaginary system. It is the relationship of Demeter and Kore. Demeter, goddess of the earth, has a little girl, Kore, who is grievously manipulated. She is given by Zeus to his brother Hades, king of the underworld, both as a bond between them and as an impossibility of a bond because one is in the sky and the other is in the underworld. One day, a crevice opens up under Kore's feet; she is abducted by Hades. The little girl is thus separated from her mother. At that moment she loses her voice and she changes her name; she becomes Persephone. But since the patriarchal regime is not completely in effect, Demeter refuses to reproduce without her daughter. Then Hades is obliged to give back Kore for two seasons of the year: spring and summer. One sees there the separation of the daughter and the mother. One might say that at the beginning there was Demeter and Kore and that then there was a good mother/daughter relationship outside the patriarchal regime. One sees how this rapport was destroyed and how there was still a resistance, that is to say, Demeter didn't allow it to happen completely.

That said, I think it is interesting that today this mother/daughter relationship is questioned because it is the most obscure and most explosive relationship in patriarchal culture. If one were to succeed in creating again a good relationship between mother and daughter, women would no longer subordinate themselves. There would be a feminine identity and women would not submit themselves to what is called the exchange of women among men.

L.S./E.H.B.: What are the basic representations in the symbolic masculine world by which the oppression of women is articulated?

L.I.: Virgin, mother, whore. One might also add the mask of femininity that one sees in mythology beginning with Athena. Athena is always veiled and that is, I think, the basic ornamentation of the female body. And Athena is also called Pallas which means wound. The ornamentation becomes the veil over the wound.

L.S./E.H.B.: I was thinking just now of Oedipus.

L.I.: In reflecting recently on matricide, I thought that, for me, Oedipus is a repetition of Orestes; it is in fact a repetition of matricide. What do you mean when you refer to Oedipus?

L.S./E.H.B.:   It seems to me that the *Oedipus* represents submission to a unique system that annihilates the woman.

L.I.:   A unique system which would articulate itself on the murder of the mother and the identification with the father? If one touches the mother, one becomes blind. I would rather reverse that and say that one becomes blind because one forgets and one denies the beginning, that is to say, the connection with the mother. The fundamental blindness of our culture is there. And if this denial of the connection to the mother posits in some fashion the murder of the woman who gives us life, it is necessary to understand that one doesn't dare to touch that again without fear because it would be to participate again in the same crime. Therefore I believe that the sexual anxieties of men are explicable in great part by the fact that they are constrained in the functioning of the sole patriarchal order to kill the mother but they don't cease having the desire to return to this mother, to their birth, to their bodies, to their house of flesh. And it is at the same time a lunatic anguish because they have to kill their mother in order to become men.

*L.S./E.H.B.:*How might the language of women deconstruct the representations of which you have spoken before?

L.I.:   I want to say that that is what I have tried to do more and more in certain texts. I think it is necessary to act in two ways. First, to criticize the existing system and that is perhaps what is pardoned the least, because people are not going to accept that you might put in question a theoretical system. So it is necessary to act in two ways, to question the systems and to show how we can deconstruct them because we are at the same time inside and outside them. We have to reject all the great systems of opposition on which our culture is constructed. Reject, for example, the oppositions: fiction/truth, sensible/intelligible, empirical/transcendental, materialist/idealist. All these opposing pairs function as an exploitation and a negation of a relation at the beginning and of a certain mode of connection between the body and the word for which we have paid everything.

So when someone tells me that the beginning of *Amante marine* is fiction, I say no. It is not fiction. Or otherwise everything is fiction and the "truth" which is imposed on us is a formidable fiction. This has posed a very interesting and complicated problem in the publication of books by women insofar as they were unclassifiable. They didn't fit into the existing categories because in fact they were not exactly literature, nor were they exactly essays or theory. What were they? One didn't know where to put them. I think that one of the important functions of the publication of women would be to create a "genre," a language which doesn't adhere to the existing categories, which refuses to submit itself to the established order.

L.S./E.H.B.:   To change reality, one has to change the symbolic order. Do you agree?

L.I.:   Completely. The symbolic order is an imaginary order which becomes law. Therefore it is very important to question again the foundations of our symbolic order in mythology and in tragedy, because they deal with a landscape which installs itself in the imagination and then, all of sudden, becomes law. But that only means that it is an imaginary system that wins out over another one. This victorious imaginary system is what we call the symbolic order.

L.S./E.H.B.:   It seems—and you have already spoken about this—that the binary values are now being questioned. Does this questioning affect the masculine/feminine opposition?

L.I.:   This is at the same time a simple and difficult question. The binary values are now put into question; it is necessary that they be so, for we are the victims of this opposition. But the opposition feminine/masculine is a false opposition which doesn't truly belong to binarism, or, if it does belong there, it is to a binarism which is completely hierarchized. As with a certain number of opposing values that I mentioned before—materialist/idealist, etc.—there isn't truly an opposition. Rather, there is one pole of the opposition (the masculine) which constitutes the limit of the system and which plays with the other pole (the feminine) according to its needs. One is not able to say that this is a true binarism.

What we have to do is affirm the two poles, recognizing that the feminine will not be in the same mode as the masculine. In our present culture, to want to say that there is no difference is, I think, the politics of the neuter, a nihilistic politics in the worst sense of the term. I feel like asking how it happens that at the moment when something valuable occurs on the women's side, immediately a discourse of androgyny, of nonsexual difference arises. It is necessary to pay a great deal of attention to this because we risk being swallowed again by a new "humanism." Recently at the University of Vincennes, someone said, "We are all human beings," and I answered, "I totally refuse to be a human being. What is this abstract reality, this ideal that doesn't exist?" I refuse to be a human being because I cannot be one; I was not given the possibility of being a complete human being; therefore, I have no desire to be that. To affirm that the two poles exist is, in my opinion, liberating; it is to affirm a social, economic, cultural, religious, ideological reality which underlies everything. Once this affirmation is made, how does one find — if the earth does not blow up in the years to come, not an impossibility — a meeting place which would recast this opposition? I think it is first necessary to affirm the difference in order to find again the place of alliance between the two poles.

L.S./E.H.B.:   Can you conceive of a discourse liberated from oppression, a place where masculine and feminine would be able to coexist peacefully?

L.I.:   That continues what I was just saying. I hope so. I work for it. But that does not depend exclusively on me; that depends also on the other pole of difference. Unhappily, I fear that it's not going to happen tomorrow. To return to Nietzsche, when he says that God is dead, it seems that the collapse of this keystone of a transcendental system leads to the carriers of the phallus becoming gods themselves. Why is phallic culture so important after the fall of the gods? Because the carriers of the phallus want to be gods themselves. It is terrifying. Therefore, in my opinion, the meeting of the poles would be a type of sharing. If to be the carrier of the phallus is to wish to be an absolute power, there is no sharing. It is a very difficult question; one has to answer by means of a philosophical detour. In order that there not be a hierarchy and in order that there be a possible place of reconciliation, one has to have a double mirror, that is to say, not everybody should be obliged to look at oneself in the same mirror.

L.S./E.H.B.:   Women's language is unknown, but the masculine one is also because it is deformed by its uniform will to oppress. Women are working to deconstruct it. How?

L.I.:   There is no authentic masculine language. That is evident. Because from the moment that a pole of difference pretends to decree the universal, it says that its discourse is not sexualized. However, there are indications of sexual difference in this discourse that has pretensions to the universal. Therefore, what can we do? What I am trying to do is to discover the indices of sexual differences, to interpret and to show that the so-called universal discourse, whether it be philosophic, scientific, or literary is sexualized and mainly in a masculine way. It is necessary to unveil it, to interpret it, and at the same time to begin to speak a language which corresponds better to, and is in continuity with, our own pleasure, our own sensuality, our own creativity.

L.S./E.H.B.:   Do you know any masculine works which are engaged in the quest for a nonoppressive masculine discourse?

L.I.:   I would rather wait to answer. What I am able to say without hesitation is that when male theoreticians today employ women's discourse instead of using male discourse, that seems to me a very phallocratic gesture. It means: "We will become and we will speak a feminine discourse in order to remain the master of discourse." What I would want from men is that, finally, they would speak a masculine discourse and affirm that they are doing so.

L.S./E.H.B.:   In your work you speak about feminine autoeroticism. What role do you attribute to it?

L.I.:   It is important that women discover their autoeroticism and that this autoeroticism not imitate a masculine model, as it does in Freud's work. It is necessary that women discover their own autoeroticism, that they reveal themselves to each other and leave their rivalries, the hatreds which have been imposed on them as competitive merchandise, in the marketplace. Accordingly, women will discover the positiveness of their homosexuality, in whatever form it will take. I would also say this about men. But I don't mean that women ought to renounce their heterosexuality, for that would lead to a new cloister in which we would be enclosed, constructed by our own hands. I am sorry when I see certain women falling into a sexual moralism, for example, aggressing against women who are heterosexual. I am sorry because in a way they endorse the existing order. But I am also able to say that the heterosexuality which is mandated is almost always pathological, if there isn't also for both sexes a happy autoeroticism and a happy homosexuality, whatever be the form. For me, these are two possibilities which ought to flourish in order for something as difficult and complex as heterosexuality to succeed.

L.S./E.H.B: What elements of Freud's theory can be retained in a new psychology of women?

L.I.:   I would say everything, on the condition that one goes beyond. All of Freud's work is to be understood as the work of an honest scientist. He said of women that which he was able to say in describing what he heard, with the ears that he had, which probably couldn't hear anything else. What Freud says about feminine desire is heard on the couch. But there are other things that are heard and the problem is that he stopped at a certain point, that is to say, that he normalized woman in her role, the condition that she had at a certain moment.

There is in Freud something else also. If psychoanalysis started with the hysterics, one sees Freud change his position towards them between his studies of hysteria where he listened to them for he had everything to learn, and the case of Dora, where, having constructed his system, he bent Dora to his interpretations. This seems to me very revealing. Thus he imposes his system and doesn't want to hear the famous debate of 1932 and what people like Karen Horney, Melanie Klein, Ernest Jones are telling him about sexuality. He doesn't want to hear because he prefers his system to what is said. Notably, he wants to save the Oedipus complex, which is the keystone of his system.

L.S./E.H.B.:   How would women see men in a psychoanalysis constructed by women?

L.I.:   I feel like saying, as what they are without feeling obliged to be something else than what they are. As accepting their sexuality without a categorical phallic imperative because that makes them and us suffer with their obligation to have an erection at the right moment. I think that it is the phallocratic system that they have endorsed, which has been glued on their back. Historically, there was a division which was made, with women as guardians of the corporal and men of the sexual. I would hope that each would refind that which is body and that which is sex. Men are terribly separated from their bodies; they are sexual machines.

L.S./E.H.B.:   Simone de Beauvoir has said that she admires your work very much but reproaches you not being shocking enough. What do you think of that?

L.I.:   I am glad that Simone de Beauvoir admires what I do because she is a woman who has done a great deal, whom I admire for the direction and the risks she has taken. As for the second part of the statement, I do not understand it because I was excluded from Vincennes, put into quarantine from the analytic world (and I only give some examples). I also remember having a conference — in a progressive bookstore which the next day had a stone thrown through its window. It could be that Simone de Beauvoir does not totally identify the place from which I am shocking or maybe for her, shock is to produce shocking statements constantly. I do not say that I never speak shockingly but I think that there is a much more basic gesture to make, which consists not solely in making shocking statements or discourse but in saying from where we speak, that which permits us a certain type of discourse, that which changes deeply the position of the subject who masters the discourse.

Then too, to reconstruct a discourse in order to produce shocking statements does not interest me. One returns perhaps to the question of equality with difference. Probably and even surely, Simone de Beauvoir is much more interested in a vindication of equality than I am.

L.S./E.H.B.:   Monique Wittig and other women writers have written utopias which illustrate a new consciousness of women. Do you have a utopian vision?

L.I.:   If to be utopian is to want a place that doesn't exist yet in some of its modalities, I am utopian. That said, I only speak of this place from the sensory and corporeal experience that I have of it. Therefore it is not a simple projection of I don't know what kind of dream; it is a place that already exists and that I wish could be developed culturally, socially, amorously.

L.S./E.H.B.:   What do you hope for in the future of women?

L.I.:   That they reenter into culture and affirm their identity which is a special identity, that is, women should not be simply reproducers of the existent roles, they should also be co-creators of this world.

The interviewers would like to thank the National Endowment for the Humanities for enabling them to pursue the research for this interview. E.H.B would also like to thank the PSC-BHE Research Award Program of the City University of New York.

Jeanne Moreau

Interviewed by
Annette Insdorf

Why does a talented and successful actress like Jeanne Moreau trade meaty parts for giant risks in becoming a director? The fifty-one-year-old international star of films like Truffaut's *Jules and Jim,* Malle's *Viva Maria,* and Welles's *The Trial* offered some reasons after her second effort as a director, *L'Adolescente,* was shown at the Chicago Film Festival in November 1979.

"I'm fed up with cinema these days! As Roger Corman said, there are lots of special effects but not many ideas. There is no upheaval, no exhilaration. I try to live a kind of daydreaming and nightmaring. I want to share this creation, this visual search, with a scenarist and a strong story line, and make a film that escapes from traditional cinematic form. I'm tired of always the same images, and men who are so familiar with the camera that they treat it like an old mistress—something you pat on the ass in passing."

But *L'Adolescente* and *Lumière,* her first film, demonstrate that Moreau treats her camera more like a young lover; together they surround her characters with curiosity, affection, and desire. *L'Adolescente* is a deeply sensual and sensitive film: its themes of sexual awakening, loss of innocence, and delight in sheer living are mirrored in the rich visual texture and lyrical camera movements. Moreau's inspiration for the cinematic style came, curiously enough, from music: "Ravel. I listened to Ravel's waltz while preparing *L'Adolescente.* That's why the camera seems to envelop the characters till suddenly breaking off before a harmony."

Moreau's story, cowritten with French novelist Henriette Jelinek, takes place in the French provinces just before the declaration of World War II. The protagonist, a twelve-year-old girl (Laetitia Chauveau), falls in love with a young Jewish doctor (Francis Huster) till she discovers he is having an affair with her silent but erotically expressive mother (Edith Clever). *L'Adolescente* is graced by the fine performances of these three, as well as Simone Signoret (the generously wise grandmother) and Francis Veber (the violently handsome father). While Moreau's perspective is nostalgic and somewhat idealizing, the film is realized with the kind of intimate detail and visual fluidity that set it above the bulk of contemporary films.

On at least a superficial level, the languid pace of *L'Adolescente* and its focus on a young woman can be connected to the growing number of French films by women which have been enlivening New York theaters. Does Moreau feel a kinship with popular new directors like Diane Kurys (*Peppermint Soda*), Coline Serreau (*Why Not!*), and Yannick Bellon (*Rape of Love*)? "Our *féminité* in creating unifies us. Each of us has a particular personality but it's evident that there's a familiarity with being a woman. When it comes to cinematographic form, we are very different," acknowledged the director, in French that constantly shaded into fluent English. "But when I saw *Peppermint Soda*, from the very first shots I felt good, because the camera had a pace . . . a personal curiosity. For example, when I am in a restaurant, even with people who interest me, I am conscious of the total environment. In spite of myself, I suddenly zoom in on someone in the background. It's as if I were shooting, stealing a gesture, a crossed leg, a hand reaching toward something. I don't want to surrender this freedom."

It became apparent that for this actress-director, cinematic style is less a question of aesthetics than morality. "Great painters said it before filmmakers: a frame should be full. Auguste Renoir and Monet said it; Picasso said it in a different way. But as soon as you have the privilege of choosing for the future spectator what he should see, you have to give *generously* something to look at. This is artistic integrity. Not just a beautiful shot for its own sake—that's a rupture of rhythm, and a betrayal." When I asked whether her inspiration might be the deep-focus style developed by Jean Renoir in films like *Grand Illusion* and *Rules of the Game*, she nodded emphatically and added, *"la tolérance* . . . and you can imagine how important a close-up becomes when depth of field is the context. It's a dramatic point, like in music," she exclaimed in her throaty voice.

Music recurred often in our conversation, invoked by Moreau to illustrate varied points. (Her versatility includes singing, and she has recorded four albums.) For example, when asked whether her work belongs to the category of "women's films," she found the term "a qualifier against which I react a bit. It's like in a symphony: there are wind instruments and string instruments, an equilibrium. In Mozart, sometimes there is less wind, but no one would say Mozart's music is feminine. In Beethoven's Seventh Symphony, Second Movement, there's this androgynous melange — two themes which for me are masculine and feminine," continued the actress who, appropriately enough, incarnated the somewhat androgynous Catherine in Truffaut's memorable *Jules et Jim*. "All male creators have a strong feminine side, and vice versa."

Moreau's refusal of the adjective *feminist*, however, stems from her vigorously antipolitical stance. "I'm not an activist. I hate organization — probably because I don't like politics, which is a deformed world, purely masculine. No, masculine is too kind a word to describe politics: it's the exercise of power at its most brutal, vulgar, and dishonest, a kind of manipulation of the human being, whether male or female. I understand that feminists needed to organize but they fell into the same traps." Moreau continued to voice a distrust of generalities: "I wanted to speak of things I know intimately. For example, rivalry among women is a lie. It exists only inside of masculine organization. Friendship between women is profound and easy. There are no rituals to undergo, no power relationships to establish — like putting your feet up on the table or blowing smoke in your interlocutor's face. We are the mirror of each other, whatever the age. Physically, women all feel (which is stronger than understand) the transformations of the aging body; there is a complicity. I want to share this with people because it's important to live in truth," she stated simply.

These concerns are particularly palpable in *Lumière*, Moreau's first attempt as a hyphenate, writer-director-actress. She played Sara Dedieu — the actress who is "the thread linking all the characters" — only because none of the actresses that she envisioned for the role were available. "I wanted Audrey Hepburn, and wrote the screenplay thinking of her. But she was already working with Richard Lester. Then I tried to get Bibi Andersson but she was rehearsing a play with Bergman in Stockholm. So I tried to get that marvelous Swedish actress Gunnel Lindbloom, but she was directing her own film. I wanted Anouk Aimée but she was involved in a relationship in the U.S. and didn't want to fly over. Finally, my producers and distributors were nervous — we were to start shooting in three weeks. 'Why don't you do it?' they asked. So I directed the film from within. It was tiring, but good preparation: whatever happened after that seemed really light."

And yet, *L'Adolescente* was not such a simple matter. Because of a limited budget, the cast and crew became a cooperative. "Each person worked for the lowest wage, and became a coproducer after a certain point of financial return. The accounts were open to everyone; all could verify exactly where the money was spent." This sharing on a business level was an extension of the collaborative spirit during shooting: "We rehearsed a lot, improvising together. I rehearsed with the cinematographer as well as the actors, so that we needed only two or three takes after all this rehearsal. . . . Instead of omnipotence — 'I want this or that' — we grew together."

But one collaborator who didn't quite grow in Moreau's direction was the editor, whom Moreau eventually replaced with herself. "He was bullying me, trying to make me feel guilty, with a destructive attitude toward film. It's true that after seven weeks of shooting, your material is not always perfect, but one should not allow another person to make you feel down all the time. Oppressive," she mused while puffing at another Dunhill. "So with a lot of courtesy, we had to part." Fortunately, Moreau was no newcomer to the role of montage: "As an actress, I was always fascinated by the processes of editing, mixing, recording of music — like watching a flower bloom."

The petals of *L'Adolescente* grew during forty-two days of shooting in the light of Aveyron, a French region that Moreau described with passionate intimacy. "In a world gradually invaded by technology, even imperceptibly, pouf!" — here, she raised her arm, gesturing like a deft magician — "you notice a television antenna between two chestnut trees. Pouf! You see an enormous electric tower emerging from a forest . . . so when you discover a place where none of this exists, you feel like Robinson Crusoe on an island. At moments one is exalted by its purity and beauty. At other moments there is fear, as if one were under a spell. This place is so far away from ordinary life that the impression depends on the movement of the sun: changing shadows can create fear. This region provoked in me that desire to . . ." She paused for a moment. "The desire for desire," she offered with a laugh.

Moreau will return to this same region for her next film, *Désirs*, since Aveyron "carries within it a mystery and violence that I was not able to explore totally in *L'Adolescente*." She is writing the screenplay for Robert De Niro, with whom she costarred a few years ago in *The Last Tycoon*. Although the location will be French, the script will be in English, and Moreau plans to work with an American screenwriter. She seemed especially excited about the music, whose composition will precede shooting: "I'm interested in a crazy Englishman who lives isolated on an island, researching the music of the Vikings. He works with a variety of primitive instruments made from natural things—wood, rock, natural strings, shells, etc. —with eight different tonalities. It's strange because it rejoins Chinese and Japanese musicality. The beats are from the skin of animals, and the sounds are obtained from the vibration of original materials like bones and silk."

"I need music and paintings when preparing a film," she continued in her direct and articulate manner. "The main reason I went to the Moscow Film Festival with *L'Adolescente* was to see the Pushkin Museum—the original Gauguins, Van Goghs, sublime Monets, and Millets, especially *L'Angelus*." Did they have an effect on her film preparation? "These made me realize how essential depth of field is, and the richness of all that is not inside the frame. They helped me with the position of objects and characters, even secondary, and the idea of movement: in great paintings, immobility doesn't exist. You feel a sense of what happened before and what will happen after."

Moreau's gentle insistence on continuity—in terms of character and camera—was reminiscent of Truffaut's early declarations, but she felt any influence would have to be instinctive rather than intentional. After working with Welles, Buñuel, Losey, and Antonioni, "all you can get from them is an unconscious knowledge of what is bad and pointless. You have so much responsibility when you start a film that it's like going to war. You're in such a state of emergency that you cannot remember what other directors have done." She leaned forward intently. "You know that beautiful saying of Cocteau—'we are all thieves.' We don't do it on purpose, but our daily bread is impressions: beautiful, ugly, poetic . . . painting, music, screams, whispers, lights." She pointed out the window on Manhattan's Upper East Side: "Look at the way the shadows have moved on this building just opposite since we began talking. One is like a sponge. That's why Cocteau's saying is beautiful. As long as we use well what is stolen, it's OK. Take and give. Or give and take."

I suggested that after having absorbed much of the genius of classic directors, she now gives consistently to young directors, often lending her reputation as an actress to new filmmakers in order to get them started. This is the case with her next film as a performer, *Lucien chez les barbares*, to be directed by Armand Bernardi, about whom she spoke with luminous conviction. She learned about the script through two separate sources: her twenty-eight-year-old cinematographer Pierre Godard, and her closest friend Florence Malraux (daughter of André and wife of director Alain Resnais) who is on the board of the French commission that grants funds to filmmakers. Both urged her to read this story of a woman who goes to Algeria during the war because her son is fighting there, and falls in love with a young friend of his. "I said yes immediately and we start shooting in April."

And as if Moreau didn't have her hands full, she is also costarring with Richard Harris in a Canadian film, *A Ticket Is No Longer Valid*, to be directed by George Kaczender from a novel by Romain Gary. She accepted the part of the whore who becomes a member of the Resistance, and finally a madam in a brothel, because "it brought back to my memory all the wonderful cinematic images, like Dietrich — the prostitutes who are always *romanesque* in film tradition."

The director appeared determined but patient vis-à-vis *Désiré*. "François [Truffaut] told me a few years ago that in directing my first film, I'd be very sure of myself. In the second, I'd start asking questions. And that the third film would be hell. He was right, it's getting harder and harder. I'll take my time on this one. After three drafts, I'm still at the note-taking stage, I'm soaking things up."

Her film — "about men" — will certainly flow with the curious and passionate movement of *L'Adolescente*, for her vision of filmmaking is hardly static: "In Paris, we have a subway that goes up in the air, on the level of the third floor of apartment houses. You can glimpse through windows a guy turning on a TV, another guy scratching, children scuffling . . . I've always been fascinated by this. Or on a train, if you have a harassing journey, you see houses with lovely lights and think, 'Oh! if only I could enter this strange house,' and imagine relaxing in a bed inside. There is curiosity, and the desire to be another, and the desire to enter someone else's life."

There seems to be a renewed sense of freedom and adventure in Jeanne Moreau, freshly divorced from American director William Friedkin. "The privilege of age is really that you're allowed to *not* pretend, to say and do what you think is right. I have a sense of morality that I want to express in my films. Jean Renoir would have used the word tolerance. For example, *L'Adolescente* focuses on the girl, but I could have made a film about each character in it. . . . A director is all the characters."

Selected Bibliography

Maya Angelou

MEMOIRS

I Know Why the Caged Bird Sings. New York: Random House, 1970.
Gather Together in My Name. New York: Random House, 1970.
Singin' and Swingin' and Makin' Merry Like Christmas. New York: Random House, 1976.
The Heart of a Woman. New York: Random House, 1981.

VERSE

Just Give Me a Cool Drink of Water 'fore I Diiie. New York: Random House, 1971.
Oh Pray My Wings Are Gonna Fit Me Well. New York: Random House, 1975.
And Still I Rise. New York: Random House, 1978.

PLAYS

Cabaret for Freedom, with Godfrey Cambridge. New York: Village Gate Theatre, 1960.
The Best of These. Los Angeles: 1966.

SCREENPLAYS

Georgia, Georgia. (1972).

TELEVISION

Blacks, Blues, Black (1968).
Assignment America (1975).
The Legacy (1975).
The Inheritors (1976).
Sisters (1978).

Joan Barton

VERSE

The Mistress and Other Poems. Hull, Sonus Press, 1972. Reprinted in *A House Under Old Sarum.* Harry Chambers/Peterloo Poets, 1981.
Ten Poems. Perdix Press, 1979. reprinted in *A House Under Old Sarum.*

A. S. Byatt

NOVELS

Shadow of a Sun. New York: Harcourt Brace, 1964.
The Game. New York: Scribner, 1968.
The Virgin in the Garden. New York: Knopf, 1979.

UNCOLLECTED SHORT STORY

"Daniel," in *Encounter* (London), April 1976.

OTHER

Degrees of Freedom: The Novels of Iris Murdoch. New York: Barnes and Noble, 1965.
Wordsworth and Coleridge in Their Time. New York: Crane-Russak, 1973.
Iris Murdoch. London: Longman, 1976.

Margaret Drabble

NOVELS

A Summer Birdcage. New York: Morrow, 1964.
The Garrick Year. New York: Morrow, 1965.
The Millstone. New York: Morrow, 1966; reprinted as *Thank You All Very Much*. New York: New American Library, 1969.
Jerusalem the Golden. New York: Morrow, 1967.
The Waterfall. New York: Knopf, 1969.
The Needle's Eye. New York: Knopf, 1972.
The Realms of Gold. New York: Knopf, 1975.
The Ice Age. New York: Knopf, 1977.
The Middle Ground. New York: Knopf, 1980

SHORT STORIES

Penguin Modern Stories 3, with others. London: Penguin, 1969.

UNCOLLECTED SHORT STORIES

"Hassan's Tower," in *Winter's Tales 12*, edited by A. D. Maclean. New York: St. Martin's Press, 1966.
"A Voyage to Cytherea," in *Mademoiselle*, December 1967.
"The Reunion," in *Winter's Tales 14*, edited by Kevin Crossley-Holland. New York: St. Martin's Press, 1968.
"The Gifts of War," in *Winter's Tales 16*, edited by A. D. Maclean. New York: St. Martin's Press, 1971.
"Crossing the Alps," in *Mademoiselle* (New York), February 1971.
"A Successful Story," in *Spare Rib* (London), 1973.
"A Day in the Life of a Smiling Woman," in *In The Looking Glass*, edited by Nancy Dean and Myrna Stark. New York: Putnam, 1977.

OTHER

Wordsworth. New York: Arco, 1969.
Virginia Woolf: A Personal Debt. New York: Aloe, 1973.
Arnold Bennett: A Biography. New York: Knopf, 1974.
For Queen and Country: Britain in the Victorian Age (juvenile). New York, Seabury Press: 1979.
A Writer's Britain: Landscape in Literature. New York: Knopf, 1979.

Marilyn French

NOVELS

The Women's Room. New York: Summit, 1977.
The Bleeding Heart. New York: Summit, 1980.

OTHER

The Book as World: James Joyce's Ulysses." Cambridge: Harvard University Press, 1976.
Shakespeare's Division of Experience. New York: Summit, 1981.

Germaine Greer

The Female Eunuch. London: MacGibbon and Kee, 1970.
The Obstacle Race: The Fortunes of Women Painters and Their Works. New York: Farrar, Straus & Giroux 1979.

Luce Irigaray

CRITICAL WORKS

Le Langage de déments [The language of Schizophrenics]. The Hague: Mouton, 1973; also in *Approaches to Semiotics 24,* 1973.
Speculum de l'autre femme [Mirror of the Other Woman]. Paris: Minuit, 1974.
Ce Sexe qui n'en pas un [The Sex Which Is Not One]. Paris: Minuit, 1977.
Et l'une ne bouge pas sans l'autre [And One Does Not Stir without the Other]. Paris: Minuit, 1979.
Amante Marine [The Sea Lover]. Paris: Minuit, 1980.

ARTICLE

"When Our Lips Speak Together," in *Signs* (New York), Autumn 1980, and in *New French Feminisms,* edited by Elaine Marks and Isabelle de Courtivron. Amherst: University of Massachusetts Press, 1980.

Diane Johnson

NOVELS

Fair Game. New York: Harcourt, Brace & World, 1965.
Loving Hands at Home. New York: Harcourt, Brace & World, 1968.
Lesser Lives: The True History of the First Mrs. Meredith. New York: Knopf, 1972.
Burning. New York: Harcourt Brace Jovanovich, Inc., 1973.
The Shadow Knows. New York: Knopf, 1974.
Lying Low. New York: Knopf, 1978.

OTHER

Terrorists and Novelists. New York: Knopf, 1982.

Erica Jong

NOVELS

Fear of Flying. New York: Holt, Rinehart & Winston, 1973.
How to Save Your Own Life. New York: Holt, Rinehart & Winston, 1977.
Fanny, Being the True History of Fanny Hackabout-Jones. New York: New American Library, 1980.

UNCOLLECTED SHORT STORIES

"From the Country of Regrets," in *Paris Review*, Spring, 1973.
"Take a Lover," in *Vogue*, April 1977.

VERSE

Fruits and Vegetables. New York: Holt, Rinehart & Winston, 1971.
Half-Lives. New York: Holt, Rinehart & Winston, 1973.
Here Comes and Other Poems. New York: New American Library, 1975.
Loveroot. New York: Holt, Rinehart & Winston, 1975.
The Poetry of Erica Jong. New York: Holt, Rinehart & Winston, 1976.
Selected Poems. London: Panther, 1977.
At the Edge of the Body. New York: Holt, Rinehart & Winston, 1979.
Witches. New York: Abrams, 1981.

Alison Lurie

NOVELS

Love and Friendship. New York: Macmillan, 1962.
The Nowhere City. New York: Coward McCann, 1966.
Imaginary Friends. New York: Coward McCann, 1967.
Real People. New York: Random House, 1974.
The War between the Tates. New York: Random House, 1979.
Only Children. New York: Random House, 1979.

UNCOLLECTED SHORT STORY

"Hansel and Gretel," in *New Story 2* (New York), 1951.

OTHER

V. R. Lang: A Memoir. Privately Printed, 1959; in *Poems and Plays,* by V. R. Lang. New
York: Random House, 1975.
The Heavenly Zoo: Legends and Tales of the Stars (juvenile). New York: Farrar, Straus &
Giroux, 1980.
Clever Gretchen and Other Forgotten Folk Tales (juvenile). New York: Crowell, 1980.
Fabulous Beasts (juvenile). New York: Farrar, Straus & Giroux, 1981.
The Language of Clothes. New York: Random House, 1981.

Jeanne Moreau

FILMS (AS ACTRESS)

Ne Touchez Pas au Grisbi (1954).
La Salaire du Péché (1956).
Le Dos au Mur (1957).
Lift to the Scaffold (1957).
Les Amants (1957).
Le Diologue des Carmélites (1959).
Les Liasons Dangereuses (1959).
Five Branded Women (1960).
Moderato Cantibile (1960).
Jules et Jim (1961).
La Notte (1961).
La Baie des Anges (1962).
The Victors (1963).
Peau de Banane (1963).
The Trial (1963).
Will of the Wisp (1963).
Diary of a Chambermaid (1964).
Mata-Hari, Agent H-21 (1964).
The Train (1965).
Viva Maria! (1965).
The Yellow Rolls Royce (1964).
Chimes at Midnight (1966).
Mademoiselle (1966).
The Sailor from Gibraltar (1967).
The Bride Wore Black (1967).
Immortal Story (1968).
Le Corps de Diane (1968).
Great Catherine (1968).
Monte Walsh (1970).
Alex in Wonderland (1971).
Compte à Rebours (1970).

Mille Baisers de Florence (1971).
Nathalie Granger (1972).
Chère Louise (1972).
Joanna Francesca (1973).
Souvenirs d'en France (1974).
Making It (1974).
Le Jardin qui Bascule (1975).
Mr. Klein (1976).
The Last Tycoon (1976).

FILMS (AS DIRECTOR)

Lumière, 1975.
L'Adolescent, 1979.

Robin Morgan

VERSE

Monster: Poems. New York: Random House, 1972.
Lady of the Beasts. New York: Random House, 1976.
Depth Perception: New Poems and a Masque. New York: Doubleday, 1982.
Anatomy of Freedom: Feminism, Physics, and Global Politics. New York: Doubleday, 1982.

OTHER

Editor, with Charlotte Bunche and Joan Cooke, *The New Women.* New York: Bobbs-Merrill, 1970.
Editor, *Sisterhood is Powerful: An Anthology of Writings from the Women's Liberation Movement.* New York: Random House, 1970.
Going Too Far: The Personal Chronicle of a Feminist. New York: Random House, 1977.

Grace Paley

SHORT STORIES

The Little Disturbances of Man: Stories of Men and Women in Love. New York: Doubleday, 1959.
Enormous Changes at the Last Minute. New York: Farrar, Straus & Giroux, 1974.

UNCOLLECTED SHORT STORIES

"Dreamers in a Dead Language," in *American Review 26,* edited by Theodore Solotaroff. New York: Bantam, 1977.
"Somewhere Else," in *The New Yorker,* 23 October 1978.
"Friends," *The New Yorker,* 8 October 1979.

Christiane Rochefort

NOVELS

Le Repos du guerrier [Warrior's Rest]. New York: Doubleday, 1958.
Les Petits Enfants du siècle [Children of Heaven]. New York: McKay, 1962.
Une Rose pour Morrison [A Rose for Morrison]. Paris: Grasset, 1966.
Printemps au parking [Spring in the Parking Lot]. Paris: Grasset, 1969.
Archaos ou le Jardin étincelant [Archaos or The Glittering Garden], Paris: Grasset, 1972.
Encore heureux qu'on va vers l'été [At Least Summer's Coming Soon]. Paris: Grasset, 1975.

OTHER

C'est bizarre, l'écriture [Writing is a Strange Experience]. Paris: Grasset, 1970.
Les Enfants d'abord [Children First]. Paris; Grasset, 1976.
Ma Vie, revue et corrigée par l'auteur [My Life, Revised and Corrected by the Author]. Paris: Grasset, 1978.

May Sarton

NOVELS

The Single Hound. Boston: Houghton Mifflin, 1938.
The Bridge of Years. New York: Doubleday, 1946.
Shadow of a Man. New York: Rinehart, 1950.
A Shower of Summer Days. New York: Rinehart. 1952.
Faithful Are the Wounds. New York: Rinehart, 1958.
The Birth of a Grandfather. New York: Rinehart, 1957.
The Small Room. New York: Norton, 1961.
Joanna and Ulysses. New York: Norton, 1963.
Mrs. Stevens Hears the Mermaids Singing. New York: Norton, 1965.
Miss Pickthorn and Mr. Hare: A Fable. New York: Norton, 1966.
Kinds of Love. New York: Norton, 1970.
As We Are Now. New York: Norton, 1973.
Crucial Conversations. New York: Norton, 1975.
A Reckoning. New York: Norton, 1978.
Anger: A Novel. New York: Norton, 1982.

VERSE

Encounter in April. Boston: Houghton Mifflin, 1937.
Inner Landscape. Boston: Houghton Mifflin, 1939, with a selection from *Encounter in April,* London: Cresset Press, 1939.
The Lion and the Rose. New York: Rinehart, 1948.
The Leaves of the Tree. Mount Vernon, Iowa: Cornell College, 1950.
The Land of Silence and Other Poems. New York: Rinehart, 1953.
In Time Like Air. New York: Rinehart, 1957.
Cloud, Stone, Sun, Vine: Poems, Selected and New. New York: Norton, 1961.

A Private Mythology: New Poems. New York: Norton, 1966.
As Does New Hampshire and Other Poems. Peterborough, New Hampshire: Richard R. Smith, 1967.
A Grain of Mustard Seed: New Poems. New York: Norton, 1971.
A Durable Fire: New Poems. New York: Norton, 1972.
Collected Poems 1930–1973. New York: Norton, 1974.
Selected Poems, edited by Serena Sue Hilsinger and Lois Byrne. New York: Norton, 1978.
Halfway to Silence. New York: Norton, 1980.

PLAYS

The Underground River (1947).

SCREENPLAYS

Toscanini: The Hymn of Nations (1944).
Valley of the Tennessee (1944).

OTHER

The Fur Person: The Story of a Cat. New York: Rinehart, 1957.
I Knew a Phoenix: Sketches for an Autobiography. New York: Holt Rinehart, 1959.
Plant Dreaming Deep. New York: Norton, 1968.
The Poet and the Donkey (juvenile). New York: Norton, 1969.
Journal of a Solitude. New York: Norton, 1973.
Punch's Secret (juvenile). New York: Harper, 1974.
A World of Light: Portraits and Celebrations. New York: Norton, 1976.
A Walk through the Woods (juvenile). New York: Harper, 1976.
The House by the Sea: A Journal. New York: Norton, 1977.
Recovering: A Journal 1978–1979. New York: Norton, 1980.